FAT SASHA

AND THE

URBAN GUERILLA

FAT SASHA

AND THE

URBAN GUERILLA

*Protest and Conformism
in the Soviet Union*

by

DAVID BONAVIA

ATHENEUM   1973   NEW YORK

Copyright © 1973 by David Bonavia
All rights reserved
Library of Congress catalog card number 73-80743
ISBN *0-689-10562-2*
Manufactured in the United States of America
Printed by the Murray Printing Company, Forge Village, Massachusetts
Bound by H. Wolff, New York
First American Edition

To Judy, who also experienced it, and
made it all possible

Contents

Acknowledgements

FOR assistance, advice and additional information in the preparation of this book, my sincere thanks are due to Mr James Yuenger, Mr Anatol Goldberg, Mr Peter Reddaway, Mr and Mrs James Peipert, Mr Peregrine Fellowes and Mr John Gittings; to several colleagues and acquaintances who would prefer not to be mentioned by name; and above all to my wife.

My thanks also go to *The Times* for entrusting me with the post of Moscow Correspondent, and for subsequently granting me the leave of absence which enabled me to write the book. All the views expressed in it are my own, and do not necessarily reflect those of the Editors of *The Times*. The responsibility for any errors or inaccuracies also rests entirely with me.

DAVID BONAVIA

Preface

THE author would like to state that this book is not a novel, but a factual account of real people, conversations, situations and events in the Soviet Union, observed mostly in the period 1971–72, but some of them dating back to 1969.

To protect many of the people concerned, it has been necessary to blur their identities and change their names. Essential facts about their characters and behaviour have been retained; but alterations of detail have been made to render this book unacceptable as prosecution evidence even at a Soviet political trial. Soviet officialdom can only regard it as the 'lies and inventions of a mercenary bourgeois scribbler'.

Much of the book consists of conversations, recorded as direct speech. These are meant to be condensed versions of what people said, remembered as fairly and accurately as possible. Writing from memory after an interval of months, it is impossible to achieve the word-perfectness which would be aimed at in a news story. But two of the longest passages are slightly edited transcriptions from tape recordings.

FAT SASHA
AND THE
URBAN GUERILLA

Khrushchev's Funeral

KHRUSHCHEV'S funeral was an event marked mostly by mud, and by the umbrellas of foreigners.

To a passing bird, the scene must have appeared unusual. The vast Novodevichy Cemetery, final resting place of so many figures of the Soviet establishment, usually crowded with visitors, was entirely empty save for a small knot of people at the very far end. Normal visitors, and people who had come unknowingly to tend graves, were turned away.

A bird with a more than passing interest in these matters would also have observed the thin, grey line of uniformed militia (police) around the cemetery, and the lorry-loads of soldiers standing by discreetly in side-streets, in case of trouble.

The precautions, in the event, were unnecessary. The majority of Russians were learning only that Monday morning of Khrushchev's death on the previous Saturday, when the Soviet correspondent of the London *Evening News* had first disclosed to the outside world his final heart failure. Moscow people had their jobs to go to anyway. Goods trains drawn by diesel engines rumbled along the embankment between the cemetery and the Lenin Stadium.

Nikita Sergeyevich Khrushchev, who ruled the Soviet Union in a totally personal style from the mid-1950s until 1964, died before completing his seventh year of retirement, on 11th September 1971. For the Soviet public, he had already become a non-person, his name banned from the newspapers until he was called on to issue an ambiguous repudiation of his Memoirs, which were printed in the West less than a year before his death. (All Khrushchev actually said in his 'repudiation' was that he had not handed any Memoirs to any publishers, and that the methods of Western propaganda were well known.)

This was almost the first that most Russians had heard of Khrushchev after his deposition at a special meeting of the Communist Party Central Committee in 1964, and his replacement by the three-man leadership of Leonid Brezhnev, Alexei Kosygin and

Nikolay Podgorny. They were still, apparently, firmly in power a year after his death. Throughout his retirement he was spotted in public only once every year or so, when he came into town from his country villa near Moscow to vote at local 'elections'.

None the less, Khrushchev remained a legend, and the subject of endless jokes and anecdotes. One of the most striking things about the dull leadership style of his successors was the way it dried up the flow of popular political anecdotes. Most of those current at the end of the 1960s were left over from the Khrushchev period. People said: 'Life under Lenin was like travelling in a train: there was one man at the controls, and there was light at the end of the tunnel. Under Stalin, it was like a tram: one man driving, and the passengers all being jolted and flung about inside. Under Khrushchev, it was like an aeroplane: one man in the pilot's seat, and all the others feeling sick.' As an afterthought, was added: 'Under Brezhnev, it is like a taxi: the further you go, the more it costs.'

Why should people joke that they 'felt sick' under Khrushchev's leadership? Did he not free them of the terror by which Stalin ruled? Did he not abolish the Stalin cult and seek better relations with the West? Did he not permit a brief flowering of honesty in Soviet literature, and recognise that Communism would stand or fall by the amount of food and consumer goods it produced? If he did all these things, why did people seem so cold and indifferent at the news of his death? Only a few of the more free-thinking people sighed and thought of 'the good old days under Nikita Sergeyevich'. The mass of the population seemed to remember him as the leader who made them look silly.

Under Stalin, however vast the mechanism of terror, the Soviet Union achieved heroic deeds, in industrial construction and the defeat of Germany. If a whole generation of politicians and intellectuals was simply scythed aside, this was a matter of small concern to the working masses, who accepted the Stalin cult at its face value. After all, their great grandfathers had been serfs who defied the Tsar.

Khrushchev let them down. He let them feel how sheepish and blind they had been in their worship of the monster, Stalin. This called in question the value of their sacrifices, as much as the integrity of Khrushchev's own career. He clowned in front of foreign leaders. He blustered over Cuba, and then gave in. He made coarse jokes, and humiliated other leaders in public. To paraphrase the old saying, there was no need to scratch Khrushchev to find a peasant. People were often amused by him, many even believed his promises about catching up with America. They were heartened by Russia's first triumphs in space. The younger intellectuals were thrilled by the new freedom of expression which he allowed them, though often shocked by his own philistinism. But the final judgement on him was that he let too much out of the bag. When Brezhnev and Kosygin began blurring the Party history to sooth the memories of Stalin's Terror, most Russians accepted it with relief. They, too, bore a share of the responsibility for the Terror.

Monday's Moscow newspapers marked Khrushchev's death by printing the briefest of announcements, consisting of a few lines expressing anonymously and collectively the regret of the Communist Party and the Government at his passing. There was no proper obituary notice, and on the Sunday evening no one had thought to call off a fireworks display around the entire Moscow skyline, marking some annual celebration or other.

The only wreath signed in person by a Soviet leader came from the old Armenian politician, Anastas Mikoyan, who not only worked closely with Stalin, but stayed by Khrushchev's side right up till the moment of his disgrace, and still got away into an honourable retirement. He has written a series of published but widely unread Memoirs, and still totteringly visits the theatre in public.

None of the other leaders—not even Leonid Brezhnev, whom Khrushchev made Head of State and who succeeded him as chief of the Party—saw fit to express their condolences in a personal and at the same time public manner. If they telephoned the widow, it was never learnt of.

To Soviet people, there was nothing strange in this. A disgraced leader is a disgraced leader. Nowadays, he has the good fortune to be given a big *dacha*, allowed to keep a town flat, and doubtless receives a generous supply of *Stolichnaya* vodka and Armenian brandy, as well as that increasingly rare commodity, sturgeon caviar. A K.G.B. lady discreetly guards the gates of his mansion against unwanted visitors (unwanted by whom?). Previously he could have simply disappeared overnight, for ever or for fifteen hellish years, or gone through the mind-wrecking humiliation of a show trial and mock confession. To the average Russian's way of thinking, Soviet politics have become almost unbelievably humane.

Still it was a shock to see that among the past and present leadership only Mikoyan had sent a personal wreath. It would have been less striking had there been none from any of them. But Mikoyan's gesture seemed a reproach to the present leaders, who had been so obsequious towards Khrushchev while he was still in power. Or perhaps the loneliness of his wreath should be seen as an irony of history, following Khrushchev's own betrayal of the Stalin whom he apparently worshipped during the dictator's lifetime. There is a treasured item among Moscow collectors: a 78 r.p.m. record of a speech which Stalin gave at a banquet not long before his death. It begins with the words: 'Comrades, I did not intend to speak tonight, but Nikita Sergeyevich has persuaded me . . .' Such ironies are the life-long companions of a career in the Soviet Communist Party.

A smallish crowd of Russians had gathered outside the cemetery to catch a glimpse of the funeral, doubtless consisting of people who had heard the news by rumour, or by listening to the often-denounced but popular foreign radio stations, and who by coincidence had the chance to take the morning off. A few months previously, the entire city, including the leadership, stopped work on a dazzling summer's day, and mounted police were called out to control crowds milling round the lying-in-state of three spacemen, killed on re-entry after a month in earth orbit. This event received extensive press and television coverage, whereas Khrushchev's funeral was completely ignored by the official Soviet media. People wishing to learn details of it had to tune into a sporadically-jammed Russian service of the B.B.C., or to Radio Liberty, the American-backed propaganda station, or the official Voice of America.

The much smaller crowd which turned out for Khrushchev was at first confined to the forecourt of the 'Beryozka' Foreign Currency Store, which had been closed for the day. This was yet another irony. Not only did foreigners make up a substantial proportion of the small number of people allowed to attend the funeral itself; but even those Russians who turned out of their own accord had to wait by a shop patronised by foreigners, and by those of their countrymen who had access to foreign currency. It was sheer coincidence, of course. But it seemed to emphasise symbolically Russia's rejection of Khrushchev's memory, until the time when a more fair-minded generation should restore him to his niche.

A special militia cordon had been dispatched to hold the sight-seers back from the roadside directly opposite the cemetery gates. There was much grumbling about this. People kept asking the militia officers: 'But *why* can't we go, just to look?'—to which the answer would be a shrug, or: 'Move back there.' This went on until, inexplicably, two men in civilian clothes suddenly walked down the street beyond the cordon, and one of them turned and shouted: 'Come on Comrades!'

Who the men were is a mystery. But there was an immediate surge forward which caught the militia off guard, and the crowd succeeded in reforming on the pavement, on the side of the road opposite the cemetery. In the face of temporary *force majeure*, the militia decided to tolerate this new situation, rather than calling out the khaki from behind the 'Beryozka' shop. They may have had instructions on no account to provoke incidents which might recall the hysteria of the crowd scenes at Stalin's funeral, and which would have done Khrushchev too much honour in the eyes of his successors.

The newly-dug grave was at the farthermost recess of the Cemetery, alongside the headstones of a physicist and some other, recently-deceased minor notables. It was a grey morning which threatened drizzle, and the first to arrive at the scene—about two hours early—were mostly Japanese correspondents. They had apparently not been informed of the previous lying-in-state at the suburban hospital which is popularly known as the 'Kremlin Clinic' (because of those who are allowed to use it). It had been expected that there would be speeches at the small, brick funeral parlour there, and a veritable convoy of foreign correspondents' cars, huge and small, had rendezvoused outside the Ukraina Hotel. Together with a few Soviet political dissidents, they were guided to the 'Kremlin Clinic' (which is quite difficult to find unless one knows Moscow very well) by a Soviet photographer who worked for the Moscow bureau of an American news agency. He had evidently not received instructions to the contrary from the Soviet authorities. As it happened, there were no speeches at the funeral parlour.

Back at the cemetery a few inquisitive Russians began poking their heads over the wall, and were stared back at and even photo-graphed by Japanese correspondents. These Russian idlers were shooed away by a Soviet militiaman, but from time to time, when his back was turned, a few heads would pop up over the wall again, like a child's puppet show, and watch the Japanese, who were now taking pictures of the empty grave.

The large number of Japanese present might seem surprising, since Japan barely figured in Khrushchev's foreign policy. But the Japanese presence in Moscow by the early 1970s was enormous, in terms of diplomats, correspondents, businessmen, airline representatives, and presumably the odd spy. It rivalled the American, British, French, Italian and West German presences, among those of the capitalist world.

For anyone present at the cemetery, the temptation to pick up one of the reddish pebbles from the grave as a souvenir was excruciating; but good taste seemed to forbid it. In fact, no one would have objected. The only visible representative of authority, so far from the cemetery gates, was the militiaman trying to keep the heads down from the wall.

A few correspondents were duly joined by some diplomats from N.A.T.O. Embassies (British and American, mainly), though in an unofficial capacity, and none above the rank of Secretary, unless one counted the wife of the British Counsellor. None of the Soviet-block countries sent so much as a reporter, nor was any journalist of a Russian newspaper openly present. (A Bulgarian student, who probably got into hot water for associating with Westerners in Moscow, and was eventually sent home, once remarked: 'I spent nearly my entire schooldays being told that Khrushchev was the wisest and best person in the world.') The Chinese for their part, had hated Khrushchev, and blamed him for the Big Schism between the Chinese and Soviet Communist Parties; so they sent no representatives to his funeral.

By this time the drizzle had begun, and people began either gathering round those with umbrellas, or demonstratively not doing so, and defying the rain to stroll among the headstones trying to recognise the odd name or two. The graves in that part of the cemetery were mostly those of people fairly distinguished in their own right, but no one of Khrushchev's stature.

Russians, who had been naively asked by foreigners why a former Head of Party and Government was not being buried at the Kremlin Wall, merely laughed in astonishment. They expressed the opinion that, all things considered, he was lucky to get into the Novodevichy. One of his neighbours in the graveyard—though far away on the other side—is Stalin's second wife, mother of Svetlana, to whom Khrushchev refers in his Memoirs.

Burial at the Kremlin Wall is the final accolade of a Soviet career, and presumably well worth it, considering that there is supposed to be no after-life for Communists. You either go in the Wall, as in the case of a cremated cosmonaut's urn, or—a greater honour—get one of the few remaining grass plots in front of it. Stalin has had a grass plot since his removal by Khrushchev from the Lenin Mausoleum, so he came off better in the end than his posthumous rival and former close helper. A plain memorial slab marked the grave since his expulsion from Lenin's tomb, until the erection of a bust in 1970, which was one of a number of moves taken around that time to repair Stalin's reputation from some of the damage done to it by Khrushchev.

All Khrushchev himself got was a photograph on his simple headstone—the picture being changed at least twice after the burial, to show him at different ages. Whether this was a deliberate move on the part of the family, or the result of some dispute over the most tasteful way to represent him, remains as obscure as the family itself, which now consists mostly of women.

The cortège finally arrived in the rain, with the wreaths on an open, green-painted lorry, and the body in the usual converted bus which serves as a hearse. The handful of political dissidents who had gone to the funeral parlour had more sense than to try to get past the militia cordon at the cemetery. So the crowd which came slowly up the alleyway with the coffin consisted mostly of relatives, close friends, and foreign correspondents and photographers who had been at the clinic—together with a sprinkling of K.G.B. men (security police) in their characteristic short raincoats and tight-fitting hats. They evidently came just to make sure no one made too inflammatory a speech. There was also a small and rather mediocre band, which kept playing the same funeral march over and over again.

The bird, if still watching, would have been puzzled by the apparent desire of the crowd to enter the grave before the body. The pressure towards the graveside, where the coffin lay on a platform, was terrific. Those standing on the edge of the muddy hole were in real danger of being pushed into it. The relatives wept and pleaded, but it did no good. Photographers were reduced to lifting their cameras over people's heads and pointing them downwards at Khrushchev's bare face, now beaded with rain, which a weeping daughter would wipe away from time to time. The face looked like a pale, rumpled pumpkin with a wart.

It was a funeral like other funerals—perhaps unusually undignified because of the poor arrangements, but distinguished by the genuine and deep feeling of so many of those present. The few speeches—including one by Khrushchev's son and another by a young man whose father was posthumously 'rehabilitated' by him—were moving. The son, Sergey, is a mature, fair-haired man with spectacles, said to be an engineer. Little is known about him. He was wiping away tears when he came to speak by the graveside. His oration was short and sincere, with a trace of bitterness. People might like his father, or not like him, he said. But no one could pass him by without turning to look. Sergey said that all the world's newspapers and radio stations, *with notable exceptions*, had commented on the death. This seemed as far as Khrushchev's son dared go in criticising the public treatment of his father. Every word would be reported.

An old, small lady at the back of the crowd was in a near-panic because she wanted to get through. 'Comrades, what can I do?' she pleaded, 'I am supposed to make a speech.' Everyone cleared a passage for her, among the K.G.B. raincoats and the foreign umbrellas, and she spoke in a shaky voice of Nikita Sergeyevich's good deeds as a Party worker when he was a young man in the Donbass. She was an Old Communist herself.

The speeches were at an end. Somehow the relatives managed to organise the mourners into a queue to pass around the coffin and take a last look at Khrushchev. Relatives and close friends bent and kissed the damp face, and the crowd jostled them past. The mud became thicker from the many shuffling feet. Then workmen hammered down the coffin lid with its red cloth covering. It was lowered unsteadily into the grave, and the first spadefuls fell on it with a sound like distant explosions. The grave was filled in quickly and flowers piled on top. Foreign correspondents and photographers began hurrying towards the cemetery gates, checking facts and names with each other. On the street, some of them broke into a run to get to their cars. The Russian crowd on the opposite pavement looked on stonily.

A few weeks later, a rumour circulated briefly that Georgian nationalists had robbed the grave and desecrated Khrushchev's body in revenge for what he did to Stalin. Inspection showed the grave undisturbed, with a party of West German tourists taking photographs, while their Intourist guide waited impatiently to get back to the bus.

The Direct Approach

WHAT now seems like a million years ago, under Khrushchev, there was a generation of youngish, well-educated people who felt that Soviet society was being purged of the evil of Stalinism, and was going somewhere. People had come out of prison camps, and were doing the unthinkable: writing about it, talking and even singing about it. This seems to have been a relatively optimistic generation which felt it could work with, not against the system, though there were sure to be some frictions. To it the West looked with a hope which was disturbed by the treatment of the novelist and poet Pasternak, the various international crises, and, after Khrushchev's fall, the case of the writers Daniel and Sinyavsky. The general trend of thinking in the West—thoroughly shaken by the Czechoslovak business in 1968—was summarised by a senior diplomat at the French Embassy in Moscow, who even after the invasion said that he was determined to regard Russia as '*un pays comme les autres*' (a country like any other).

But even in the optimism of the Khrushchev period, when many Russians also looked to the West with the hope of genuine *détente* and exchange of ideas, there were signs that 'Destalinisation' had gone too far. There were still too many people around who bore complicity for the massacres and mass deportations of the 1930s, the blunders early in the War, and the repressions which took place in the post-war period, including the persecution of returned prisoners of war. This complex series of oppressive acts was matched by murderous strife in the leadership, and it was this above all that the post-Stalin leaders really wanted to put a stop to. The killing of Beria, Stalin's last police chief, was a much more significant act of Destalinisation than the subsequent poetry readings by the popular Yevgeny Yevtushenko. (Beria's Moscow house, where many of his victims were said to have been tortured, is now the Tunisian Embassy. A series of accidents and deaths in this Embassy has led to a superstition that the house is haunted.)

True Destalinisation would have meant a massive series of trials, involving hundreds of thousands of culprits—false informers, prison camp guards, police and Party officials, and many others—some of whom were by then reaching the height of their undisturbed careers. Destalinisation had to stop, because it was making things too hot for too many people. Alexander Solzhenitsyn's novels—banned in Russia but printed in the West—are the symbol of what the post-Khrushchev leadership had to put an end to, by turning back the political clock. At the same time, the Leadership seem to have come to an agreement among themselves never to return to the system of mutual liquidation which Stalin favoured under his own aegis; and this is only sensible from their point of view.

The 'turning back of the clock', which is a slow process and was still going on in 1972, faced the 'optimistic generation' with a terrible dilemma, as they slowly realised what was happening. Not in their effective lifetime would it be possible again to print a realistic account of prison-camp life, and the other evils the country had gone through, thus purging it, and leading it on to a kinder future.

So for millions there was a choice to be made. The majority of the 'optimistic generation' simply did what they would have done in any other country, and took the attitude: 'If you can't lick 'em, join 'em'. Many came to lead a double existence, publicly loyal, and even members of the Party, building careers and having a child or two; but keeping a circle of friends—three, sometimes as many as five—who would not inform on each other. They could occasionally get together to vent their shame and frustration, and their growing anxieties at a repetition of Stalinism, by listening to protest songs or passing around typescripts of clandestine literature. Others, more numerous, joined the establishment body and soul.

There were still others, relatively few in number, who decided to live by their consciences and take a stand of principle, come what may. There was always the chance that a change for the better might occur after all, and their choice would be vindicated. The Daniel-Sinyavsky trial, the subsequent persecution of other intellectuals, and above all the invasion of Czechoslovakia in 1968, gave them ample opportunity to make their stand. The result was predictable. Most of them lost their jobs. Some were exiled. Some were jailed or sent to 'psychiatric hospitals'; some have already even ended their stretches. A small group remained, for the time being, at liberty.

It seems likely that around 1968 some clever officials persuaded the Communist Party's ruling caucus, the Politburo, that the best course was to leave a few political dissidents around to act as barometers. This idea could have originated in the powerful administrative apparatus of the Party Central Committee, or among the senior police agents of the K.G.B., or in an influential faction drawn from both. Their argument probably was that dissidents, as shown by the results of the Daniel-Sinyavsky trial, were dragon's teeth: one thrown aside could give birth to several others. And besides, their groups could always be infiltrated, and some of their members secretly subverted, so that the K.G.B. would be amply informed on their activities.

A disadvantage, this argument must have conceded, would be that it would be mildly embarrassing for stories to reach the outside world of the acts of oppression being pursued daily in Soviet society, since oppression is not a state or condition, but a series of deliberate actions. On the other hand, it may have seemed that the influential political circles of the West were fed up with political dissidents, having plenty of their own, and would be more interested in doing business with the Soviet leadership than in trying to encourage internal opposition in Russia. They could more easily prevent war and reduce arms spending if they dealt with a stable Soviet leadership. Dissidents would also help Russia's image in the outside world by giving the impression that her society was tolerant, liberal and open—which could not be farther from the truth.

The biggest mistake in this policy was probably a result of self-indoctrination, which addles the brain more effectively than any other drug. The outside world simply did not lose interest in dissidents, or merely see them as a hopeful sign for Russian society. On the contrary, the more it learned, the more intrigued it became, the more it wanted to know about them and the tales they had to tell. Even the Italian Communist Party is interested in the Soviet dissident scene. Italian reporters are among the most active in Moscow. A country which has a serious chance of getting a Communist-controlled government in the future wants to know what other Communists do when they are in power. And of course the dissidents' reports of oppression were seized on by all right-wing, socialist or even Maoist forces which disliked Soviet Communism (or rather Socialism, as the present stage of Soviet society is officially named). This did not make the dissidents' reports any less true.

In other words, the freedom with which dissidents were getting information out—a telephone call, followed by a quickly-dialled Telex message to a newspaper office in the West—was all becoming too much for the leaders. This was evidently the reason for the crackdown which took place in 1972. A policy had failed, and was being changed. Unfortunately for the K.G.B., the security police who had to cope with internal dissidence, they probably had contradictory instructions from the Party leadership, something in the nature of: 'Shut dissidents up, but do it without any fuss.' This, by definition, was impossible, since the dissidents reported all moves against them to the Western press, and another series of oppressive acts was chalked up to the discredit of the Soviet regime.

The dissidents have mostly already been extruded from Soviet society—sacked from their jobs or dismissed from their institutes. They no longer see the possibility of changing society from within, so they walk around it, beating at it with their fists, and calling on the world to examine it more closely.

*

Two of the most intelligent people in Moscow are Valery and Vera Chalidze. Vera is also one of the city's most charming women, and she is a direct descendant of the early 'Soviet aristocracy' largely massacred by Stalin. She is petite, has a mop of black, rather curly hair, an almond-shaped face, and the closest thing imaginable to what used to be called an 'ivory complexion'. Her grandfather was Maxim Maximovich Litvinov, one of the most distinguished of Soviet diplomats in the between-the-wars period, and indeed for a long time Commissar for Foreign Affairs, i.e., Foreign Minister.

Vera's English grandmother (Maxim Maximovich's widow) is at time of writing still alive, although 83 and perhaps already 84. Ivy Litvinov lives in a huge, Edwardian-looking block of flats on an embankment of the Moscow River, though it was built much later than the Edwardian period in which she was brought up in London and Cambridge. There are mock stone chessmen on the roof. Vera herself speaks and understands English excellently, though she has a noticeable Russian accent and is not completely bilingual. Those who follow the genealogy of Soviet society will realise that she is the cousin of Pavel Litvinov, sentenced to five years' exile in Siberia for protesting on Red Square against the invasion of Czechoslovakia.

Maxim Maximovich, though his career never recovered completely from the shadow cast over it at the time of the Great Purges, was fortunate enough to escape the fate of many other distinguished figures of the early Soviet period. He was restored to active service under Molotov for the wartime and post-war period, was made Ambassador to the United States, and died in retirement in 1951.

Valery professes to speak nothing but Russian and Polish, but this could be because he is too proud to attempt to speak a language badly. He becomes irritable if Vera passes more than a few words of English chat with any visitors without translating for him. He is of mixed Polish and Georgian ancestry. He says he does not remember much Georgian, though his surname is from the Caucasus and not from Poland. He detests associating seriously with people who cannot speak Russian (or presumably Polish) with reasonable competence, though Vera is perfectly capable of acting as an interpreter for English, and sometimes does. He says that, in meeting foreigners, he wishes to be introduced only to a '*Kul -turnaya publika*' (roughly translatable as 'people who know the score').

Being trained as a physicist, Valery has an exaggeratedly pedantic and literal mind, which he probably cultivates deliberately in his self-appointed cause of enquiring into and 'advising the Soviet Authorities on' matters concerned with Human Rights in the Soviet Union. He is the main driving force behind the totally unofficial Soviet Human Rights Committee set up in November 1970, and sometimes known as 'The Sakharov Committee'. By 1972, this Committee consisted of Chalidze, Academician Andrey Sakharov, the nuclear physicist, another scientist called Andrey Tverdokhlebov, and—most interesting perhaps—Igor Shafarevich, aged 48, still active as Professor of Mathematics at the Moscow State University, and in 1971, despite his association with the Human Rights Committee, actually re-elected a member of the Lenin Prize Awards Committee. The authorities indicated that they regarded the Human Rights Committee as illegal, but hesitated to move against it.

Shafarevich's position is one of the most significant in the entire dissident movement. Here is a man who not only appends his signature to protest documents, and attends dissident gatherings, but is apparently not persecuted for it, and has maintained an extremely prestigious job. It is possible that he has been talked to privately by his superiors at the University, but this has never been reported. He may also have had urbane interviews with K.G.B. representatives, but sometimes people prefer to keep quiet about such cosy chats.

How long this situation can last is anyone's guess. Professor Shafarevich appears to be a pleasant man of wide interests, who speaks good English (he has travelled abroad), and is prepared to discuss frankly such questions as comparative higher education, which most Soviet intellectuals would rarely talk about freely with foreigners, for fear of saying the wrong thing and having it reported.

The only person in a remotely comparable position is Academician Sakharov, acknowledged in the Soviet Union to be one of the country's most distinguished scientists and the principal brain behind the Soviet H-Bomb. Perhaps he suffers from a political conscience as a result of his discoveries in this field; at any rate, he is thoroughly fed up with the entire state of things in the Soviet Union—from the facilities for research workers to the status of the national minorities. He says so openly in signed tracts periodically circulated privately in Moscow and eventually published in the West, though not in the Soviet Union. He also makes a point of sending these tracts to the top Soviet Leaders for their personal attention (which an Academician should merit). But he has never received any reply or acknowledgement from them.

For several years the authorities left or seemed to leave Academician Sakharov alone, because of his truly exalted position in the scientific community. He was allowed to attend political trials to which all others but a few of the defendants' relatives and some K.G.B. stooges were denied entry. His political tracts, though of course not printed in the Soviet Union, were also tolerated, and the Leadership may actually have found some of his suggestions interesting. As to his repeated signature of protest documents, this merely led to a slow process whereby even people in the West would have become less interested in his opinions, or so the authorities may have thought. At any rate he was not prosecuted or expelled from the Academy. The idea, apparently, was gently to let him become a bore.

The turning point came on a cold day in January 1972, when Academician Sakharov was refused permission to attend the 'public' trial of Vladimir Bukovsky, a young dissident who had given the world details of the horrific conditions in Soviet 'special psychiatric hospitals', where sane political dissidents are confined with real lunatics and subject to the brutal 'attentions' of convicted criminals recruited as male nurses. Bukovsky, after a brief period of liberty in 1970–71, was re-arrested, and tried at a Moscow suburban court in January 1972. All independent observers were banned from the courtroom, but the proceedings at the trial eventually got out, through the tireless efforts of his friends, and caused an international scandal. The defence had been virtually denied the right to present a case, and the prosecution's case was made up of a political, anti-Western tirade culled from the pages of Party propaganda journals. Bukovsky was given seven years in prison and labour camp, and five years in exile to follow, partly for giving a secret television interview to William Cole, a correspondent of the American C.B.S. network who was subsequently expelled from the country. Cole later described Bukovsky as a delightful young man who enjoyed taking a drink, liked girls, and longed to travel the world. But he had taken a stand of principle on the issue of the 'psychiatric hospitals', and despite a heart complaint which might grow worse in prison, he was determined to contribute his mite to what he called the 'spiritual enlightenment of Soviet society'. He is one of the most tragic and pitiable victims of the whole series of persecutions against dissidents in recent years.

Bukovsky's friends, who weathered the trial grumbling and complaining in an ante-room, report that Academician Sakharov was literally beside himself and shouting with rage. Only someone who has lived in Russia or studied Russia can understand the prestige which is accorded to an Academician, and which falls little short of that of a member of the Central Committee of the Communist Party. For such a man to have to rant at a crude cop in 1972 was a deeply symbolic event.

Already in the previous year, secret Party meetings were being told that Academician Sakharov had indeed 'merited something' in the eyes of Soviet science, but had recently 'gone a bit daft' and started associating with anti-Soviet elements. In 1972 this secret campaign (of the type described so well by the banned novelist Alexander Solzhenitsyn in his interview of March that year with the *New York Times* and the *Washington Post*) sought to persuade influential sectors of the public that the real Sakharov died several years ago, and that the person now using his name and authority is an imposter. A photograph, apparently emanating from official sources and purporting to show Sakharov, was published, with certain reservations, in a Dutch book. Who this person was it is impossible to say, but he did not look like Sakharov. The real Academician Sakharov, who came with his wife to my farewell party on May 11th, in Moscow (apparently a deliberate decision on his part to associate for the first time with foreign correspondents) was instantly acclaimed by other authoritative Russians present. This man, as several senior British diplomats and others may confirm, is on the tall side, perhaps just under six feet, middle-aged, with fair and slightly thinning hair, and tends to squint somewhat. He is shy and soft-spoken. His wife is more lively, is rather stocky, in the sense of broad-shouldered, and has a notably aquiline nose. She is bright-eyed, and does a good deal of his talking for him.

Some of Academician Sakharov's wisest and most incisive statements were made in a document which he circulated in June 1972, and which reflected a bitterness and anger not so noticeable in his previous writings. Before, he had seemed mainly concerned with international relations, peaceful co-existence, and the reform of Soviet society as a means of making it more competitive and efficient. But in 1972 he wrote:

'I believe, as before, that it is possible to overcome the tragic contradictions and dangers of our age only through convergence and mutual transformation of capitalism and of the socialist order. In the capitalist countries this process must be accompanied by a further strengthening of the elements of social defence of the workers' rights, a reduction of militarism and of its influence on political life. In the socialist countries it is also essential to reduce militarisation of the economy and messianic ideology; it is vitally important to reduce extreme instances of centralism and Party-State bureaucratic monopoly, in the economic sphere of production and consumption, as well as in the sphere of ideology and culture.

'I ascribe, as before, decisive importance to the democratisation of society, the development of free expression, legality and the provision of basic Human Rights.

'I hope, as before, in the evolution of society in these directions under the influence of technological and economic progress, although my predictions have become more reserved.

'At present, it seems to me still more than before that the only genuine guarantee of the preservation of human values, in the chaos of unregulated change and tragic upheavals, is the freedom of human convictions, and Man's moral urge towards good.

'Our society is infected with apathy, hypocrisy, narrow-minded egotism and hidden cruelty. The majority of representatives of its upper crust—the Party-State administrative apparatus, and the highest and most advanced strata of the intelligentsia—keep firm hold on their overt and covert privileges, and are profoundly indifferent to violations of Human Rights, to the interests of progress, and to the security and future of Mankind. Others, disturbed in the depths of their souls, cannot allow themselves any "free thinking", and are doomed to torture themselves with internal conflict. Drunkenness has taken on the proportions of a national catastrophe. It is one of the symptoms of the moral degradation of a society which is sinking deeper and deeper into a state of chronic alcoholic poisoning.'

This despairing note in Academician Sakharov's latest tract indicates the sort of considerations that motivated him in risking the total loss of a prosperous career and in aligning himself with Chalidze and the others in the Human Rights Committee.

The Chalidzes live in the very shadow of the Foreign Ministry, though the hideous and fantastic structure now existing is not the one Vera's grandfather worked in as the head of the Soviet pre-war foreign service. But what Valery is trying to do has little direct connexion with Soviet foreign policy. It would have been more appropriate had they lived, say, beneath the Ministry of Internal Affairs, the Prisons Administration, the Serbsky Institute of Forensic Psychiatry, perhaps even the K.G.B., or the Party Central Committee itself.

One or other side of the family has owned the flat for many years, though in 1972 Valery and Vera seemed to be living in only one room of it. Presumably it had been split up and turned into a 'communal apartment'.

Valery says he seldom goes out, preferring to let people come and visit him. Unlike many dissidents, he declines to visit foreigners' apartments, considering this an invitation to the K.G.B. to mount *provokatsii*. He spends quite a lot of time re-arranging the furniture of the bed-sitting room, and Vera does not seem to mind. The room is clean, but very dingy, as so many Russian flats are, and it is absolutely cluttered with books, a desk and chair, curios, a divan bed, scientific objects. There is a small easel for oil painting, and Valery has recently started making modernistic *objets d'art* in heavy cast metal.

Valery is not just a physicist, but a very talented one, as the authorities recognised by appointing him head of a plastics research team (a subject in which Russia desperately needs to catch up with the West). He left the job for political reasons, as briefly noted in Issue No. 16 of the clandestine protest journal, *The Chronicle of Current Events*, but for some reason he prefers not to discuss that subject. For a while he did not work, but that could have put him in danger of being exiled from Moscow for 'parasitism'. However, if his wife worked, as perhaps she did, this would have been less feasible. She could support him, and the rights of men and women to do domestic or other work as they please are apparently equal under Soviet law.

Towards the end of 1971, Chalidze got himself some sort of a job within his *spetsialnost*'. Dissidents frequently refuse to accept work outside their sphere of academic qualification once they have been dismissed from their jobs for political reasons. They do so, not necessarily because the work offered them is always of a menial nature, but because it is seldom very interesting, and because they wish to demonstrate the injustice of their dismissal or removal, and the wastage of their qualifications. They may be hounded from job to job, or denied any work at all except as night watchmen or stokers, through the *Otdely Kadrov*, the K.G.B. departments which supervise the personnel of every Soviet establishment much above the status of a bottle-collection point. Chalidze apparently found a niche for himself in a spectrological laboratory associated with an icon-restoring establishment—a rather nice job, one would have thought.

Valery required Vera to remain with him most of the time when he was at home, not only perhaps because he was a fundamentally lonely figure, but in order to have someone else with whom he could work at his Human Rights projects, have translations of English materials prepared, and spin the web of inner freedom which kept them both so alive and fascinating despite their depressing surroundings.

Once, when it was suggested that she might go out to meet somebody on a particular day, he said with indignation: 'But I require you here.' She said: 'Yes, but it'll be in the daytime.'

'Oh, that's all right,' he replied. 'I thought you were going to leave me alone in the evening.'

Vera's look showed that she would never have contemplated

such a thing, so there seems to be a slight difference of approach between the Soviet Human Rights Movement and the Women's Lib Movement in the West.

The house they live in is very dilapidated, though clearly it was once quite grand, and is in that Moscow street which occurs in many Russian-language text-books for its strange name, Sivtsev Vrazhek. There are broad, shallow staircases, and the Chalidzes live at the very top, on the fourth or fifth floor, so that visitors who are afraid of getting stuck in the lift usually arrive breathless. This puts Valery at something of a moral advantage with them, though it is not his fault.

Valery's work on the Human Rights Movement from 1970 onwards has been of a strictly investigatory and advisory capacity, as he puts it. His reason for collaborating in the formation of the Committee was simplicity itself: 'There was no other'. He regards the task of the Committee as the investigation both of the theoretical problems of Human Rights, and of their application in the Soviet Union in accordance with standards laid down by the United Nations (with the active participation of the Soviet Union). He also sees the Committee as 'advising' the authorities on the results of its investigations. In addition, the Committee has taken it on itself to issue formal, signed protests in cases of violation of Human Rights in the Soviet Union in individual cases.

Chalidze was the compiler of an unofficial journal called '*Social Problems*', which published materials related to these questions. It was not a rival to *The Chronicle of Current Events* (which at the time of writing has gone through its 25th typescript issue since 1968, despite active K.G.B. efforts to suppress it). '*Social Problems*' was not supposed to be a chronicle, but an academic journal.

Valery made no secret of his editing it—he published his name and address on the title page—or of the fact that he contributed a goodly proportion of the articles in it. It was not, to be frank, a very readable journal, because it was often very legalistic and theoretical. Around April 1972 Valery announced that he was ceasing 'publication' on a regular basis because it was not achieving much, in his opinion, and the others associated with the Committee were not doing enough to contribute to it. Ironically, or perhaps for purely practical purposes, he used as the cover of the final issue some pages from an English-language technical journal describing very advanced, computerized business equipment, such as Soviet commerce and industry will not know on a wide-spread scale for decades.

This does not mean that Valery was allowed by the authorities to do as he pleased with his Committee. Much of his foreign mail, and probably his Soviet mail as well, was intercepted and confiscated, and he once at least protested officially to the Ministry of Communications about the refusal of a telephone operator to let a call through to him from a Human Rights worker in New York. His telephone was disconnected during President Nixon's visit to Moscow in May 1972. However, in general he succeeded in continuing to make international calls or to receive them—something which shows how anxious the authorities still are to adhere at least outwardly to international postal conventions, even while applying strict censorship in practice and frequently suppressing or simply 'losing' mail.

Valery's concern for rights extends not only to human ones. He and Vera own a young ginger–and–white tom–cat which they call Geoff, of which they seem very fond. As it matured, it began to want mating and became very miserable because the owners did not know how to find a female and perform the process in a one-room flat. Someone suggested that they have the cat castrated, so that it should spend the rest of its days happily getting fat, sleeping, being affectionate, and occasionally playing, as neutered cats do. Both Valery and Vera were instantly indignant: 'How can you suggest such a thing?' Vera demanded. 'How would you like it if someone did that to you without your consent?'

Valery said: 'The cat has a *right* to do *it*.'

The same cat, when still half a kitten, was the cause of acute embarrassment to two foreign journalists who had heard Chalidze's reputation for brusqueness and pedantry, and were nervous of meeting him, quite apart from the question of possible *provokatsii* or even assaults by K.G.B. men on that ill-lit street. Throughout the discussion, which was on an extremely serious and analytical level, and during which Russian thoughts of some complexity had to be mentally and simultaneously translated and taken down in legible English shorthand, the cat kept coming to perch on one visitor's shoulder and stare into its master's face, as though to ask: 'Is he making sense?' This made the visitor want to giggle, and Vera kept trying to drive the cat away. But the serious expression on Valery's face, and the relentlessness with which he pursued his topic, made the interview almost unbearable each time the cat decided to resume its perch. Nonetheless, it would have been bad manners to shoo off the hosts' beast, and it was a nice cat.

Geoff, the cat, was probably also present, in constant danger of being trodden on, at Chalidze's birthday party in 1971, to which a large number of dissidents and a few foreign correspondents came. It was a scene which will live sharply in the memory for a lifetime.

One of those present was a quiet-spoken and good-looking young man, a political prisoner who had just emerged from the dreadful conditions of a cell in Vladimir gaol, which he had shared with several others, suffering the perpetual misery of cold, close confinement and semi-starvation. Before being let out, he had been fattened up a bit, and his hair was beginning to grow. His wife, a charming and attractive woman, and their pretty young daughter, had come hundreds of miles from the place where they lived, to welcome him and bring him home. When asked what his daughter was going to do when she grew up, he looked at her affectionately, and said with the utmost simplicity: 'She will destroy the K.G.B.' With an impossible combination of tenseness and serenity, he actually seemed to be missing the prison from which he had just emerged, and which, through all the Russias, is still the most feared of punishment centres, though located in a favourite venue for foreign tourists. He said he could never rest in his mind till his friends were released from there, too. All the time in gaol, he had been hungry and able to think of little but food. Now, from nerves and fatigue, he could barely eat.

Professor Shafarevich was at the party, talking freely and articulately to foreigners and openly demonstrating his alignment with the dissident movement. He expressed willingness to receive telephone calls from foreigners at home—a very rare thing for a person in such an official position.

Everybody had tried to bring a present for Valery or some drink, but people saw that the drink would not last, and were going easy on it. Valery himself drinks little—'he will nurse one all night,' a friend said—but a Russian party usually breaks up when the drink is finished. Most of the correspondents left early, sensing that the Russians would prefer to talk things out on their own.

Some of the Russians must have felt that next year, the Leap Year, there were bad things coming. There is a superstition among Russian intellectuals that the worst things happen in Leap Years.

In 1952 there was the 'Doctors' Plot', by which Stalin had plotted an anti-Semitic purge before his death; in 1956 there was the invasion of Hungary; in 1960 Pasternak died; in 1964 Khrushchev was ousted, and in 1968 there was Czechoslovakia. Of course, one could have found good things in those years as well as bad, and plenty of bad things in other years, too. But the mere existence of the superstition probably affected K.G.B. tactics in their campaign against dissidents, and the first few months of 1972 certainly seemed to be vindicating the soothsayers.

In that year, Valery appeared to become more shy of contacts with foreigners, or perhaps he just gained the impression that they wanted to steer clear of *him*. It was the period after a wave of house-searches, interrogations and arrests in Moscow, Leningrad, Kiev, Riga, Lvov, Vilnius and elsewhere, in January.

Chalidze adhered firmly to the principle that if correspondents wanted to talk to him, they should telephone him openly and arrange an interview without secrecy. He even agreed with a light heart when a wry Canadian correspondent suggested an interview arranged through the Foreign Ministry, and Valery proposed a request for an official interpreter. The project never got far, but it showed up a few lies in the system. The Canadian's official contact man had told him he could interview 'any' Soviet citizens, provided they consented. But the request for an official interview with Chalidze—whose Committee had already been recognised by similar bodies in other countries—was met with a stony silence. When the Canadian persisted, he was told first: 'We neither know this man, nor want to know him.' He persisted again, and finally got the grudging reply from the Foreign Ministry: 'We are not in harmony with the aims of this organisation.' That at least was true.

Chalidze became involved, in a minor way, with one of the American Congressmen who came to Moscow early in 1972, because the Congressman wanted to come and talk to him, and he agreed as a matter of principle. These people later caused a fuss by handing out religious literature (which is implicitly forbidden by the Soviet Constitution) and by visiting Jews seeking to emigrate.

Izvestia published an attack on them, in which it mentioned 'a certain Chalidze' (always an ominous turn of phrase). But Valery insisted that he had never been mentioned in the newspaper, because there were plenty of Chalidzes, and the actions ascribed to him bore no relation to his real activity.

The K.G.B. will have a hard time with Chalidze, if they ever try to prosecute him. He knows his rights, both in Soviet law and under International Conventions, to which the Soviet Union is a solemn partner, a good deal better than they do. He is known and has friends in the outside world, and he will fight to the last micrometre of principle and legality on every issue involved. Whether his connexion with the Litvinovs will help to protect him is problematical, since the family's name is already associated with political dissent.

In late 1972 Chalidze was given an exit visa from the Soviet Union and went to lecture in the United States. While he and Vera were in New York, a Soviet consular official informed him that he had been stripped of his Soviet nationality, and confiscated his passport. However, Valery declared that although he preferred exile to imprisonment, he intended to fight the decision and return to the Soviet Union one day. This is why the account of his life and activity in Moscow has been left in the present tense.

Pavel

THE person who will be referred to as Pavel had intended to be present at Khrushchev's funeral, perhaps even to try to make a speech. He had arranged to guide the correspondents' convoy from the Ukraina Hotel, and it was only when he failed to turn up, and wristwatches were being anxiously checked, that the American-employed Soviet photographer agreed to take over. One minor political dissident got cold feet at the last moment, and stood alone in the windswept forecourt of the hotel, as the Chevrolets and Volkswagens drove off up Kutuzovsky Prospect.

The speculation at the time was that Pavel—who had a menial job in some academic institute—had failed to get the necessary permission to absent himself. In fact, he was arrested the moment he stepped outside his flat in northern Moscow that morning. He was taken to the local police station, held quietly for a few hours, and released only when a phone call came through to the effect that the funeral was over.

Pavel is a character who belongs half to Milton, and half to Kazantsakis. Milton would have recognised in him the forces of light and dark in constant battle. Kazantsakis might have appreciated his attitude towards politics, which resembles the great Zorba's attitude towards life. At the time of writing, Pavel is under arrest and probably going to be put away for a long stretch. But he is a live human being, and therefore to be referred to in the present tense.

Pavel is regarded both by the K.G.B. and by many Soviet dissidents as the *vozhd'* (Great Leader) of what has come to be known as the Democratic Movement, or, more simply, the Movement. It is theoretically distinct from the Jewish Emigration Movement, the Lithuanian Catholic Movement, the Ukrainian Nationalist Movement, the Crimean Tartar Return Movement, the Baptist Initiativist Movement, and others. But they all have their links, and at times assist each other. Together, they make up a generalised movement for more personal, religious and national freedom in the Soviet Union.

Until his arrest, Pavel's arrival on the scene sometimes recalled the appearance of the King of the Sea in Rimsky-Korsakoff's opera 'Sadko'. A shaggy and menacing figure, he seemed to rise up with prophecies from a world at whose nature mortals could only guess. It was alarming enough when he rang, demanding a meeting. One person was nearly frightened out of his wits when Pavel evaded the police guard at a foreigners' compound, and suddenly struck his shaggy mane in at the window. Symbolic of the supernatural powers which one sensed in Pavel was the fact that other people, told of this sudden appearance, unhesitatingly asked what floor it was on. It was, in fact, on the ground floor, but no one would have been particularly surprised to see him materialise at the sixth or even the fourteenth storey.

Pavel is in himself a necessary phenomenon in Soviet history. The Stalin period, and its political hangover, went against human nature. Human beings tend to be indiscreet, unpredictable, unreliable, and different from each other. The Stalinist and post Stalinist ideology have tried to turn them into reserved, programmed, predictable, similar machines. This has merely made people excessively suspicious of each other, and still more suspicious of strangers.

Pavel's openness, combined with his tremendous force of personality, make him seem unusual in the Soviet context. He has sought to free people from neo-Stalinism by direct challenge, and by an act of faith towards each other. If the Soviet state system tends to make people inwardly draw away from each other, Pavel has dared them to trust each other, speak their minds, and do what they think is right. Such a person had to see the light of day even in Soviet Russia, and encourage others to do like him, if the country was not to fulfil the worst Orwellian predictions about its future development. So although Pavel's arrest and probable imprisonment are a bad sign, the fact of his existence can be interpreted as a good one. He himself has always proclaimed an unshakable optimism about the Soviet Union.

This was the origin of the Democratic Movement in the late 1960s. It took the promises of Soviet socialism literally: it saw that the Laws and Constitution guaranteed certain freedoms, and it claimed them in the name of the entire country. If the State broke such people and threw them aside for doing so, it was only accusing itself of lying. The lie became more evident, and the Movement gained more strength, if only a little more.

When some people accused Pavel of 'making too much noise', and spoiling things for those who were allegedly trying to change the system quietly from within, he retorted with an anecdote: 'A man is walking through a marshy forest, when he finds another up to his waist in dirty bog-water, washing himself. "Let me give you a hand out," says the traveller. "No thanks," says the other. "I live here".'

There are specialists on Russia who consider that the Movement which Pavel in particular represents has little importance, because there are relatively few people involved, and because it is a superficial phenomenon brought about by the aftermath of the Khrushchev and Stalin periods. To them, 'the dissidents' are just a small group of seedy men who hand out stories which are printed by foreign news media.

This attitude is a perfectly natural and understandable result of the restrictions accepted by Western diplomats. With rare exceptions they decline to mix with people of whom the Soviet authorities might strongly disapprove, for fear of being accused of interfering in the country's internal affairs. And, of course, Soviet diplomats must not be given the excuse to mingle with 'subversives' in Western countries. A clearer failure of the policy of reciprocity could hardly be imagined since Soviet representatives in the West mix with whomever they please. It is not the fault of the Western diplomats in Moscow, many of whom would dearly love to become more 'involved'; they have their orders from their Governments, and the Governments have yet to be convinced that the Democratic Movement in Russia is worth fooling with, especially when you can read all about its doings in the newspapers anyway.

There are also those who shun Pavel as *pyushchy* (a drinker). And there can be no question that until his arrest he drank heavily, as a man has a right to, whose father was murdered by the secret police, who met his wife and had a daughter in prison camp, and who has lived in daily fear of house search, arrest, shadowing by car-loads of thugs, detention and other forms of harassment. By Russian standards, Pavel is no more than a steady drinker. He is not an alcoholic, because he can do without drink when he has to, and then the Miltonian angels begin to sparkle in him. The more he drinks, the more he topples into his own bitter anger and frustration which turn as much against his friends as against the Powers who rule the country. 'You just want to get all your information from

Jews,' he may say scathingly when drunk (although he is a Jew himself). Or he may warn people against considering others reliable, though he has not been totally reliable himself. Before his arrest, he used to have a frightful habit of telephoning suddenly to demand late-night meetings and lifts home.

In a perverse way, the K.G.B. may have done Pavel a good deed by arresting him so early in the 1972 drive against dissidents—which, according to him, was decreed by a special session of the Central Committee at the year's eve. To have been left alone, while his friends and supporters were arrested around him, might have broken him more quickly than labour camp or prison.

Some of Pavel's friends were worried about his habit of taking bottles of vodka from foreigners from time to time, and the K.G.B. tried to use this to discredit them all. But this was not a transaction, because he gladly rendered up any information he had, without any vodka being involved, simply because he wanted the world to know about it. Exchanges of presents are in accordance with a Russian custom. Russians can be insanely generous, and it is bad form to visit a Russian home for a meal without bringing a present. If it is not the season for flowers, drinks are the most appreciated gift, especially vodka. Similarly, Russians will bring flowers which they can ill afford, and even valuable old books and curios, or folders of prints, to give to a foreigner, who could buy the equivalent much more cheaply in his own country. It is sincere and very touching. Russia is in fact one of the few countries where most foreign correspondents are *not* prepared to offer money to private individuals for information, because it could be used to discredit them and their contacts.

Pavel led the Movement, in the eyes of the K.G.B., because he was one of the first to get in touch with Western correspondents in the late 1960s, and start helping them to get to know what was really going on in the country: the extent of the oppression not only in Moscow, but from Eastern Siberia to the Baltic States.

All who knew Pavel at liberty will remember him in a totally personal way. One's relations with him were never fixed. One quarrelled with him, laughed with him, drank with him, got angry with him, or admired and marvelled at him. He seemed to want drama around himself, and he certainly got it.

One evening he rang at short notice and asked to be brought into the foreigners' compound for a talk. He had two admirers in tow: an other-worldly religious artist and his wife, to be called the Zhukovs. They were among Pavel's supporters, and they were both active in the Democratic movement, though they later left the country under severe threats from the K.G.B. Pavel demanded to tape-record a statement on the occasion of some anniversary or other considered important in the Movement. They were always celebrating anniversaries, a habit which they took over from the Soviet State itself. But Pavel rudely insisted that he make the recording on his own, in an adjoining room, while his friends patiently waited for him. About halfway through the recording, they crept in quietly and sat on the floor to listen. He would break off his statement to rage at foreigners for their indifference to what was happening in Russia, and their eagerness to reach compromises with the Leadership. 'You're all reptiles,' he said at one stage. Eventually he ran out of steam, and sank into a morose lethargy, from which it was possible to ease him out and send him home.

Episodes such as this made people fear visitations from Pavel, particularly since they were usually unexpected, and arranged at the last moment when there were other things also requiring to be done. But when he wanted, he could charm the daylights out of anyone. He rang one sunny afternoon in early spring, a few months before his arrest, and said: 'Can you lend me thirty Roubles?'

This was a foolish request, since foreigners dislike financial entanglements with dissidents. Rebuffed, he said: 'Never mind. Come down and meet me now. I want to talk to you.'

He was sauntering along the street by the official House of Cinema, wearing an old windcheater, his eyes twinkling above the grizzled beard. 'Sorry if I alarmed you,' he said. 'I just thought it would be a plausible way to get you out for a chat. Let's go to the market. It's Easter soon. We ought to buy some catkins.'

He was serious, rational, prophetic. He talked about the Leadership's motives, and the campaign being cranked up against the dissidents. At the market he got some catkins for himself and his family, and an extra bunch for the Zhukovs, who lived nearby. 'Remember,' he said as he took his leave on the street, 'if they expel you from this country, it'll be for using your head, for lying on your bed sometimes and thinking. That's what they don't like.'

Then he would disappear from one's horizon for weeks at a time, either taking offence, or concentrating on some other foreigners. But when he surfaced again, he made it seem as though the last meeting had only been a few days ago. 'Have you been angry with me, or something?' he would say disarmingly. He was totally absorbed in what he was doing. Foreigners came and went, on longer or shorter postings, but they all had one thing in common: they left in the end. So did some of his Soviet friends, given the opportunity. He stayed behind.

A Westerner who saw a lot of Pavel, in the months immediately before his arrest, gives this estimate of him:

'Like everyone who ever knew him, I was aware that he was a man of tremendous personality. I used to go to his apartment, I guess once or twice a week. Sometimes I would just show up on the spur of the moment. He lived in an apartment building with two elevators —I never did know the actual street number. It was facing a boulevard, and what I used to do was drive along it, go all the way along one side of the boulevard to the next corner, keeping a sharp eye out for someone who might be watching, some kind of K.G.B. car, or informer sitting on the street looking suspicious.

'You got into his apartment, and you walked down a longish corridor past the kitchen and then turned right into his sitting room. Along one side there was a sofa where he slept, and on another side was a corner where his wife slept. There was yet another large room, next to that at the rear of the apartment, where he kept most of his papers.

'I think that the real end came after B. was sentenced. He had already been sentenced to twelve years, but he hadn't yet been sent off to the nether regions of the Soviet Union. Pavel heard from him somehow that B. knew, someone had told him—some official, or some papers he had seen—that he, Pavel, was next on the list. And they were going to get him.

'Of course this came after what we now know to have been a tremendous campaign (in 1972) to wipe out underground literature at all costs. And Pavel for a couple of days really went berserk, he was worried to death. He was almost pathological. He was convinced that any hour they were going to come and nab him and just send him away for the rest of his life. Well . . . not the rest of his life, precisely.

'I asked him: "What do you expect?" And he said: "Fifteen years for treason," flatly. He expected that. He was very, very nervous and he was drinking quite heavily, and I asked his wife: "What do you think?"—and she said—it was very strange, very ironic, she said: "Oh, it'll be a month yet." This was strange, coming from this woman whom he had met in camp and all that; but she figured he had a month's grace.

'This was late at night, it must have been about two o'clock in the morning. And he got out some of his memorabilia from his camp years, and started showing them to me, and of course he's very fond of them. It's a strange sort of thing how people treasure the memories of their meanest years.

'He said: "I will be ready, I will go. I know prison. They have done all they can to me. They can do nothing more to me. If they beat me or kill me you will know, because I have friends."

'That night we were both pretty high on vodka—I remember I'd bought over some canned fish—I said: "Pavel, we can go outside on the staircase and talk about this, or take a walk, or do it whichever way you want: but I'm astounded by the fact that you're not deep in a camp somewhere already. What is your source of safety?" And he said: "I have very many friends in the French and Italian Communist Parties."

'I was absolutely astounded by this, but then I started thinking back to the time when B. was arrested, and Pavel issued a flaming statement, and nothing happened to him. There were rumours in the diplomatic circles that the French and Italians had told the Russians that to arrest Pavel at that time, when they were starting their so-called Peace Offensive, would be a tremendous mistake in terms of their image, of world opinion. Anyway, that was what he said to me his main source of protection was.

'I'm sure there was more to it than that—I'm sure there was a lingering reluctance to arrest someone whose father had been killed and then rehabilitated twenty years later. After a couple of weeks, after he had had his message from B., he calmed down a little bit, and of course everybody was waiting for the other shoe to drop, for *him* to be arrested. They had put, I think, literally hundreds of security agents on this whole business of the underground literature, to try and stamp it out, but they never succeeded. And Pavel became a little more bold in his contacts with me and other foreigners.

'It took a couple of months (before he was arrested). In the meantime, I saw him again and I said: "Well, what's happening? They haven't arrested you yet. You were so worried. Do you think yo were just being overly fearful, or what?" And he said: ' No, no;

but I have prepared myself. I am ready to go." This was at a period when the whole dissent movement was falling apart. A lot of the young people, who would otherwise have been very interested in joining the Movement, were being scared off. Once he had called me and someone else to his place, saying there was something important, and it turned out to be nothing, and he asked us to give him a lift somewhere, and we were very angry. We pulled up in the car, and he said: "Now just wait a moment. I know that you people are very involved with the Jewish question. But you have to remember that *we* stand for something" (i.e. the Democratic Movement as such).

'He was almost pleading. Although in a mood, he was quite sober. And he said: "Remember that we are the last flame." This is not an exact quote, and I shouldn't exaggerate it, but he said: "We are the Russia of the future, we are the ones who are holding the true Russian tradition . . . And just don't forget our existence."

'So we chatted on a while, and he was in a very depressed mood, because he could see what was happening, people were being scared off.

'And people were tailing him all the time. As a matter of fact, a week earlier than that I had gone out for a drive with him on a Saturday morning, and we were followed by two cars for sure, each with several men in them, and possibly a third one. They just followed us all over the place. We chattered and chattered into my tape recorder while we were going. But they were there, and it was really tough.

'The main room in his apartment was very interesting. He had a lot of drawers in it, and he'd take out these memorabilia of camp life—sketches, drawings, some quite beautiful, done in the camp; old photographs, including some of his father, that he had saved for thirty years. And on the wall there was something he was very proud of: a picture in stark black and white, showing four people who had been thrown into the camps, I forget exactly who they were.

'And there was a picture of a Soviet prison camp, with a high barbed wire fence and a watchtower, and in English the slogan: "Come to the Soviet Union for free psychiatric treatment." He liked that so much he kept it on his wall.

'As I recall, there were a great many icons that he kept there, some of which were very valuable, I'm sure—quite ornate, intricate ones. And I always had a strange feeling, sitting there underneath all this old stuff, seeing this man who was aware of the past, but was always concentrating on the future.

'This, I think, was the chief thing about Pavel. He had taken the past, as applied to himself and his family, not only his personal past, but the past of Russia, and he was always looking towards the future, always thinking of changing things, knowing that in actual terms the Movement wasn't terribly important, in the sense that it had no broad base of popular support—but with the feeling that if the flame could be kept burning, there would come a day, there would be a day when what he was doing would contribute to a change of Russia, to change in Russia.

'And this is why I wasn't surprised when a rumour cropped up that he was about to be offered the chance of leaving Russia or getting arrested and being sent off for a zillion years. That dissident girl whose father was a K.G.B. Colonel was given the same choice. He had, a day or two earlier, actually gotten an invitation from some kibbutz in Israel. I heard about this, and I called him up one night, when he was asleep. I said: "Is this true?" And he very drowsily answered: "Yes, it's true." So I asked him: "Where did it come from?" And he said: "The devil knows." And I said: "Pavel, do you want to leave the Soviet Union?" And he replied in deliberately ungrammatical Russian: "I don't wanna go nowhere." Knowing that he was sleepy, I just cut off at that point. A great many other people have left, but he was determined to stand his ground.

'It is important that he, really more than anyone else in Moscow, was the cement for the activist part of the movement. There were other people like Shafarevich and Chalidze, and so on. But the young people especially, who were the only people who could keep the movement alive, were attracted to him simply by his sheer force of personality; and had he not been there . . . .

'If Pavel had not existed, much of the actual work that was done in getting the news of the dissident movement out to the West simply could not have taken place. Because the young kids, who didn't know their own minds, just wouldn't have joined up. But he was the flame that attracted them. And actually his dark side contributed to it, because the others were too correct for a lot of the young people seeking something. He was earthier, he had more immediate *rapport* with people. And as a simple human being he appealed to people. And now that he's gone—and I'm convinced that he *is* gone—the Movement for the time being is going to fall apart.

'Pavel may be gone, but someone else, I think, by the very nature of that society, is bound to spring up who is like him. And for all their current depression about the way things are going, the Movement will have someone, and they shouldn't feel too terribly badly.

'There was a very important thing about his drinking that very few people recognised. Two drinks, two slugs of vodka, and he'd be off. His system simply could not tolerate alcohol. He could have two glasses of vodka and be shot for the night. He'd start getting worried. The point is not only that he drank heavily, which he did, but that it took very little to touch him off, and that's why people sometimes got the wrong impression. He would at first get very jubilant, and then the nastiness would set in.

'I don't think at all that he's headed for a physical or mental crisis. He always talked in terms of going to prison. One night I was giving him the cold shoulder treatment because of all his demands, and he said: "What's the matter?" And I said: "Well, we're kind of tired." And he said: "We're tired too, but we sleep in prison."

'My personal impression is that when he gets to prison he's going to feel, horrible as this sounds, that he's home again. He's going to be reliving his whole childhood and it will increase his determination not to be broken. If they put him away for fifteen years, he's a man of what—fifty?—unless they use drugs on him to break his mind, he'll come out of there just as fierce as ever at sixty-five.

'My Russian wasn't quite good enough to catch the precise meaning, but he said once, talking about prison: "I'll die there." But he said it in a kind of ironic tone, and his wife looked at him and I thought she was going to be shocked and frightened and everything, but she wasn't really worried. I'm still not quite certain how to explain all this.

'The people who got put away and then shied off the Movement when they came out? His attitude to them was typical of him. His mood was one of understanding and of deep regret. He got angry at the young kids who got frightened off. But he always appreciated that people who had been through the mill, and still felt that they could create things—they had paid their dues. In a sense, they were grown, and they had been through it and could make their own decisions. He would regret it very deeply, but that was that. And of course there was also the simple geographical problem that all these people (who served their terms and were released) were being sent to towns way off in the boondocks, and the whole problem of communication was much tougher. As it was, to get a letter across the country out of a camp sometimes would take a couple of weeks, sometimes a couple of months.

'No, his mood was never one of anger when it came to someone who had really been through it. He was constantly trying to recruit new people. I never understood, and I didn't particularly want to know, how he did this. Maybe friends through friends through friends. But at the end he wasn't succeeding very well.

'The group around him was kind of interesting in the sense that some of them were not true dissidents, they were attracted by the notion of doing something exciting. But when it came to any kind of understanding of what the dissident movement meant, in terms of Russian history, they were real dopes. They may have had some practical use in passing on messages or making phone calls and passing information. But some of them were really quite stupid.'

The following is an account, recorded by Pavel himself, of a fairly typical day in his struggle against the K.G.B., until the moment when they finally arrested him, as he knew they would:

'Today was the anniversary of the day Sinyavsky and Daniel were arrested. For the first time, people had come to Pushkin Square in a group to protest against an illegal arrest. So each time in subsequent years, at 6 p.m., people came to commemorate this, simply by standing in silence for a minute with their hats off. People who were, so to speak, still in a position to struggle.

'Last year there were foreign correspondents who came too, as well as the other people. Though actually not too many people come—about 50 or 60 usually. The K.G.B. photograph everyone, including the correspondents. K.G.B. come in different guises— as uniformed militia, as *druzhinniki*, or as plain clothes men.

'Today they asked my friend Vanya "Where is your *Vozhd*" (Great Leader)?' I went with Vanya to the market to get some beer. When we got there, we saw two K.G.B. cars were following us. There was a big queue at the beerstall, so Vanya stayed for beer and I came home on the bus. When I got to the stop and wanted to board the trolleybus, two K.G.B. agents came up and one of them said to me: "Hello, Pavlushka" (This is an insultingly familiar use of the diminutive by a stranger).

'I said: "Hello".

'They said: "Where are your friends today? Where's Viktor G.?" '
(An economist recently returned from exile in Siberia, who shortly afterwards returned there voluntarily, when his wife, in her turn, was exiled. She had done the same for him.)

'They said: "Where's your girl Inessa?" (detained for nearly a year in an Interrogation Prison in 1970). ' "Will you see them today?"

'I said: "Yes, and I'll see you, too."

' "No, you don't need to see us," they said.

'Today was the anniversary of my late mother's birthday, so I went with my wife to the cemetery. That was about 4 p.m. The same K.G.B. cars. It was dark already. I thought they would come in the cemetery after us, but they just surrounded it and didn't go anywhere. So we stood by the grave and paid our respects to my mother and went back. We had to be at the Square by 6 p.m.

'Vanya and some other friends had stayed at our place, and came out after us and went to Pushkin Square. We got into a taxi, and it turned out that we were too early. My daughter said: "Let's go straight to the Square, sit for a while and then show ourselves."

'But you have to be there exactly on time.' (Otherwise the demonstration will be broken up before it takes place.)

'So we're off, and I say to the driver: "Pushkin Street, opposite the *Dom Soyuzov*" ' (an official building). 'As we drive around towards the *Detsky Mir*, two K.G.B. cars overtake us and tell us to pull over. The taxi driver was scared.'

(The *Detsky Mir*, or 'Children's World', is the biggest children's clothing shop in Moscow and is directly opposite the Lubyanka, K.G.B. Headquarters for the Moscow Region, on the square named after Dzerzhinsky, founder of the Soviet Secret Police. So, with grotesque irony, the K.G.B. Lubyanka building is sometimes nicknamed *Detsky Mir*.)

'The K.G.B. men opened the door and a man in plain clothes said: "Pavel Pa'lich, I hope you're not going anywhere today." I said: "I'm going to see some friends just now, and at 8 p.m. I'm going to the crematorium (my cousin had died)—nowhere else."

'So we drove off to Pushkin Street, went up and saw some friends, had a snack, went to the toilet, and at 5.40 p.m. my wife and daughter just happened to find a taxi. So we got into this other taxi and went to the Square. We paid him off, and he turned to go. As we got out, some men in plain clothes jumped us and started dragging us into a car.' (Other demonstrators were also being forcibly detained at that moment.) 'They took us off and we didn't know where they were taking us.

'I began to play up a bit. I bashed the driver, who had seized me by the arms, and I said: "What are you doing?" They didn't answer. They had twisted my arms when they pushed me into the car. The driver was going to answer, but his chief hushed him up.

'We saw they were taking us to the police station where we live, but they didn't know the way. I started giving them directions. My daughter pulled me by the arm and said: "Dad, who are you talking to? Do you think you're a tour guide or something?" I was only showing them the way because they were lost.

'So we got there, but I didn't know what had happened to my wife. They took us to the same police station as they did on the day of Khrushchev's funeral.

'Straight away, the militia men on duty sent my daughter one way, and me the other. My daughter said: "I'm not going anywhere else just now, even if you kill me." So they took us to a room, and she stayed in the corridor and I was taken inside. There was a plain clothes man in there. I said: "Look here, you know we're fed up fighting with you all the time." He said: "Let's talk man to man. Why did you have to go (to the Square) today?" '

Then there was a long discussion about why Pavel was what he was, and why he should 'give it all up'. (The K.G.B. were always advising him to 'give it all up'. Now they have just taken the simpler course of depriving him of the opportunity to continue.)

Pavel went on: 'My daughter, who was sitting in the corridor, heard two of the other K.G.B. talking. The one I had hit said: "I'll take him to court." But his Chief said: "Be quiet, he's been through a lot."

'The one who was talking to me also says: "I understand, you've been through a lot. You were in prison. But you've got to realise that everything's marvellous now."

'We were supposed to go back to the cemetery at 8 p.m. But at 7.02 they took us home in an official car, and we stayed at home.'

The Listeners

IN THE United States and other parts of the Western world, the development of advanced electronic bugging methods has caused serious public concern. In the Soviet Union, the technology of the bugging process has long been familiar to the police, and is probably as patchily developed as are most sectors of Soviet industry. It is the psychology of the process which is particularly important in Russia, whereas its technology still remains a subject of many myths and assumptions.

The most popularly held idea in Moscow is that the telephone, whether on or off its receiver rest, is used as a bugging device: either directly, to monitor phone calls, or indirectly, when the receiver is replaced, to listen in to conversations in the room. Whether this is technically feasible is a matter for an expert. But there are many occasions during conversations in Moscow flats when someone will shy off a particular topic by gesturing towards the inert telephone; it is also thought that to jam the dial halfway round its travel, with a pencil or other such object, blocks the entire apparatus as a bugging device.

Clearly the idea of bugging through telephones with replaced receivers would have great advantages from the point of view of the police. It would mean that any telephone subscriber could be bugged at a moment's notice without installing special equipment in his home, or in some adjoining premises. It also means that the bugging device can be innocently installed, indeed solicited, by the future victim, and its maintenance paid for by him.

It is only natural that foreigners, for their part, should assume their living quarters to be bugged. Embassies have special rooms with noise-making devices which make it possible to conduct a conversation securely, if not very conveniently. Foreigners and Soviet dissidents alike communicate particularly sensitive information to each other by writing it down—either on slips of paper which are then destroyed, or on eraser pads, which cannot be bought in the shops and have to be specially brought in from abroad. They are highly prized possessions among dissidents, for there is a paper shortage, and safe disposal of much paper can present a problem.

Other forms of communication in flats are sign-language and private idioms or expressions comprehensible only to those using them. 'You know who' and 'our friend' are among the most frequently used phrases in such conversations, and special gestures are evolved to indicate particular people. For instance, a pinching motion at the chin would suggest a beard, which would probably be enough to make it clear who was meant.

Some gestures are widely known: for instance, crossed hands with spread fingers means bars, hence 'imprisonment'. Others may be evolved for use among as few as two people: one such was a double flick of the left shoulder with the right hand, indicating epaulettes, and thus suggesting that the person referred to was a member of an intelligence service, either Eastern or Western.

It is clearly impossible for the authorities to install bugging devices in every room of the home of every suspect person. For one thing, there are too many potential suspects. For another, it would require too many workmen in the know, and would become too widely talked of. In addition, microphones in walls may only have a certain lifespan, after which it may be difficult to repair them discreetly. One Western diplomat found a grubby hand-print high on the wall of one of the rooms in his flat, for which there could be no rational explanation other than the secret repair of a bugging device during his absence. The Soviet maid seemed embarrassed when asked about it.

There is little point in going around trying to locate microphones in walls, and tear them out, although the Japanese Embassy did disclose that it had found some. Removal or destruction of a microphone would merely encourage the authorities to install another one somewhere else, more cleverly concealed, or use long-distance bugging techniques.

An American correspondent related that he had once been complaining in his flat about the fact that he believed an electric point in the wall concealed a bugging device. A day or so later, he came home to find the fitting hanging from the wall, with no microphone behind it, and a stranger's screwdriver lying beside it. Was this a K.G.B. joke?

Ample circumstantial evidence confirms that telephone conversations are monitored and acted on. When a person's phone is being given particular attention by the police, the quality of the line often deteriorates sharply, and there is sometimes a regular bleeping sound. The police sometimes send agents to break up meetings which they could not have learnt of except by listening in to the telephones. And anyway, it is such an obvious thing to do that it would be lunacy to assume that it is not done in a totalitarian state.

A person who believes his phone calls are being watched with particular attention will call his friends from public call boxes. However, this is a laborious process, because of the chronic shortage of two-kopeck pieces needed for calls, and the large number of call boxes which are vandalised by petty criminals and rendered useless.

Electronic monitoring is not, of course, the only form of surveillance. Foreigners can employ Soviet maids, interpreters, secretaries and drivers only through U.P.D.K., the official organisation which is a by-word to many Russians as an arm of the K.G.B. These employees have to attend regular political meetings, and are expected to report without fail on any suspicious activity on the part of their employer. They also denounce each other for such petty misdemeanours as begging foreign currency from their employers and spending it in the special shops. This mutual suspicion is one reason why a housemaid frequently may dislike, or seem to be afraid of, an interpreter or driver.

It is, in fact, a crime not to denounce a person observed doing something illegal or making a politically 'undesirable' statement. The K.G.B. even use this as a means of 'provocation' to test people out, or to frighten them. For instance, two Russians may conduct an 'anti-Soviet' conversation in the presence of a third, who simply wants to go away and forget about it all. The next thing he knows, he is denounced by one of the parties to the conversation, for not having reported it!

Since Soviet employees may spend every weekday in the foreigner's office or home, answering the telephone when he or she is out, and able to look at any papers or other objects not specially locked up, there is little need for them to be too obvious about their surveillance. It is useless for a Western resident to try and combat this by bringing in special strong boxes or locks for drawers in his flat—this would merely attract attention and invite the K.G.B. to have a closer look when the occupant was away for a few days. (In the nature of the posting, foreigners frequently have to leave their Moscow homes unattended.) One policy, though not an infallible one, is to conceal sensitive papers on the "needle and haystack" principle—for instance in the sleeves of gramophone records. But there is a danger that a document may then be forgotten about entirely, or one may forget precisely which record sleeve it was left in, and it may turn up at the wrong moment. All such systems are subject to constant human error and carelessness.

So the best policy for a foreigner involved with Russian dissidents, and wishing to protect them as much as possible, is to destroy their written materials immediately after use. This may not be necessary for the sake of the content, if it is intended for publication in the West. But it may be wise to prevent the K.G.B. from obtaining copies of typescripts or handwriting which would enable them accurately to identify individual people or typewriters seized in searches at the homes of dissidents. This is a more important point than it may seem, for the K.G.B. spent the first half of 1972 in an all-out campaign to track down and arrest the people responsible for editing and reproducing underground material.

On the other hand, if it is clear that the K.G.B. are aware of the nature of a foreigner's contact with a Russian, and are merely allowing it to continue in the interests of seeing how far it will go, there is little point in concealing written materials, except in the most elementary fashion so as not to invite too much special attention all at once.

From the psychological point of view, close surveillance and bugging are both counter-productive and helpful for the police. On the one hand, the authorities have a perfectly legitimate interest in knowing whether suspects—Russian or foreign—are engaged in genuine espionage and subversion, or merely in exchange of information not forbidden by the Soviet Constitution or Criminal Code (though often it is decided to interpret certain Articles distortedly in order to prosecute the Soviet citizens involved).

The effectiveness of bugging is limited by the widespread awareness of its existence. One may not be able to guarantee that a conversation cannot be overheard (as in Orwell's '1984', where there may be a microphone in the middle of a field), but one can certainly make things very difficult for the eavesdroppers.

However, the psychology of bugging is well developed. Its most important characteristic is the victim's inability to discover whether and when and where he is being bugged and is not being bugged. The intangibility of the process makes people careless. A person who lives naked in a glass box soon stops worrying about decency. And a person who lives constantly with bugging can save himself the inconvenience of evading it, by simply persuading himself that he is not telling the eavesdroppers anything important, or anything which they do not know already. He may even develop a confession psychosis, which makes it a relief for him to give away things which he knows would be better kept to himself.

On the other hand, the knowledge of the ever-present surveillance, or at least the constant possibility of it, must make espionage, at all levels, ten times more difficult for the Western spy in Moscow, by comparison with the opportunities available to his Soviet counterparts in the relatively open Western societies. Indeed, the K.G.B. foreign intelligence section seems embarrassed by the sheer amount of information lying around at its disposal in Western countries. They have to send in huge teams of agents simply to cope with the flow, and this is what led to the large-scale expulsions of Soviet officials from London in 1971. So to some extent, correspondents and other people not working for intelligence services may be *excessively* suspicious about the amount of surveillance to which they are exposed in Moscow. Once the K.G.B. has established to its own satisfaction that a foreigner is not involved in truly criminal activities such as espionage, speculation on a large scale, or subversion, it is liable to relax a little and merely play a vague watching role over further contacts with Soviet citizens. Thus, the more open a correspondent can be about his work in Moscow, the better, as long as it does not infringe published laws.

However, the foreigner usually has the easy way out, of leaving the country when things get too hot. So it is only fair to respect the wishes of his Russian acquaintances about the manner in which the relationship should be conducted, for it is they who must "carry the can" in the end. Their views differ widely, and sometimes individuals change their views or are simply not consistent in their behaviour. They are only human after all.

One person would say: 'These get-togethers in flats with lots of drinking and chattering are no good. It is necessary to maintain some *konspirativnost* (secrecy)'. Another would say: 'Who cares? They know I pass on information anyway. Let them do their worst.' Another view: 'Going to foreigners' flats is inviting provocations (frame-ups) by the K.G.B.'. Still another person would disagree: 'Why should we not visit a foreigner's flat, if it is not forbidden by the law?' The whole question is confused and full of inconsistencies, for all those concerned.

In other words, the Western observer of Soviet society has to float in its water, drifting where his acquaintances take him, and shying off only when someone seems to be becoming too reckless or indiscreet, or when his purpose becomes clearly irrelevant to the foreigner's own functions. For instance dissidents, like any other Russians, may try to persuade foreigners to buy them things abroad or at Foreign Currency Stores. This is an infringement of the existing rules on 'speculation' as they are generally understood, if Roubles change hands. Russians are often very generous to each other, and if they have a foreigner as a friend, and he has easy access to things they badly need, they see nothing strange in asking for them. The acid test is whether they are prepared to take 'no' for an answer. It is only those who persist, against a foreigner's reluctance, who have to be shied clear of.

The feeling of living completely exposed to surveillance is more than some foreigners can bear, presuming that even the most intimate parts of their private lives at home can be overheard by some policeman at the other end of a bugging device. Such people simply cannot 'take' Moscow, and usually leave after about a year, for the most understandable reasons. Most people put the overall question of bugging out of their minds, as far as possible, and settle surprisingly quickly into a routine of platitudes, sign language, discretion in telephone calls and letter-writing, serious conversations during walks in the country or on city streets, and the use of Diplomatic Bags, as far as the mood or practice in a given Embassy permits. Some Embassies are freer than others about the use of their Bag for non-diplomatic purposes, and it is generally assumed that the world champions in this practice are the Soviet, Bulgarian and other East European Embassies in foreign countries. The whole question of Western Embassies observing the rules governing use of the Bag is somewhat farcical when one takes this into account.

Everybody, at some stage or other, has occasion to wonder just what sort of a scene it is at the places where electronic bugging devices are monitored. In hotels, a special room, or even a floor, is believed to be given over to this work. But what about the K.G.B. linguists who have to listen in, day and night, to the doings in the flats of particularly 'suspicious' foreign residents?

An imagined scene: A long room like a telephone exchange, lit by naked bulbs hanging from the ceiling. Ashtrays and half-empty tea glasses everywhere. Men in shirtsleeves, with headphones on, or simply watching the monitor light of a tape recorder, yawning, ready to resume listening as soon as the occupants come home or wake up. Occasional phone calls, relayed from militia posts at the entrance to foreigner's compounds: 'So and so's just come back. He seems to be quarrelling with his wife.' Or: 'X has just brought in two Soviet citizens in his car.'

Time for change of shift. An English-speaking monitor arrives with his packet of sandwiches for the early morning shift. His colleague stretches and removes the headphones.

'Zdravstvui, Sash'. *Anything happening?*'

'Ni-che-vo. *(Absolutely nothing). They came home late from a party, and they weren't speaking to each other for a while. Then he had another drink, and she came and joined him and they made it up and launched into one of their usual tirades about us. There was a tit-bit about the Ruritanian Ambassador's wife being slightly cracked and trying to get off with a student from her country at the University. Nothing much to it, I'd say. Then they went to bed and made love, and I can tell you their style is starting to bore me. Then he got up again and had another drink and typed a bit, and came to bed and snored a lot. Look, you can see the snoring now on the monitor light. They won't be awake till his alarm goes about 9.00. I wish you luck. But they're being very careful, and obviously using a lot of sign language. He went out yesterday evening before the party, and seems to have met a Soviet traitor somewhere for a short while, but Borya knows more about that, because he was on that shift. I think we could give this one a rest for a while, personally. Concentrate on some of his Soviet friends. But the chief'll have to decide. Anyway, I'm off. Best of luck to you. What's the weather like?*'

'*Minus eighteen. Bit of a wind, too. You'd better get going, old son'.*

'Nu, poka (*'bye, then).*'

'Bud' zdorov (*keep fit).*'

People often ask what sort of 'provocations' the K.G.B. are capable of mounting against foreigners. Here are two examples drawn from life.

Foreigner A, who could be a Western businessman or correspondent, is reading a three-day-old copy of a newspaper from home in his flat one day, when he receives a telephone call from someone who refuses to give his name, but asks to meet him to discuss 'something important'. Foreigner A, being cautious, refuses a street-corner rendezvous, and tells the caller to brave the police guard and come to his office. The caller agrees and fixes a time.

At the appointed time, a nervous and shifty looking man, badly shaven and smelling of cheap spirit, arrives at the front door. He is already suspect, because he has successfully run the gauntlet of the guard at the gate. He takes off his shoes and tip-toes in, gesturing that the radio should be turned on, so that the conversation can be obscured by background noise. Foreigner A declines, feeling that he should not try to conceal anything that transpires in a first conversation with such a stranger. The visitor consents to talk normally.

'My name is Weill. I have information for you,' he says, after some hedging and aimless chit-chat. He pushes across a technical drawing in blue pencil, which looks harmless enough, but could be anything. Foreigner A pushes it back. 'I have no interest in such material,' he says. 'I do not even understand what it is about.'

The visitor tries another tack: 'I have transcripts of some conversations on the telephones of the Japanese Embassy.' More suspect still. Foreigner A, if he has any sense, refuses to have anything to do with such material. But the visitor is persuasive and loquacious, and shows signs of being hard to get rid of. 'Let me give you my telephone number', he says, 'in case you decide to contact me.' In order to be rid of the fellow, Foreigner A consents to take the number. 'Call me,' says the visitor, 'on such and such a day, between 7.45 and 8.00 p.m., at this number.' Foreigner A says he will do so if he feels the need.

The visitor is eventually persuaded to leave, and the door is closed firmly behind him. Foreigner A, suspecting something fishy, looks at the telephone number doubtfully. Then he takes it into the kitchen, burns it with a match, and washes the ash down the sink.

A week or so later, Foreigner A is lying in on a Sunday morning when there is a ring at the doorbell of the flat. He thinks the post has come early. But when he opens the door, there is a man in a duffle coat and motoring cap, a complete stranger, poised with a pencil and eraser pad. He writes: 'I am an assistant military attaché at your Embassy. I must talk to you urgently. I shall be walking with my family today in such and such a park, at such and such a spot. Can you meet me at 3 p.m.?'

Foreigner A, frightened and upset, nods. He spends the rest of the morning in a state of nerves, uncertain what is happening, and afraid that he may be about to be warned of some frightful plot to frame him up. He is unable to eat his lunch, and arrives at the rendezvous early, looking around him anxiously. At 3 sharp, he spots the man from the Embassy. They walk off among the trees.

'We have had a telephone call from a person named Weill,' says the man from the Embassy. 'He says he has information for us. He asks us to call him at a certain time, and says you have the telephone number. We don't like to involve you in such things, but it is our job and we have no alternative but to check all lines of enquiry.'

Foreigner A says: 'I no longer have the number.' And suddenly it dawns on him that only the act of burning the number and forgetting it has saved him from the Soviet frame-up. Supposing he had the number still in his pocket. Asked by a member of his own Embassy, his first, trusting gesture might have been to hand it over unthinkingly. The Embassy, following its own line of duty, would have made the call, 'just to check'. The K.G.B. would have ensured that this was a once-only telephone number, and therefore the mere fact of the Embassy call to it would prove that Foreigner A had acted as a go-between for a spurious 'Soviet traitor' and a foreign intelligence service. All it might need after that would be a visit from a couple of men in raincoats, and a 'promise' that the whole indiscretion would be overlooked if Foreigner A supplied them with one small piece of information to which he had access through his own Embassy or other channels.

Provocation No. 2 goes as follows: Foreigner B, a student, has made a few Soviet friends, whom he likes and trusts. One night he goes with them to a restaurant. Some strangers come and sit at a nearby table, and seem interested in Foreigner B—a natural reaction on the part of many perfectly innocuous Russians. One of them gets up, seemingly overcoming his shyness, comes over, and asks: 'Where are you from?' Foreigner B tells him, and an amicable if platitudinous conversation ensues. The stranger asks him to take a glass of vodka, and it seems rude to refuse. He pours two vodkas out of the same bottle from his own table.

The next thing Foreigner B knows is when he wakes up, fourteen hours later, in a strange bed, completely naked, with his clothes folded neatly beside him. One of his Soviet friends comes in, evidently worried but relieved to see him regain consciousness. 'I don't know what happened to you last night,' he says. 'You suddenly passed out. We sort of humped you out of the restaurant, making out you were just drunk, and when we got you onto the street and sitting on a bench, an ambulance was already arriving to pick you up. We somehow got you into a passing taxi and brought you here before they got you into the ambulance. We put you to bed.'

Foreigner B may still trust his Soviet friends and believe that they have saved him from a frame-up. But for the rest of his life he may have the lingering suspicion, despite himself, that they too were 'in on the act'. In that case, he does not know how many photographs the K.G.B. now have of him, naked, unconscious but seemingly enraptured, in bed with an anonymous female or male. Such photographs can be produced at any time for the next decade or two when he is at a sensitive stage of his career or his marriage, and when he has access to information of interest to the K.G.B. Tired Embassy officials admit in their franker moments that such things happen frequently to their nationals in the Soviet Union. But they hush them up as a matter of principle, because that is what the victim usually prefers. It is a bad policy, like negotiating with political kidnappers—expedient at the time, but merely perpetuating the risk of further such attempts.

An intelligence service, like any industry or ministry, only has finite resources in terms of personnel, money, time and equipment. Constant decisions have to be made about how to allocate these resources, or how to obtain more from the national policy makers. Therefore even the K.G.B. cannot collect every scrap of potentially useful information on everyone in Moscow, let alone file it coherently and retrieve it when it is relevant.

Consider the difficulties involved in surveying a single foreigner. His mail has to be carefully opened, using methods which will not leave obvious traces. Then it has to be read (often overcoming difficult handwriting, and expressions whose meaning is known only to the persons corresponding). People he writes to in a dozen countries may have to be checked up on, to make sure they are not fronts using codes. Soviet employees, if he has any, have to be regularly briefed, disciplined, insured, pensioned off, and generally kept in working order, so that a huge personnel department is required merely to cope with foreigners' drivers, interpreters and so on, and another such department to cope with *it*. If the foreigner is under close surveillance, every one of his telephone and Telex calls, within Moscow and to foreign countries, must be recorded, examined and weighed for possible hidden meanings. Still more laborious, his flat has to be bugged in several rooms at once; his comings and goings have to be surveyed. If he is to be tailed for purposes of intimidation, it may require two cars and between six and ten men, possibly more. If he is to be tailed discreetly, to find out what he is up to, another few men will have to be put onto him. Then his Soviet acquaintances, if he has any, will have to be checked up on. The most vulnerable can be interrogated, formally or informally, intimidated or infiltrated, and then all the information about them and their activities has to be added to the mounting pile. Everything has to be collated, and in the end someone has to take the responsibility of deciding what, if anything, ought to be done about the person under surveillance.

The Soviet administrative system—which can hardly fail to be reflected in the K.G.B.—usually tends towards one of two extremes: massive concentration of resources on a single project, liable to yield maximum results or prestige; or inefficient squandering of resources on bureaucratic procedures, in which no one is anxious to take the responsibility for any single decision.

A Soviet dissident hazarded the guess that, to judge by its current behaviour, the K.G.B. has become ultra-cautious, at least in Moscow itself, about making decisions which may give the Party Leadership grounds to accuse it of being too crude, ignoring public opinion or too obviously infringing Soviet laws. The F.B.I. and C.I.A. have had similar problems. Alternatively, the professional K.G.B. agents may be 'working to rule' under their present boss, Andropov, who is a Party functionary and not a career policeman.

There is the feeling of an organization not pulling its weight somewhere. There were so many things which the K.G.B. could have done to check the flow of information from dissident sources to the West in the period 1968–72, and which it did not do, that one is forced to the conclusion that this was either a deliberate matter of policy, or a case of K.G.B. sulks. In the latter case, the security police may simply have required detailed, written instructions from the Party Central Committee or the Politburo, even on relatively trivial matters, such as how to deal with an individual dissident or foreign contact. Such an attitude could have resulted from Party rebukes about bad publicity caused in the international press by rough, old-fashioned police methods. It would explain why certain dissidents were allowed to do the most damage to the image of the Soviet system in the eyes of the world *before* they were arrested and put away, let alone the damage resulting from their 'trials', once they had already become known of.

There is also the possibility that the K.G.B. was simply following a policy line worked out in conjunction with advanced Party theorists, who believed in having some dissidents around to improve the Soviet Union's image as an open society, and keep check on others.

A further explanation of the combined inefficacy and overkill of K.G.B. tactics is that this is an organisation which has simply failed to move with the times in its methods of internal control. Its brightest people—for instance, its best linguists—are probably moved quickly on to the foreign espionage side. The classic methods of social control by the Soviet secret police are mass terror, secrecy and lawlessness, and the modern K.G.B. is able to play on lingering fears from an earlier period. But Khrushchev at least established a tradition whereby such methods should be applied much more sparingly than under Stalin, and his successors have tried to adhere to it to a large extent, if only in the interests of self-preservation. Left with mainly traditional methods which have gone out of fashion, the domestic K.G.B. may not even be at liberty to modernise itself efficiently: this would mean telling the Party that many more resources were needed, because things were getting out of hand politically—a confession of failure, and a doctrinally unacceptable argument which could be fatal to the career of the person who put it forward. (In the same way, Soviet criminologists are not allowed to state openly that there is an increase of crime in Soviet society, as this is a point emphatically denied by Soviet official dogma. Thus, when calling for more advanced methods of crime prognosis, they are not even permitted to state in their learned journals why this should be necessary.)

Denied its former right to carry out mass murder and deportation, the K.G.B. has to resort increasingly to its other classic tactic, secrecy. All its doings are swathed in enigma. The veil is only lifted from time to time when a Soviet dissident has something like a normal conversation with his K.G.B. interrogators (they are human, too), and reports it. But this mania for secrecy—which may lead K.G.B. officers to pretend fatuously that they are members of the Criminal Investigation Division, when making a political arrest—is a source of vulnerability.

Similarly, the desire to keep a superficial appearance of legality

leads the K.G.B. into monstrously bureaucratic procedures and
pretences. The sheer labour which goes into preparing the protocol
for a single house-search is considerable. The weight of the Soviet
bureaucracy may bear down heavily on the individual, but it can
also be brought to bear on the bureaucracy itself, if the individual
is clever and well informed enough to use it, judo-like, against
itself. Of course, numbers and force will win for the time being.
The years 1970–72 saw some of the boldest dissidents subdued.
As a K.G.B. man was reported to have told one of them in a moment
of frankness: 'Some of you we will bend, some we will break, and
others we will expel.'

The great problem is that dissidence in Soviet society is a
phenomenon with deep roots, even if the present activists may not
make up more than a tiny percentage of the population. So mere
suppression does not solve it, only delays the day when it will
have to be faced up to. In this sense, the K.G.B. is the instrument
of a contradictory policy, and can only be expected to behave in a
contradictory fashion. The overkill tactics sporadically used against
contacts between Jews and foreigners in 1971, and against the
Democratic Movement in 1972, may be effective in the short run.
But for every dissident put away on fabricated or loosely formulated
charges, there are several people who may be inclined towards
dissidence out of disgust at watching the process.

The person who will be called Ilya Gorbachov in a later chapter
put it like this: 'The Soviet intelligentsia, one might say, are
ranged in seventeen ranks. In the front rank are those who expose
themselves by openly calling for more freedom. In the second
rank are those who more or less actively support them, but do not
expose themselves so much. In the third, fourth and other ranks
are people who sympathise with them in varying degrees, or not
at all. Now when the first rank is put away, the likelihood is that the
second rank will step forward to take its place.

'Those first people who signed protests and stood out against
the system in the late nineteen sixties—like Pavel Litvinov, for
instance—those were real heroes. In the West you have freedom
of expression, so you may not understand this. But for a person
brought up in this sort of society, with all the weight of propaganda
and official pressure on top of him, to break through it all and still
keep an independent spirit, needs a mind baked as hard as diamonds
by that million-ton pressure.

'At the centre of Russia's political life, there is such an extreme electrical tension that most people cannot bear to come close to it. Only those of the strongest will can stand the tension at the heart of things in this country.

'Dissidents are like fish in a pond, with the K.G.B. watching them from the bank. As long as the watcher can see their positions, he is satisfied. Down there, somewhere, he sees Solzhenitsyn, and some other fish have gathered around him. Over there, he sees someone else. But sometimes the fish are beginning to jump a little, and then he must reach out and knock them on the head so that they go back under the water again.'

The future of the K.G.B. depends on the future of Soviet society as a whole. The most recent experience suggests that it is not an organisation with the resources or even the real will to plug all the loopholes of discontent and protest. So as Soviet leaders seek closer ties with the West, in order to modernise their economy and insure themselves against long-term enmity with China, they will have to learn to live with a certain level of chronic protest. Whether they accept this, and whether the protest eventually swells strong enough to change the system; or whether they merely continue knocking it on the head through the K.G.B.'s frightening but inefficient methods, is one of the big questions which govern the future of the Soviet Union and its allied states.

On ledges halfway up the outer walls of the K.G.B. Lubyanka building, television cameras are installed to watch the street at any moment of the day. There is no attempt to conceal them. They are said to be monitored with particular thoroughness when Chairman Andropov arrives for work, and when he leaves the office, in case of an assassination attempt.

The cameras are symbolic of an attitude maintained by the political leaders in the Central Committee building close by. Enclosed in their well-guarded offices, they view the world through special mental cameras, selectively and suspiciously. Unfortunately, the cameras are one-way devices, and the world can learn little by peering into their lenses.

The Closed Circle

MANY people have remarked on the similarity between the Soviet system of ideas—claimed in Russia to be the only true form of Marxism—and the systems worked out by various schools of Christian theology, from Jesuits to Fundamentalists, or even the mature stages of Confucianism and Buddhism. All these systems have one thing in common: they claim to provide an answer to every question. What is unanswerable in their terms, they ignore or set aside as irrelevant.

The Soviet Union has an elaborate system of public relations, which enables its rulers to represent themselves as liberal and broad-minded when this is desirable for foreign consumption. But the domestic propaganda is quite unequivocal in rejecting liberal attitudes (the very word 'liberal' is derogatory) and in insisting that there can be only one true answer to any problem or question. The Soviet citizen is supposed to live within a completely closed circle of ideas. To try and step outside it can lead to rebuke, ostracism, demotion and even imprisonment. The political parallel with Confucianist China or past Christian theocracies should be clear.

The Soviet citizen is not only denied the right to hold a view opposite to that of the leaders (unless he keeps it strictly to himself); he is deprived of the prerogative to doubt, or even to suggest the possibility of several alternative and equally valid answers to problematical issues. This applies in every social sphere: politics, foreign affairs, religion, morals, economic development.

Under Stalin, it was even applied to science, particularly biology, but the disastrous practical consequences of dogmatism in research led his successors to allow scientists a greater measure of intellectual liberty within their own field. Such liberty is denied to scholars in the humanitarian disciplines, because they are more closely related to politics, and this helps to explain why independent political thinking is more often found nowadays among natural scientists than among historians and philosophers in the Soviet Union, though there are exceptions. Free thought can barely survive in the atmosphere of a Soviet humanitarian faculty: but it is a sheer necessity for the men who keep Soviet science abreast of the most up-to-date world developments, and sometimes ahead of them.

Not only have most philosophers in the West come to reject closed systems of ideas, but many have even cast doubt on the adequacy of human language to express anything but an approximation of truth. Soviet philosophy points to these mounting doubts and qualifications as a symptom of the decadence of Western thought, compared with the allegedly robust and comprehensive 'science' of Marxism-Leninism. Russian scholars are supposed to study Western philosophy as a biologist examines a microbe; with a detached interest, or possibly with the aim of rendering it harmless. There is not the slightest suggestion that Soviet social thought has anything to learn from the West or from anywhere else, for it is regarded as perfect already in principle, and requiring further research only to flesh out its details and adapt it to man's changing economic and technological circumstances.

The biggest concession Soviet thought makes to reality is its recognition that the path of world revolution is tortuous, and that human society may go through stages only dimly foreseen by Marx, before the final revolution which will bring the spanner-wielding industrial proletariat to power in all countries of the globe. (Such an event, by the way, has yet to take place in the Soviet Union or in any other country.)

The use of a closed system of ideas to explain every phenomenon, or to prevent discussion of the inexplicable, excludes direct communication between the rulers and the ruled, because it excludes the desirability of impromptu questions to which no answer has been prepared in advance. It is exactly this which explains the stultifying nature of Soviet 'press conferences', at which questions are expected to be submitted in writing, so that the most awkward can be sifted out and ignored. Only real professionals like Premier Kosygin, and Culture Minister Furtseva are capable of fielding questions off-the-cuff from foreign journalists, and retaining some measure of authority or credibility in the process. Khrushchev fancied himself a master at this art, but often his impromptu answers humiliated his colleagues by their frankness or flippancy. This was almost certainly one reason why he was removed, and his system of free-and-easy contacts with Soviet citizens and foreigners alike was abolished by his successors, who live completely secluded existences.

Another feature of closed ideological systems is that they need a special caste of people whose task is to interpret them to the masses, and work out their application to unforeseen phenomena. In Confucian China, these were the scholar-administrators, who enriched the country's literature while they attended (somewhat amateurishly) to its economy. In the Christian Church, generation upon generation of theologians has striven to reconcile dogma with reality, to such an extent that Christianity has ceased to be a closed ideological system. In the Soviet Union, it is the Party propagandists who fulfil the role of interpreters.

Propaganda is two things: a means of communication, and a means of persuasion. It can be used to communicate information and ideas through public media to only a small group of initiates or to the entire population at once, almost overnight. It is also used to make sure that there is no deviation from the officially sanctioned concepts, until the leaders themselves consider it necessary.

It is hard to convey to most people, who have not read Soviet newspapers, the fantastic lengths to which they go to maintain the closed circle of ideas. By comparison with *Pravda* or *Sovietskaya Rossiya*, the British Communist *Morning Star* is a lively little sheet with an attractiveness of presentation and a freedom of commentary impossible in Russia. The same applies to other Western Communist papers, and also, in varying degrees, to the press of East Europe, which in some cases is so much freer in tone than the Soviet press that the Russians use it to float contentious or advanced ideas. (This has been especially the case with discussion of China in the East European press. And in August 1972 the Russians used the Hungarian press to reveal the extent of their displeasure with the Egyptians for expelling Soviet military advisers.)

Soviet propaganda is, in fact, struggling against severe disadvantages in its attempt to fit every phenomenon to its own system of ideas. The ease of communications in the modern world, and the bewildering variety of new political attitudes at the personal and national levels, make it a very creaky process. This is why the Soviet news media are usually hours or days behind their Western counterparts in reporting important events, sometimes even at home as well as abroad, or may ignore them completely. It is also the reason why *Pravda* is almost letter-perfect in typography throughout an entire year of publication: the newspaper goes to press so early, and is so thoroughly scrutinised for political content, that typographical errors are caught like salmon in sardine-nets. (Human error, however, still cannot be excluded, as when *Pravda* reported a Soviet message of solidarity sent to the General Secretary of the British Mineworkers' Union, Mr Euston Road—actually the union's London address.)

A typical issue of *Pravda* consists of six and sometimes only four pages of print—minute when compared with a major Western daily newspaper, even if allowance is made for advertising. This small size makes it easier to check that all the printed facts and ideas conform to the model. None the less, *Pravda*'s complete staff is said to number about 700. Other daily newspapers except *Izvestia*, the organ of the Council of Ministers, have to be content with a daily quota of four pages, because of the national shortage of newsprint. They are expanded only for special issues, which carry full or partial texts of speeches considered particularly important.

Pravda's front page is seldom its most interesting. There is invariably a long editorial, usually on domestic policy, of an optimistic and orthodox tone, with such stereotyped headings as: 'The Duty of a Communist', or 'Harvest Toils'. Relatively seldom will *Pravda* devote a front-page editorial to foreign affairs, unless it be a matter of total orthodoxy, e.g.: 'Get Out of Indochina', 'Europe's Hopes', or 'Soviet-Arab Friendship'.

Much of the rest of the page will be given over to 'up-beat' economic news, such as the completion of a new hydro-electric power plant, or the start of work on a blast furnace somewhere. The ordinary Soviet citizen is supposed to take an informed interest in these matters, although in the Western press they are regarded as matters for businessmen or specialists, and are consigned to special sections of the paper, or special papers.

This is the cause of much misunderstanding and ill-will between Soviet and Western journalists, although the more sophisticated Soviet journalists, who have travelled abroad, understand the situation perfectly well. No newspaper in the West could ever acquire a substantial readership by covering its news pages with stilted and optimistic progress reports on industrial construction projects, either in their own countries or in the Soviet Union. Yet the Soviet press is perpetually complaining that Western 'propaganda' overlooks Russia's achievements in industrial development, and concentrates on the failings. In fact, this is exactly the way Western newspapers cover their own countries: economic stories usually only make news when there is a crisis or major difficulty. Otherwise the economy is merely expected to do its job by feeding and clothing people, and providing them with cars or radio sets or foreign currency.

At the same time, Western observers in Moscow can retain their intellectual self-respect only through an attitude of extreme scepticism about Soviet official claims, since important failings are discussed so rarely and so obliquely in the Soviet press. This has led to an '*odnako* syndrome'—*odnako* is the Russian word for 'however'. The most informative content of a Soviet newspaper article frequently comes towards the end of an otherwise highly optimistic passage, in a paragraph or two preceded by the word *odnako*. So it is easy to get into the habit of skimming through the platitudes in a Soviet article, up to the point where a glimmer of frankness or new information is apparent.

Pravda also tends to pad its front pages with seemingly meaningless exchanges of congratulatory messages on the occasion of national holidays, anniversaries, and so on, with friendly or moderately friendly states. The sending of a Soviet message of congratulations will almost always be followed up a few days later by the publication of the 'message of gratitude' of the recipients—but not *vice versa*.

Foreign news has a foothold on the front page, usually only a small one, running over to the foreign columns inside. These are in the main divided between news from other Communist countries, news from the rest of the world, and longish, highly repetitive commentaries on foreign policy.

In 1972, Russia seemed to regard the Communist countries as falling into three blocs: those with which it had relations supposed to be totally satisfactory (East Germany, Poland, Hungary, Czechoslovakia, Bulgaria, Mongolia, North Vietnam and North Korea); those with which its relations left something to be desired (Yugoslavia, Rumania, Cuba); and those with which it had downright bad relations (China and Albania). The inclusion of North Vietnam and North Korea in the first group is deceptive: both countries are torn between loyalty to Moscow and to Peking, but Russia prefers not to discuss this, for fear of embarrassing their leaders or forcing a showdown.

An attentive reader can tell when Soviet relations with another

Communist country—say Rumania—are deteriorating. The Soviet press will then permit itself to print stories about *bad* things which happen in that country, be it only a question of a train crash or a flood, disclosed through the sending of a 'message of sympathy'. Or it will reveal the existence of certain 'problems' in the country's economic and political life. It is not considered correct to print stories about bad things or 'problems' in any of the first group of Communist countries—even a major national disaster will be passed over as fleetingly as if it had taken place in Russia itself. And in Russia, big accidents and natural catastrophes are only scantily mentioned—usually some time after they have happened, and often only in a tone of self-congratulation at the way in which they were coped with. Information about their true extent is spread only by rumour.

Another sign of deteriorating or improving relations can be spotted from year-by-year collation of the messages of congratulation and other formal exchanges among leaders. The substitution of the phrase 'friendly relations' for 'fraternal relations' with another Communist country would imply a crisis: 'fraternal' is a dogma word, whose omission would signify something seriously wrong.

Conversely, a certain restraint has to this day been maintained in discussing the role of Maoism in China, and the sharp deterioration of Sino-Soviet relations in the 1960s. The Soviet press has always stopped short of saying that China is irretrievably lost, for the foreseeable future, to Soviet-style Communism. And when forced to deal with the smaller but closer problem of pro-Peking Albania, it has done so by keeping quiet about that country almost completely.

The widest fluctuations are shown in commentaries about countries like Rumania and Yugoslavia, which pursue relatively independent policies. When Russia is wooing one or other of them, it treats it like a 'first category' country. When it is at odds with them, it prints articles about their 'problems', and the exchanges of formal messages show a cooling-off in vocabulary. In 1968, Czechoslovakia was also a 'second-category' ally.

Why go to all this trouble to convey information about Russia's relations with other Communist states in an oblique fashion, when it could just as well be stated openly? The reason is that this is the easiest way to avoid violating sacred dogmas about the overall fraternity among Communist countries, and the contention that their unity and progress are unshakable in the long run. It also enables people with a legitimate interest in these matters—local Party officials, for instance—to 'get the message' quickly about some trend in foreign policy, because they are used to the 'signals'. The masses will not read the press systematically enough, or are simply put off bothering about foreign policy at all by the obscurity of the code, and by the monotony of the articles if read for their face value alone. It is a great advantage for any political leadership to be able to pursue its foreign policy without any but the broadest reference to public opinion.

The above is not meant to be a comprehensive review of the Soviet system of propaganda. But it gives some examples of the art in its first capacity, as a form of communication. Its second task, persuasion, shows it at its worst from the intellectual and ethical points of view.

If a government had a totally persuasive policy, it would not need intensive propaganda to put it across. The less attractive its policies, the more propaganda it needs. The more lies it tells, the more it has to accuse its opponents of lying. These simple principles have been elaborated into a complex system of misinformation and distortion in the Soviet press. Here are examples of the tactics used:

Exhaust your opponent with sheer volume of words: Having control of all except certain clandestine information media, the leadership can fill them completely with its own points of view. If the viewpoint is too simplistic, it can be repeated endlessly, or phrased so long-windedly that an opponent cannot even be bothered to read it all. This is the first step towards the opponent's not replying, which is the first step towards his acquiescing.

Render your opponent speechless with anger: By telling a big enough untruth, as loudly and colourfully as possible, you can make your opponent so indignant that he will literally fall silent; and this at least is something gained. The favourite means is to accuse him hotly of doing exactly what he is angry with you for doing. Thus, if you have plotted a coup in some country, fill the press with protests about 'imperialist plots' against it.

Indignantly refute non-existent accusations: Attribute certain thoughts to your opponents, when they have never been expressed, and point out how wicked they are. For instance, if someone says Russia has had difficulty in attracting foreign investment for a big industrial project, furiously accuse him of calling for a restoration of capitalism.

Attribute your own views to your opponent, saying he has been 'forced to admit' them: For instance Tass, the official Soviet news agency, may say that the latest routine meeting of Warsaw Pact Foreign Ministers is a milestone on the path of European security. A Western news agency will quote Tass's words, to give some idea of the importance the Russians are attaching to the meeting. Tass will then re-quote its own words, attributing them to the Western agency, and pointing out how the attention of the world is 'riveted' on the meeting, which may have done no more than issue yet another platitudinous statement. Somebody, somewhere, will be impressed.

Repeat, repeat and repeat again—in the press, on television and radio, in the cinema, in lecture halls, schools and factory discussion groups. Bombard the public with the same ideas, dressed in the same jargon, to avoid confusing it. Keep the agitators minutely informed of the current line through special periodicals, closed background briefings and if necessary secret instructions. The biggest untruths need the most repeating.

Ban all your opponents' arguments, and penalise those who attempt to study them in any but the officially distilled form. Jam foreign radio stations, when technology and costs permit. Suggest that it is treacherous for anyone even to express doubt about your own pronouncements, and carry out some exemplary prosecutions.

Make your opponent feel guilty: This is the easiest part. Perfectly innocent people may feel guilty at the mere sight of a policeman, even in an open society like Britain. Most people suffer from guilt or anxiety to some degree or other, simply as a psychological state. This is multiplied in countries with closed ideological systems, which cut across natural inclinations or doubts. Even by conforming to the State's demands, a person may feel guilty for having gone against his own conscience—for instance, by denouncing an acquaintance. This breeds a nation of people with guilty secrets, who are correspondingly easier to control.

Deprive the accused person of the opportunity to defend himself: When writing about domestic affairs, the Soviet press frequently holds individuals or groups of citizens up to public scorn and hatred for having behaved in an allegedly anti-social or immoral way. It names them, but they are denied the right to reply in their own defence. Since the press is the voice of authority, it is expected to be infallible, and to prove it wrong would fly in the face of that authority. Thus when even a smaller newspaper criticises a Government Ministry for inefficiency, it will be doing so with the sanction of a senior Party organ, and the Ministry will have no alternative but to print a confession of failure and promise to do better. It is not supposed to justify itself. It is even more unheard of for an individual to bring a successful libel action against a major newspaper, because the one thing the authorities cannot bear is to be shown to be wrong. This engenders a Kafka-like situation, where a person publicly accused of wrong-doing can only admit his 'guilt' and ask forgiveness; no one will listen if he tries to defend himself; and he has no access to publicity, except through channels which are in themselves treated as illegal (e.g. clandestine tracts). In court, the function of the judge is often no more than to support the prosecution by ruling all defence contentions out of order: this is particularly the case in political trials, of course. But it would also be the case in any trial where the individual's behaviour presented a serious challenge to the Party or the police.

It is only natural that, within this closed circle, a person who tries to set a foot outside it should be regarded as either criminal or schizophrenic. A person who challenged the ideology of a theocratic state would be regarded as both a criminal and a sinner. In an atheist state, there is no fixed distinction between these concepts, nor is there any real distinction between the legislature and the executive. The State can find articles in the Criminal Code which can make virtually anything a crime without spelling it out; thus the right to strike is cancelled out by 'anti-sabotage' laws, and the right to express a free opinion is denied by the laws against 'anti-Soviet propaganda'. If a person should defend himself too vigorously for the comfort of the police and the Public Prosecutor, he will simply be sent to a psychiatric institute, declared schizophrenic, and put away in an asylum with genuine lunatics until he renounces his views. Even that may not be enough to secure his release, if the State regards him as a particular threat to its own authority.

Consider, then, the position of the individual in the Soviet political framework: by agreeing with everything the State says, and repeating it loudly when told to, he can avoid confrontations with authority, rise high in his job, acquire a fair measure of comfort and security, raise a family, and even obtain the right to travel abroad occasionally. He may be called on to do things which go against some deeper form of morality than his 'official' conscience: for instance, he may be asked to acquiesce in the persecution of another person for political reasons, and to tell lies to further the process. If he resists, he will himself be suspect. He is on a slippery ladder, because the more official mistrust he incurs, the less promotion he will be given, and the less prosperity he will enjoy; this may increase his sense of injustice and dissastisfaction, and drive him into the arena of open dissidence, which leads to imprisonment or the mental asylum.

Since dissidence is treated as a crime, it can be tackled with all the resources at the control of the Soviet police organs, which also tackle conventional crime. Western visitors to the Soviet Union have commented favourably on the lower incidence of crime in that country, and Americans are struck by the relative safety with which one can walk the streets. Often this is held up as an argument in favour of the Soviet system, to some extent justifying its low level of material prosperity and its lack of personal freedom.

Western societies could also reduce crime by learning some lessons from the methods used in the Soviet Union. Perhaps their legislatures and Home Affairs Ministries would care to consider such measures as the following:

(1) Drastically reduce the value of money, so that its attraction for criminals is less. This can be done by introducing bottlenecks in the supply of consumer goods and services, which mean that money alone is frequently not enough to secure them. It is necessary to have privilege, either through access to foreign currency certificates, or through political seniority. However, this does tend to increase some forms of crime other than straight theft—black-marketeering and bribery, for example. A special police force can be set up to deal with them: inspectors go round shops to make sure the assistants are not holding back scarce goods for their friends, investigate countless frauds in public institutions, etc.

(2) Make it impossible to leave the country without elaborate visa procedures; strictly control all foreign exchange transactions; patrol all frontiers with armed guards and dogs, and print pictures of them frequently in the press as reminders. Make it a serious crime, even a form of treason, to attempt to leave the country without official sanction. When people are given permission to leave,

forbid them to stay away for longer than a certain period of weeks or months and hold their relatives hostage.

(3) Make sure that almost everybody's whereabouts are known at any given time. Introduce police control of residence permits in the cities, and forbid strangers to stay in them for more than three days without reporting to the local militia. Put a policeman in charge of every sizeable personnel department at places of work.

(4) Increase the number of crimes for which the death penalty is applicable. Shoot people for large-scale economic speculation and for crimes construed as treason, if necessary in peacetime. Make the death penalty almost automatic for murder, and introduce it as a sanction against mutinies in prisons or labour camps. Justify the increased number of executions by saying that they are 'exceptional' measures.

(5) Step up surveillance and documentation of every aspect of the individual's life. Increase the volume of form-filling and other bureaucratic procedures needed to perform any social or economic act.

(6) Blame all crime on 'remnants of the past and bad elements'. Rule out any discussion of social conditions as a factor contributing to crime. This prevents public sentimentality about the criminal's motives.

By applying these six simple rules, Western societies will be able to make their streets somewhat safer to walk on, and will reduce the number of criminal gangs and bank robberies. Whether they consider that they have made a net gain in the process is for them to decide, and perhaps vote on by referendum after an experimental period.

An Argument

MOST Westerners who have contact with official or orthodox-minded Russians end up by having an argument, or a whole series of arguments, on basic differences. A typical one might go something like this:

Russian: 'Well, how do you like our country?'

Westerner (say British): 'It is very interesting.'

R. 'Yes, but how do you like living here?'

W. 'I personally am quite well off. I cannot say I am uncomfortable.'

R. 'Of course, you have so much *valyuta* (foreign currency). I expect you live better here than at home?'

W. 'In a few ways, yes. For instance, Scotch whisky is much cheaper for me in your special foreigners' shops than it would be in London. I employ a housemaid for my wife, which I would consider an extravagance at home. But in general I cannot say foreigners live better here.'

R. 'In what way do you live worse?'

W. 'Since you have asked me that question, I would say that there is less to buy in the shops, even in the foreign currency shops: when we have to use your ordinary shops, we find them very bad and very expensive. The theatre and the cinema are less interesting than at home, and the public transport is more crowded. If our car breaks down, it is difficult to get around Moscow.'

R. 'Well, we Russians use our own shops and our own public transport, and I cannot say they are perfect, but we are proud of the progress we have made. As a foreigner, you are so much better off with your big flat and your foreign currency. This is a courtesy which our government extends to you. But are you not struck by the greater justice of our economic system?'

W. 'I can't say so. What strikes me about your economic system is how inefficient it is, and how low the average standard of living is.'

R. 'What do you mean by *average* standard of living?'

W. 'You can work it out in terms of average purchasing power per head of population, but of course there are wide differences among different sectors of the population, in our country as in yours. The differences are somewhat wider in our country, but then we do not try to conceal them, as you do.'

R. 'What concerns us is the living standard of the working man. Our workers are clearly much better off than yours.'

W. 'I would disagree. Remember that our workers are paid their entire wages in what you call *valyuta*—that means that they can buy any of the things which you are prevented from buying in the foreign currency store here, within the limits of their earnings.'

R. 'That is ridiculous. You are talking about some shortages and problems in the supply of consumer goods in our country, which are of a temporary nature and will be solved. But our workers enjoy free health, education, pensions, and many other benefits.'

W. 'Are you aware that Britain also has a National Health Service, an old-age pension and free state education? That even prescribed medicines are subsidised by the state, and textbooks are provided free in schools?'

R. 'Oh, come. What is this Health Service you are talking about? Everyone knows your workers have to pay for every kopek worth of medical attention.'

W. 'On the contrary. Everyone in Britain pays a small sum each week into a national fund, and out of it the free Health Service is financed.'

R. 'If you have to pay a sum each week, it is hardly free, is it?'

W. 'But the population as a whole always pays for Government services, through some form of taxation. You pay for it through high consumer goods prices, and through an inefficient system of production and distribution.'

R. 'Why do you keep saying that our system is inefficient? Your economic system is perpetually suffering from crises, unemployment, inflation and rising prices. What is efficient about that?'

W. 'There is nothing inherently efficient about inflation or unemployment. But they are the prices which a capitalist economy pays for its greater overall efficiency, and the higher overall standard of living which it provides. As to crises, this is a matter of definition. You could say that capitalist economies live in a state of perpetual crisis, because they are always striving to find ways to use more resources, and this leads to perpetual re-adjustments. Whereas your economy is in a state of chronic stagnation through excessive planning and dogma. That is a crisis, too.'

R. 'You are playing with words. There is no unemployment in our society. Everyone has a job, and can look the world in the face. That is the working man's right.'

W. 'I have heard of secret reports prepared by your Government on the existence of a serious unemployment problem outside the larger cities, in which the police control the size of population.'

R. 'I have never heard of such a thing, and I am sure it cannot be true. I have a cousin in a small town in the Ukraine who has not had a job for some months. But that is because he will not move to another part of the country, or learn a new speciality. There is plenty of work available. In the big towns, the factories are crying out for manpower. And there are the new towns, too.'

W. 'Well, let us look at it from the point of view of living standards. Many of our workers consider it quite feasible to own a car, for instance. That is very difficult and expensive for a Soviet worker.'

R. 'It is no secret that our automotive industry is in need of development. But we have had to attend to other things. A huge amount of our housing and industrial capacity was destroyed during the war. Not all that damage has yet been repaired.'

W. 'You can say the same thing of West Germany, and yet now it is one of the most prosperous countries in the world, and its workers have one of the highest living standards in the world.'

R. (bitterly): 'That is because of the Americans. Look at all the aid they poured into Germany, the former enemy, just to set her up again as a threat to the Soviet Union.'

W. 'Russia could have had post-war aid from America too, if she would have accepted it.'

R. 'What, make ourselves dependent on the capitalists and imperialists? We are not that stupid.'

W. 'You depended on America for many of your supplies in the war, and you have still not paid for them.'

R. 'We paid with our blood to defeat Hitler, while you were safe across the seas. My father died at the Front.'

W. 'I am sorry about your father. Britain and America also fought in the war. In fact Britain fought almost alone from 1939 until Hitler attacked you in 1941, after you had concluded a friendship treaty with him.'

R. 'How did you fight? You just sat in your islands.'

W. 'Have you ever heard of the bombings of British cities, the Battle of Britain, the Dunkirk evacuation, the war in South East Asia and North Africa, and the war in the Atlantic? Or the convoys to Murmansk?'

R. 'I have heard of these things, of course. But they are tiny compared with the war which we fought against Hitler. Half our country was ravaged by him.'

W. 'People in the West would generally recognise that Russia suffered more in the war than other Allied countries. This was partly for geographical reasons, but it was also due to Stalin's purge of the General Staff before the war, and his failure to foresee the German attack.'

R. 'About the *purge* you mention, I know nothing. There were certain repressions, which included military officers, in the period of the personality cult, but they have long since been exposed and repudiated by the Party. And if you look in the latest Party history, you will see that Stalin's decision not to fortify our Western borders more strongly was aimed at staving off the German attack for as long as possible, by not provoking Hitler. Of course we knew he would attack in the end. And then we had to wait so long before you opened the Second Front in the West. *We* paid for that delay.'

W. 'Well, we can argue about the war all night, but it is getting off the subject. If one looks at it from the material point of view alone, people generally live better in the West than in Russia. But one must also take into consideration the amount of personal freedom which people in our countries enjoy, and which you do not.'

R. 'We have all the freedom we need. Do you mean we need the freedom to take drugs or organise criminal gangs?'

W. 'No, I mean the freedom to express your opinions in speech and in print, and to travel abroad when you feel like it.'

R. 'The freedom of speech and print is guaranteed by the Soviet Constitution, and as for . . .'

W. 'Oh, come on, now . . .'

R. 'And as for the freedom to travel, I have myself visited foreign countries. More and more of our people are now travelling abroad. But naturally we must save *valyuta* for more important things, such as importing foreign machinery to build up our economy.'

W. 'If you want to go to France tomorrow, can you do so?'

R. 'Of course not. I must get a French visa, and an exit visa. That will take time.'

W. 'Have you a passport for foreign travel?'

R. 'No, why should I need it before I have been given visas? I shall receive one when I receive my visas, and hand it in again when I return. It is the same for you.'

W. 'On the contrary. I can leave my own country any time I please without an exit visa.'

R. 'I am sorry, I do not believe you. Every country controls its frontiers.'

W. 'I am sorry, but it is true.'

R. 'Let us pass on. I have heard your propaganda broadcasts, and they are always talking about a handful of renegades like the writer Solzhenitsyn, who have sold their motherland for a foreign bribe. No one in this country wants to read Solzhenitsyn. I have seen some of his stuff. He is a clever writer, but he has no socialist principles. He has betrayed socialism.'

W. 'It was your society which produced him. But why are you not allowed to read foreign newspapers?'

R. 'I am allowed to. I have often seen your newspaper *Morning Star*.'

W. 'But very few people in Britain read that paper, which is the mouthpiece of the British Communist Party. You cannot read our main newspapers, because your Government does not allow it.'

R. 'Why should we waste a lot of *valyuta* buying your propaganda? Your big newspapers are simply mouthpieces for the monopolies. Everyone knows that. The monopolies own them. How can it be otherwise?'

W. 'Our *better* newspapers have a tradition of independent comment and reporting which often puts them above questions of ownership. That is something you cannot understand.'

R. 'I cannot understand it because it is impossible. Every newspaper will serve the political interests of those who own it. That is obvious.'

W. 'Then how is it that big newspapers owned by the monopoly capitalists, who are supposed to be behind the Vietnam War, have frequently come out against that war?'

R. 'This has all been explained in our press. It is a question of rivalries among the monopolies. Some do better out of the war than others. And since you mention Vietnam, how can you defend a political system which has led to such a result, the maiming and killing of women and children, the trampling of a nation's aspirations?'

W. 'There are few people in the West now who believe that the Americans set about the Vietnam War in the right way. There are many who believe America's motives were evil from the start. I personally believe that America became committed to a war which she did not understand, through a desire to stand by an ally in the face of what appeared to be a new aggression on the Korean pattern.'

R. 'The only aggression in Korea was by the United States and its henchmen. The result is the division of the country and the creation of a fascist regime in South Korea.'

W. 'Have you seen any North Korean propaganda magazines lately? The Kim Il Sung personality cult is outstripping even that of Mao Tse-tung, which your press is always denouncing.'

R. 'I do not read Korean magazines, but I am sure that the great Korean people will be eternally grateful to the Soviet people for their help in defeating the American aggression.'

W. 'As a matter of fact, the United States was fighting China in that war, as well as North Korea. How do you feel about Chinese policy nowadays?'

R. 'You are asking that question with a provocative intention. Our leadership has made its views on the situation in China perfectly plain. The Chinese have been monstrously ungrateful. We fed them, they ate our bread, they studied in our universities and institutes, and now they flirt with the enemy. But we are convinced that the great Chinese people will win in the end and overthrow the Maoist clique.'

W. 'Do you not think your leaders made serious mistakes in handling the Chinese?'

R. 'No, the Chinese are entirely to blame. They were ungrateful. Now the Americans are arming them to attack us.'

W. 'But China uses almost exclusively Soviet-type arms.'

R. 'They will be given more arms by the West. We seek peace with the Chinese. But we will wipe them out if they attack us. We have the means to defend ourselves.'

W. 'No one doubts that. But why did the Soviet Union have to interfere in the Middle East, thus increasing the state of tension there?'

R. 'We did not interfere. We came to the aid of the just cause of the Arab nations. We shall continue to support them.'

W. 'They have not proved very reliable allies.'

R. 'The Arabs must learn to unite and make social and economic progress before they will be able to defeat the aggressors. We can only help them in this, we cannot do it for them.'

W. 'The Soviet involvement in the Middle East has aggravated the problem of Soviet Jewry.'

R. 'There is no such problem.'

W. 'What about the desire of many Jews to go to Israel?'

R. 'A few people have been misled by Zionist propaganda. They will regret their decision. Soviet Jews are loyal citizens of the Soviet Union, and they decisively reject Zionism.'

W. 'But over 30,000 are expected to go this year alone, and many more want to.'

R. 'Let them all go to their precious Israel if they want to! Or let them remain here and be quiet.'

W. 'That sounds like a racialist attitude.'

R. 'Racialist? What nonsense. The Russian is the most racially tolerant person in the world. We have intermarried with Turks, Georgians, Finns, Mongols, small peoples of the North, and many others. We have no race prejudice.'

W. 'What would you say if an African student wanted to marry your daughter?'

R. 'Just let him try it! African students come here to work, not to mess with our girls. Mind you, I know of some Russian girls who did marry blacks!'

W. 'Why should you object to *your* daughter marrying a black man?'

R. 'It is not their colour I object to, it is their behaviour. They should study hard and work to improve relations between our countries, instead of dancing and making a lot of noise and driving round our city in expensive foreign cars. That is not what they come here for.'

W. 'You say the Russian is racially tolerant. But what sort of situation would there be if there were, say, 50,000 coloured people living in the middle of Moscow?'

R. 'They would enjoy all the rights of other Soviet citizens. But we would never allow it. People should stay in their own countries, and work to build up their own economies and social systems. That is the road to progress. And since you raise the question of race, how can your system justify the underprivileged conditions of American blacks, the fascist regimes in South Africa and Rhodesia?'

W. 'These are grave blots, and responsible Western governments recognise their obligation to work to overcome them. But you are talking about situations which have developed historically, and which cannot be solved at one stroke of the pen, or by violence. It is a slow process. You cannot simply *order* racial justice. It has to evolve. We do not have Stalin's methods of dealing with nationalities' problems at our disposal.'

R. 'What methods?'

W. 'Mass deportation of entire peoples, and liquidation or imprisonment of all articulate nationalist elements.'

R. 'There are no such prisoners in our country, nor are there any political prisoners. Not like your Northern Ireland, or South Vietnam.'

W. 'I can show you appeals from political prisoners and nationalists, smuggled out of your labour camps.'

R. 'They must be C.I.A. fabrications. We have no political prisoners.'

W. 'Only recently there have been political trials in Czechoslovakia, which *Pravda* has supported.'

R. 'Those are criminals, not political prisoners. They plotted against the Czechoslovak state and people.'

W. 'Is that why it was necessary for you to invade Czechoslovakia in order to get them out of power?'

R. 'You are being provocative again. There was no invasion. Our armed forces and those of the other Warsaw Pact states came to the aid of the Czechoslovak people, at their request. And barely a drop of blood was spilled in the process.'

W. 'I agree that it was a very well planned operation. But why not leave the Czechoslovaks to sort out their own problems?'

R. 'Because agents of Imperialism, and, I might add, Zionism, had plotted to overthrow socialism and remove Czechoslovakia from the Warsaw Pact.'

W. 'The Warsaw Pact is supposed to be an element furthering peace in Europe. Yet since the Second World War, there have been only two invasions in Europe, and both were carried out by Soviet forces.'

R. 'What invasions?'

W. 'Hungary in 1956, and Czechoslovakia in 1968.'

R. 'The situations were similar, only Hungary was more violent. Did not the Nagy renegades *declare* that they would leave the Pact?'

W. 'Was that not their right?'

R. 'No government has a right to betray socialism.'

W. 'That is the Brezhnev Doctrine.'

R. 'There is no such doctrine, and never has been.'

W. 'What if Italy acquired a Communist government, which was then overthrown by other political forces. Would the Warsaw Pact be entitled to intervene?'

R. 'We do not seek to impose our system on you. Your working masses will win their own battle in the end. What we seek in Europe is a reliable system of security, non-use of force, and recognition of existing frontiers.'

W. 'We favour the same thing. But what about freer exchange of people and ideas? What about dismantling the Berlin Wall, for instance?'

R. 'The West should be grateful to the Soviet Union for its co-operation in solving contentious aspects of the West Berlin problem, instead of trying to interfere with the frontier defence of the German Democratic Republic.'

W. 'How can you justify the shooting of civilians by G.D.R. border guards?'

R. 'Any country will use force to prevent people crossing its frontiers illegally. But our press has never reported the shootings you talk of, so I cannot believe they took place. I hear your troops have been blowing up frontier crossing points in Ireland. Why do you continue to deny the aspirations of the Irish people for unity?'

W. 'Your press has given a grossly over-simplified view of the Irish problem. But I must admit that there are plenty of elements on the Roman Catholic side who would agree with your estimate of it. Are they not strange bedfellows for you, politically speaking?'

R. 'We respect people's right to freedom of religion. The so-called religious struggle in Ireland is only a disguise for a social and political struggle.'

W. 'If you respect freedom of religion, why do you not respect parents' rights to have their children instructed in their own religion?'

R. 'Religion deforms the mind of a child. It has to be protected.'

W. 'Your propaganda also deforms minds, and yet no Soviet parents has the right to shield his or her child from it.'

R. 'Why should parents be allowed to shield their children from education in the principles of Marxism-Leninism, the most progressive system of ideas in the world?'

W. 'If Marxism-Leninism is so obviously superior, why do you have to ban your people from reading about other systems of ideas? Surely the superiority of your system would be evident?'

R. 'We do not ban them from learning about other systems. But there are immature elements which must be protected from the cunning tricks of Western propaganda, and from its cultural and ideological poison.'

W. 'As far as culture is concerned, why is it that Soviet culture awakens so little interest in the world at large?'

R. 'That is a ridiculous suggestion. What about Shostakovich, and the Bolshoi Ballet, Mikhail Sholokhov's novels, the musicians Oistrakh, Richter and Rostropovich?'

W. 'I grant you those, although the ballet's technical mastery is hardly matched by inventiveness in modern dance. Shostakovich is greatly admired. Many people have read *Quiet Flows the Don*. Some of your musicians are indeed renowned. But there is a startling lack of original creation for a country of your size and traditions. And your best creations, such as those of Pasternak, Solzhenitsyn, and the film producer Tarkovsky, are frequently banned in your own country.'

R. 'Western propaganda raises an artificial fuss around any author who betrays socialist ideals. Soviet literature is translated into dozens of languages.'

W. 'People in the West and in many other countries can read anything they choose. And yet even intellectuals in those countries would be at a loss to name more than three or four modern Soviet authors of whom they have even heard, let alone read. Whereas everyone knows the modern writers of France, Britain, America and West Germany. Why is capitalism more productive culturally?'

R. 'It is not. It is just that your tastes have been depraved and you run after anything new. The treasure house of Soviet literature will be more abiding. Surely all your people have heard of Fedin, Aitmatov, Granin, Mikhalkov, Chukovsky, and Alexey Tolstoy.'

W. 'Alexey Tolstoy, yes. I cannot say the same for the others.'

R. 'Well, you are a bourgeois, not a worker. And the bourgeois publishers will suppress Soviet literature, I imagine. I am certain the workers know of it.'

W. 'It strikes us in the West that Soviet popular culture is very imitative of our own. Your light music is always a decade or two catching up with ours; and your clothing fashions are usually about ten years behind. Why is this?'

R. 'We compose our own popular music and design our own fashions. There is nothing strange in our sifting out the better elements of your creations, and developing them in our own way. That is just mutual influence, not imitation. Anyway, these are merely the frills of culture. They have no fundamental importance, even though they may attract young people and women.'

W. 'What are the fundamentals of culture?'

R. 'To serve the development of socialism.'

W. 'Does it have no higher ideals?'

R. 'Patriotism, morals, self-sacrifice and beauty. Are not those high enough ideals?'

Samizdat

'At the rear of the apartment, they had a very clever little photographic apparatus. I was amazed, when I first saw it, for its simplicity. They had a shelf that swung out from a table, and two fittings on it to which to attach a camera; and what they used to do was, they'd take a document, they'd put it on a specific spot on the floor, and they had two strong lights attached, and they could take a 36-frame role of film as quickly as you could click a camera and flip a page. The whole thing was rigid, so the photography was always perfect. That's the way they made photographic reproductions. They used it for a whole batch of things, novels and that sort of thing.'

This was the description given by one Westerner who had the rare experience of seeing the means by which certain *samizdat* is produced. The phenomenon of *samizdat* has been widely described in the Western press: the word means 'self-publishing', and its loose translation is 'clandestine literature' or 'proscribed literature reproduced by amateur means'.

To understand the need for *samizdat*, it is necessary to understand the situation in Soviet bookshops and libraries. The bookshops, apart from their technical and art sections, are almost entirely stocked with propaganda. Although Russia claims to be the world's biggest book-publishing country, the vast majority of what it prints consists of propaganda which no one wants either to buy or to read, except for want of anything else, or in order to get ahead politically or in a job. Anything more than faintly unorthodox or unusual is sold out immediately. The translation and publication of 'foreign literature' consists mainly of East European works, books by strongly pro-Soviet authors in the West and the 'Third World', or by authors whose comments on Western society are so negative that they can be reprinted with satisfaction by Soviet publishing houses.

The main classics of nineteenth century literature are mostly unobtainable, not because they are proscribed, but because of public demand, and because of the tons of scarce paper wasted on propaganda and reprints of speeches by the Leaders. When a book is popular in the West, it will be found in most bookshops. The opposite is the case in Russia. When a book is popular, it disappears quickly from the shelves, devoured by instant queues. At the *Dom Knigi*, Moscow's main bookshop, a queue might form for a new art book, brought out in an edition which was sure to be sold quickly. A crowd would form round the sales counter to inspect it. Then a long queue would form at the cash desk in order to obtain chits. As supplies of the book ran out, a sales assistant would walk down the queue at the cash-desk, handing out numbered slips of paper, so that there should be no arguments as to who had the right to the last copy.

The logical converse of this situation is that most of what *is* on the shelves is unwanted by the public. When a new 30-volume edition of Dostoyevsky's complete works began publication on a subscription basis in 1971, some people queued night and day in shifts, for several winter days, in order to be sure of getting their names on the list when it opened. The authorities ascribe this situation to the intellectual tastes of the Soviet people, claimed to be 'the world's most widely read nation'. In fact, it only testifies to their relative intellectual starvation.

The larger part of any major Soviet library's stocks are kept in the so-called *spetskhrany* or 'special stacks', to which access is restricted, and granted to individuals only by decree of some official organ. The books in the 'special stacks' include: Russian literature, both pre-Revolutionary and post-Revolutionary, which is not considered helpful to the Communist cause and is not so famous that it would be embarrassing to conceal it (Tolstoy and Turgenev for instance, are accessible); classics of Communism by proscribed authors such as Trotsky; any foreign literature with a content remotely opposed to the official propaganda line (i.e. the vast bulk of foreign literature); files of non-Communist newspapers and periodicals, and even some Communist ones; religious literature, Bibles, prayer-books and theology; Maoist literature; books published in earlier Soviet periods which are not in line with present-day policies—for instance, works by Stalin, or editions of the Party History which have subsequently been outmoded by the whim or needs of more recent rulers; books published in limited editions for specialists only, and too frank for the ordinary Soviet reader.

This situation justifies the over-simplified concept that 'in the Lenin Library, pornography is kept in the same section as the *New*

York Times'. It would be more correct to say that the authorities make no distinction in practice between what they regard as politically harmful literature, and what the world at large regards as pornography.

The official mania for updating, and for keeping all accessible literature in line with present-day criteria, extends to encyclopaedias. Under Stalin, publication of the second edition of the main *Soviet Encyclopædia* was begun. It outlived him, since *Soviet Encyclopædias* are all brought out volume by volume, on a subscription basis, and the entire edition takes years. But Beria, his police chief, had a page or two of biography and a full-page portrait all to himself, in a volume which came early in the Russian alphabet, and hence also in time. Subsequently, after Stalin's successors had killed Beria and denounced the dictator's policies, subscribers were sent a circular letter: it contained instructions for cutting out the pages, and it initially included substitute pages on some innocent subject, to be stuck in their place. Later, the substitute pages ran out. So although this multi-volume encyclopaedia can still be bought in second-hand bookshops—for instance, on the Old Arbat in Moscow—the pages on Beria are simply cut out, and nothing is put in their place. How many other 'undesirable' sections have been similarly excised, thus depriving the buyer of interesting historical material, is not clear. But when the author checked up on the Beria section, before deciding whether or not to buy the old *Encyclopædia*, the sales woman simply smiled and said: 'You won't find that anywhere.' A new *Encyclopædia* began publication in 1969. Its appearance gave the authorities the chance to correct such embarrassing passages in the former edition as the biography of General de Gaulle, who was described as a fascist reactionary. (The late French President was widely acclaimed in Russia after his break with N.A.T.O., and visited Moscow in 1966 with the aim of establishing a special Franco-Soviet relationship.)

The character of the Soviet periodical press has already been described in outline. So it is clear how much an independent publishing service is required; this is supplied by *samizdat*.

A typical piece of *samizdat* was issue No. 25 of the *Chronicle of Current Events*, published on May 20, 1972, clandestinely, in Moscow, in the fifth successive year of the *Chronicle*'s appearance. The number of the issue was particularly symbolic: The K.G.B. dossier on the *Chronicle*, and on those who were believed to produce it, was referred to as 'Case No. 24'. This name was given before issue No. 24 had come out, earlier in the year, and some dissidents believed that it was intended as a reminder to K.G.B. agents that No. 24 must either not be allowed to appear, or that it must be the last to do so. However, other dissidents thought the K.G.B. choice of 'case number' (disclosed during house searches of suspects) was no more than a coincidence. In any case, issues No. 25 and 26 came out, as impeccably produced as ever, and duly found their way to the West.

The *Chronicle* is typed, apparently by professionals, on foolscap-sized paper, usually thin, to allow a maximum of carbon copies. It is headed: 'The Movement in Defence of Human Rights in the Soviet Union Continues.' Under the title, it contains a quotation from the United Nations Declaration on Human Rights, spelling out the prerogative of the individual to express any views and obtain any information, regardless of state frontiers. This right is seemingly guaranteed by an Article of the Soviet Constitution, but it is flouted every day by the Soviet authorities, though their country is a signatory and partner in the drafting of the U.N. Declaration. The Declaration itself is difficult to get hold of in the Soviet Union, and is regarded as an article of faith by the adherents of the Democratic Movement. Thus, seemingly meaningless multilateral treaties, full of high-sounding phrases divorced from real practice, can give hope and encouragement to people in the most unlikely situations. Critics of the concept of international bodies and declarations should bear this in mind.

The Contents of *Chronicle* No. 25 are as follows:

Political Trials: In Odessa, two men and a woman were sentenced in May 1972 to labour camp terms, with particularly severe regimen, of two, five and four years respectively, for possessing 'anti-Soviet' literature, some of it with a Ukrainian nationalist tendency.

In Dushanbe, capital of the Tadjik Soviet Socialist Republic, a 25-year-old history student was tried for 'anti-Soviet' activity. One of the charges against him was that he had sent through the post a tract by Academician Sakharov, who has, himself, never been charged with any crime for writing it. The Republican Supreme Court sentenced the accused man to three years in labour camp.

At Sverdlovsk, in the Urals, a 34-year-old history and economics teacher had been sentenced to two years in labour camp with strict regimen for 'slandering the Soviet order'. The Supreme Court of the Russian Federal Republic, sitting in Moscow, heard an appeal in April 1972, without any defence lawyer present, and confirmed the sentence. The convicted man was a former Party member.

At Kharkov, in the Ukraine, a 41-year-old Jewish worker was sentenced, by a court sitting at his factory, to two and a half years imprisonment in labour camp with strict regimen, for having written a letter to *Pravda* in 1967 on the eve of the Six-Day-War, and for possessing, though not distributing, tape recordings of Israeli broadcasts. He had been examined by psychiatrists and declared sane.

Searches, Interrogations and Arrests: Searches were conducted at the homes of more than a dozen Moscow families, in connexion with 'Case No. 24' and other political investigations. Among the materials confiscated were an official printing of Khrushchev's 1956 speech denouncing Stalin, a copy of *Pravda* for November 7, 1952, with a speech by Beria, a volume of verses by the Soviet poet Anna Akhmatova (nowadays widely recognised and acclaimed), and a record of pension payments to a dissident whose father had been shot under Stalin.

The *Chronicle* reported that Valery Chalidze had written to the K.G.B. chief, Andropov, in connexion with Chalidze's article 'Reflections on Man', which had been confiscated by the police during house searches. He called on Andropov to use 'more academic methods to defend the official philosophy'.

In Novosibirsk (which has a suburb, Akademgorodok, inhabited by promising scientists and their families), a technician at an institute had been searched, and quantities of *samizdat* had been confiscated. The technician was arrested in March 1972.

Other searches and arrests were reported in Leningrad and Sverdlovsk, and there was a detailed record of the arrests of Ukrainian nationalists and dissidents in Kiev and Lvov in the first half of 1972. A group of Ukrainians were reported to have written to the newspaper *Izvestia*, to the Supreme Soviets of the Soviet Union and the Ukraine, and to the unofficial Human Rights Committee in Moscow. They gave a warning that the present wave of arrests in the Ukraine recalled actions carried out under Stalin in 1933, which heralded the 'Great Terror' and purges of the latter 1930s. They sent their names only to the Human Rights Committee, which could be trusted not to betray them to the K.G.B., although they stated that anonymity was obnoxious to them and was a matter of self-preservation. The letter was dated May 1972.

The *Chronicle* also printed extracts from the interview given by Alexander Solzhenitsyn, the banned novelist, to two American correspondents in March 1972, in which he accused the Soviet authorities of mounting a secret campaign to discredit him at closed Party meetings throughout the country. Shortly after the interview, a representative of the Swedish Academy was refused an entry visa to attend a ceremony in Moscow, at which Solzhenitsyn was to have received formally his Nobel Prize for Literature, and to have delivered the traditional lecture in the presence of foreign observers.

A further item in the *Chronicle* was Solzhenitsyn's letter to Pimen, Orthodox Patriarch of Moscow, accusing the state-controlled Church of conniving at the gradual elimination of religion in the Soviet Union. An Orthodox Priest, Father Sergey Zheludkov, replied to Solzhenitsyn's open letter, defending the Church's compromise with state authority and saying there was no alternative to it. The Priest said it was astonishing that so much of the Church had been preserved in the highly centralised Soviet State, since religious education was forbidden. What were priests to do in such a situation?—Father Zheludkov asked. 'Say: "All or nothing"? Try to go underground, which is unthinkable in the present system? Or get oneself incorporated somehow into the system, and use whatever possibilities are permitted at present? The Russian priesthood has chosen the second course.'

The 25th issue of the *Chronicle* continued with news of political prisoners in the huge Mordovian labour camp complex—some of them still serving obsolete 25-year sentences—and details of the persecution of the Catholic Church in Lithuania. The situation in Lithuania boiled over just about this time, with protest demonstrations and at least two self-immolations by fire. There was an account of the manner in which the police broke up a Passover celebration outside the Moscow Synagogue in March, and news of the latest move by exiled Crimean Tartars to secure return to their homeland, from which Stalin deported them to Central Asia as a group penalty for alleged collaboration with the Germans in the war. (Their former homelands in the Crimea are now settled by Ukrainians and Russians.)

In Voronezh, three history students were expelled from the

university for writing a tract which called for freer discussion of sexual problems. They had also circulated articles on censorship, and the need for greater democratisation of Soviet society. Their professor was severely reprimanded for letting such things take place in his Faculty. At the same time, the Voronezh Puppet Theatre was forbidden by the Party Committee to put on a play entitled *Three Little Pigs*, because it was not fitting just before the 50th Anniversary of the founding of the Soviet Union. The dust-jacket of a book on classical antiquities was banned and confiscated from shops because the regional Party Committee felt that a diagram of the Labyrinth of Minos in Knossos was representative of a Swastika.

The *Chronicle* concludes with random news items on police oppression, and with brief reviews of other clandestine literature, including the programme of a recently formed Estonian National Front, calling for a referendum on national autonomy.

This brief review of the contents of only one issue of the *Chronicle* gives an idea of the scope and variety of dissent in the Soviet Union, affecting people in widely separated parts of the country, persecuted for political, religious and nationalist beliefs. The actual proportion of the population directly involved may be small, but there is no estimating how widespread the tacit support they receive is, particularly in the areas outside Moscow. In the capital itself, it is a constant surprise to discover ever new ramifications of the various movements, and ever new sympathisers, mostly in the age group 25–50. Even people who have barely heard of the movements, and would not dream of associating themselves with them, are capable of expressing grievances which have led to the formation of such political trends.

It must also be recalled that it is a difficult and time-wasting process for news of a single political persecution to cross the country and be published in a clandestine journal. Trials which would immediately be the subject of dozens of editorials and news stories in a Western country may be conducted in complete secrecy in parts of the Soviet Union, without the knowledge even of the main dissident circles in the big cities of Western Russia and the Ukraine. This fragmentation of protest, and disruption of communication among actual or potential dissidents, is a strong factor working against the movements, which could only benefit from greater publicity. However, the lack of communication also means that when manifestations of dissent take place, they tend to be firmly grounded in the real grievances of an individual or group, and are therefore more tenacious and harder to cope with than the many strictly imitative forms of dissent which are so widespread in the West.

As shown by the *Chronicle*'s own review section, it is by no means the only clandestine journal appearing regularly in the Soviet Union, although it is the best known, the most reliable and the longest established. Others pop up for a few issues, then run out of steam. Religious and nationalist tracts circulate individually. One recent journal (*Veche*) was the object of suspicion among dissident circles themselves, who considered it to represent Russian chauvinist and anti-Semitic tendencies, which could even reflect unofficial thinking in certain leadership circles.

The question is often asked: how can Western correspondents be sure of the accuracy or authenticity of *samizdat* materials? How can they know that these are not just C.I.A. plants designed to bring Soviet justice into disrepute? The answer is that these materials have a consistent record of accuracy and subsequent corroboration. In the majority of cases, the Soviet authorities themselves do not attempt to deny the accuracy of the *samizdat* news items which find their way into the Western press. A Soviet official journalist told a Western colleague in 1972: 'We know you are going to report on these people. Just don't overrate their importance.' In the end, reliability of *samizdat* materials comes down to the reliability and political pedigree of the person who passes them on. If he has proved reliable in the past, or been recommended by other reliable people, it is fairly safe to use his *samizdat*.

Samizdat has been complemented by the arrival of *magnitizdat* (clandestine tape recordings) and, most recently, *kolizdat*, a more systematic form of publication involving the consistent use of photography rather than typewriters. *Magnitizdat* began with much-reproduced tape-recordings of protest songs by such people as the popular Alexander Galich, deprived of his livelihood for this reason in 1971–72 on the orders of the Party; in recent years, it must be taken to include secret tape recordings of proceedings at Party meetings, giving some insight into the manner in which decisions are taken by the political hierarchy. This violates the secrecy which is one of the leadership's great sources of strength.

Kolizdat, which appeared under that name for the first time early in 1972, is short for a Russian phrase meaning 'collective publishing'. The idea of reproducing clandestine literature photographically is particularly suitable in Russia, where most amateur photographers develop their own films because of the shortage of public facilities. *Kolizdat* may turn out to be no more than another flash-in-the-pan. But its authors appear serious-minded, to judge from their introductory article, and it strikes out in some new directions. It gives detailed instructions for the submission of materials for publication, through a chain of acquaintances, each of whom trusts the other individually, but none of whom knows who is at the end of the chain (an old revolutionary tactic). It also imposes a subscription fee for receipt of the new journal *Free Thought*, which is to be distributed by the same method.

Perhaps the most important aspect of *Free Thought*, if it is to continue publishing beyond its first issue, is the concentration on economic issues. Normally, *samizdat* has found ample material in political and religious persecutions. It has been left to the Soviet consumer to feel the effects of inefficient economic management, and to foreign economists to try and analyse the real reasons for this inefficiency. Lacking access to secret discussions and secret reports, the foreign experts have often been unduly gullible about official Soviet claims of fantastic economic progress, which fly in the face of what anyone can see, simply by walking down streets and looking in shops. The contributors to *Free Thought*—who choose to remain pseudonymous—succeed in documenting the enormous gaps in fulfilment of official economic plans, and even contribute new material on the methods by which economic statistics are falsified deliberately by the authorities in order to give an impression of fulfilment and over-fulfilment. With the advantage of a purely Soviet economic training, they also point to the means whereby economic failure can be documented from the official press itself— for instance, by doing no more than reading the right copies of *Izvestia* at intervals of five or six years.

Another new direction struck out by the first *kolizdat* journal was the publication of a letter from the secret files of the Academy of Sciences, documenting an extreme case of anti-Semitism in the procedures for election to it. Hitherto, such disclosures of the goings-on at the heart of the Soviet establishment have been the subject of rumour and speculation, rather than documentation. *Kolizdat* appears to aim at putting a foot—or at least an ear—into the official 'camp', whereas *samizdat* has tended to view the whole problem of Human Rights from the other side of the fence, from the position of those at the receiving end of persecution by the Party and the police.

It is impossible to rule out the possibility that clandestine publications which make such disclosures about the leadership's methods of control may reflect growing dissent within the ruling group itself, and tacit encouragement, on the part of one or other faction, for such materials. This must remain a matter for speculation.

Samizdat is not entirely political. Some of it is purely literary, though it may consist of literature banned for political reasons—novels by proscribed Russian authors, or translations of such Western authors as Orwell (a great favourite). Even for Russians in official positions, it has virtually become a prerequisite of calling oneself educated to have read at least some Solzhenitsyn in *samizdat*. Otherwise one is in the faintly ridiculous position of condemning something one has never read. When Solzhenitsyn's latest novel, *August 1914*, was published in the West, the Soviet press tried to pre-empt its attractiveness by printing a long, hostile review of it from a Polish periodical. This meant that Party agitators would know what to say if they were asked about it.

The most tragic forms of *samizdat* are the appeals smuggled out —by heaven alone knows what means—from labour camps where political prisoners want their desperate protests and hunger strikes to be known of. There are also materials smuggled out of the eight 'special psychiatric hospitals' where political dissidents, including people who have tried to escape from the Soviet Union, are often held indefinitely. Some of the people in labour camp have been there so long that they still believe there is some point in smuggling out appeals to the emigré 'Governments' of the Ukraine and the Baltic States.

What no one, who has ever dealt with *samizdat*, will forget, is its feel and smell. Those wedges of tissue-fine typing paper—with blurred carbon print on them, folded and re-folded, rubbed on clothing and smelling of sweat—are the lifeline of the dissident movements, just as paper is said to be 'the bread of civilisation'. Passed over at street corners or in back rooms, carried in pockets for weeks on end to keep them from the eyes of the K.G.B., they can soon accumulate into an almost indisposable mountain of paper. The material is of varying quality and interest. Of late, Russian *samizdat* has been nearly swamped in Jewish appeals, single or collective, for freer emigration, which are of a repetitive nature.

Dissidents who have petitions to send try to take care to let at least one foreign correspondent see the signatures, as evidence of their authenticity. In the case of the Lithuanian Catholics' appeal in 1972, this entailed the carrying around of packets and packets of covenant sheets, scrawled all over with thousands of signatures.

A dissident once lent a political petition to some correspondents. Within a day or two, his friends asked for an urgent meeting and said: 'That crazy fool has given you all the signatures, just when we had a chance to send them to the United Nations. We need them back tonight.'

Pythagoras

PIFAGOR is the Russian for Pythagoras, so anyone with this name is sure to end up by being called 'Piff'.

Piff is hot merchandise. His flat has been searched and he has been hauled in for questioning. He keeps the search protocols as curios. They are long, rambling documents, in which are stated: the date and time; the exact name, address and nationality of the person searched; the officers carrying out the search; the witnesses present; the visitors who arrived and were temporarily detained during the search; the case (identified only by a number), under K.G.B. investigation, which prompted the search; the documents seized, identified by their first and last phrases; other materials, such as books, clippings from newspapers, typewriters, diaries, etc., which are seized; the demand for the signature of the person searched; then usually a statement that the person searched refused to sign; protests officially made by the person searched, or any of those present; all completed in a formal, bureaucratic style of Russian, and a round, immature handwriting. One copy is given to the 'searchee' to keep.

Quite a large number of Russians and Ukrainians had such mementoes to put in their scrapbooks by the end of January 1972; and Piff is one.

He is a prickly character, whose idea of humour is to embarrass other people by pointing out the vagueness of their thought (something which Valery Chalidze does as a form of self-defence). Pifagor is identified by his friends as *krupnyi matematik* (a brilliant mathematician) who at a relatively early age had not only done valuable research work, but had published text books.

His problem was mainly one of employment. He was expelled from a major university for signing a protest about Czechoslovakia back in 1968. At first, he managed to find fairly interesting work in a technical design institute, though below his qualifications. Then he was eased out, and went to another, less high-powered organisation. His salary slumped, but fortunately he already owned a 'co-operative' flat with two or three rooms, so he was not too badly off.

Along came December of 1971, and the K.G.B. began clamping down on people associated with all kinds of protest movements, in what was supposed to be a 'once-and-for-all' campaign.

Piff was among the first to be searched, but it seems they didn't get much 'on' him. Perhaps he was careful about what he kept around the flat.

The Director and Deputy Director at Pifagor's place of work were secretly instructed not to give him any more work. But they were not actually told to sack him. So for several months he had been going conscientiously to work every day, sitting at his desk, occupying himself with whatever private jobs he had in hand, drawing his modest salary . . . and waiting.

To visit Pifagor's home was a creepy experience, especially at night, because it always seemed charged with tension, and was in a rather quiet back street.

At supper there one night, Piff's friend Zhenya came in as usual, and announced that a car with three men was waiting on the street outside. Instead of showing alarm, Piff began reminiscing about the time he had been telephoned by Seryozhka, a friend who had been called in for K.G.B. interrogation from time to time for as long as twenty years. Piff recalled: 'Seryozhka rang and said he was near my place, but there was a car watching me from a building site. So I suggested we go and inspect it. We walked towards it, and the K.G.B. men inside were so taken aback that they began to panic. They flashed their headlights and started reversing away from us across the building site. But we kept walking towards them. So they stopped. Two of them got out and came up to us, and asked us roughly: "What do you want?" I just walked round them to inspect the car's number plate. Then one of them grabbed Seryozhka by the coat and hit him in the face. Seryozhka started running away across the building site, and I chased off after him shouting: "Stop, thief." This seemed to throw them, because they ran after us a few paces, then they changed their minds and went back to the car.' That was the end of Piff's anecdote.

After supper, he said: 'Let's find out about this car.' The atmosphere had been dampened, for some of the visitors at least, by the knowledge of it sitting out there, waiting.

'We'll go out now with the dog,' Piff said, 'and watch what this car is doing. You leave in exactly ten minutes.'

On the dark street, ten minutes later, there was no sign of any car, and the whole thing seemed to be a product of Zhenya's imagination. There was a belief at the time that foreign correspondents were not being followed, as part of a K.G.B. 'hands off' policy towards them, but such a suggestion only made Russian friends laugh.

Everything seemed peaceful and normal, though the darkness was eerie.

An hour and a half later, when everyone had gone home, Piff telephoned and said: 'Well, do you still believe you are not being followed?'

'I saw no car.'

Piff said: 'The car was just around the corner with its lights off. It drove off after you as soon as you left.'

Pifagor decided to break out of his professional encirclement by applying to enter a scientific competition. For this he required a character reference from his place of work.

The Powers made sure that he got a 'stinker' of a reference. They said he was politically unreliable, had made statements denigrating the Soviet State and Social Order, and was incompetent at his work. They listed jobs he had allegedly been unable to cope with (which would probably have been the kind of work Piff would have been giving to his first-year students at the University).

Piff decided to sue them. He went to a lawyer to have photostatic copies of the character-reference notarised. The lawyer refused, on the ground that the law forbids notarisation of libellous documents. Piff would not say whether the lawyer was one of those very few who genuinely try to help dissidents, or whether he just wanted to wash his hands of the whole business.

Pifagor, with only the original copy of the character reference at his disposal, applied to his local court for proceedings to be instituted against the Chiefs at his place of employment. The court declined, in a written statement, on the grounds that this was an 'administrative' dispute which should be sorted out within the confines of the place of employment. Obviously, there had been 'secret instructions' (to which not even the Supreme Courts are immune).

Pifagor appealed this decision to a higher court, which also turned down his petition, on the grounds that the 'libellous' character reference had not been 'disseminated' (*rasprostranena*), and therefore could not be considered a slight on Pifagor's honour and dignity under the Law (the Soviet way of defining libel). When last seen, he was working out where to go from there.

In the meantime, he had taken to telephoning the K.G.B., demanding that they let him copy some telephone numbers out of a diary which had been confiscated during the search. It was inconvenient not to have his friends' phone numbers, he pointed out. The K.G.B. officer he spoke to first took it smoothly, said he would check, and asked Piff to call someone else. Piff did so, and persisted. The K.G.B. became gradually ruder, until they gave him a flat refusal.

Once Pifagor declared that he was an atheist. Some of his friends were believers, though not active church or synagogue goers, and someone asked him: 'If you don't believe in anything, why did you ruin your career for the sake of an idea of justice?'

Pifagor replied: 'Because of my conscience, of course.'

'What is your conscience?'

'It is merely my 621st gene. It is all a matter of chromosomes.'

'Then why bother to follow it?'

'It's more *udobno* to follow it.' (More convenient, more agreeable, simpler.)

Emperors of Eurasia?

WHILE the Democratic Movement was at the height of its activity in the years 1968–72, Soviet foreign policy was striking out in some important new directions, which were obviously related to the domestic situation as a whole.

The country's foreign policy had run into two major difficulties in 1968–69, with the need to invade Czechoslovakia, and the flare-up of fighting on the Chinese border about six months later. The Czechoslovak business ended an era in Soviet relations with the West: the after-glow of the Khrushchev period, when attempts at Destalinisation at home were, to some extent, matched by jerky moves towards East-West détente, through summitry and greater exchange of ideas. And the 1969 crisis effectively put an end to Soviet hopes for China's return to the Soviet bloc, linked to a cessation of open ideological warfare, though it was a year or two before the Leaders in Moscow appeared to reconcile themselves to this fact.

The importance of Czechoslovakia in relation to Soviet domestic affairs need hardly be pointed out. Apart from their alleged fears of a break-up of the Warsaw Pact, the Soviet Leaders were obviously most worried by the danger of political free-thinking infecting the Soviet Union's own population, and bringing new men to the fore, to the accompaniment of unpleasant revelations about the past. Although the invasion alienated world opinion, and disillusioned a minority of Soviet intellectuals once and for all, these were secondary considerations when compared with the danger of free thinking in Russia.

The significance of the Soviet Union's clash with China in 1969 was not so immediately obvious. Many people pointed out that the two countries had been at loggerheads secretly or openly for a decade, and that Russia was so much stronger than China militarily that the threat of war between them was ruled out. They also recalled that China remained a Communist country, and thought she would probably revert to good relations with the Soviet Union, if not full membership of the Soviet bloc, in due course.

The Russians themselves, despite their continuing hopeful pronouncements and hints, did not seem confident in the future of their relations with China, as their military build-up on the exceptionally long border between the two countries showed. This build-up had reached record size by 1972, and was matched by a similar build-up, though of less advanced weaponry, on the Chinese side. Soviet propaganda warned throughout 1970 and 1971 that the Chinese were preparing for a war against their northern neighbour—however foolish that might seem from the strategic point of view. Russia could wipe out most of China's industrial and military potential with nuclear weapons, whereas the Chinese were at most capable of destroying a few of Russia's most easterly cities, with their small nuclear arsenal, and harassing her lines of communication in Eastern Siberia.

The real importance of the break with China was not so much what it brought about, as what it prevented from coming about. Historically, the Russians had for centuries been aware of China's presence on the far side of the steppes, deserts and forests of Central Asia and South Siberia. The Mongol conquerors understood the political possibilities of this entire land mass: an empire extending from Europe to South East Asia, taking in both Russia and China. After the decline of the Mongols, Russian explorers pushed through Siberia and Mongolia and set up trading posts. Religious and diplomatic missions were established in Peking. By the second half of the nineteenth century, Russia was already a powerful competitor with the Western powers for decisive political influence in the Chinese capital, and was consolidating her territorial position along most of China's northern and north-western frontiers. The importance of China as a great rear area for Russia, and the need to bar her to the influence of the sea-going Western powers, was apparent already by the 1860s.

The rise of Japan as a powerful industrial and military state brought a further challenge to Russia's position on the Pacific coast in North East Asia and in China. After the Revolution, the Bolsheviks succeeded in consolidating the Russian position in the Far Eastern Territories, and bringing Outer Mongolia totally into their own orbit. But China remained a political and diplomatic problem of great difficulty and importance.

For one thing, the Chinese political scene was a new testing ground for Marxism in its Leninist and Stalinist adaptations: it led to some re-modelling of earlier concepts about the relative importance of the industrial proletariat, the peasantry, and the urban merchant class, in the process of World Revolution. After the initial diplomatic successes of Bolshevik policy in China, Stalin failed to understand the nature of conditions there, and even fought a brief war with China over the Russian-built Chinese Eastern Railway in Manchuria. Subsequently, he was reserved in support of the Chinese Communist Party led by Mao Tse-tung, favouring friendly relations with Chiang Kai-shek, and persisted in this policy almost to the day the Red Army captured Nanking.

Despite all the flowery expressions of fraternity in the early and middle 1950s, and the wide-ranging exchanges on the military, educational, technical and commercial planes, the Chinese Communist leadership remained suspicious of Soviet intentions, and was determined to pursue an independent course. This was not what Stalin's successors had in mind at all. They did not want China as an equal partner in the leadership of the Communist world; they had no doubt at all that Moscow must be the true leader, and the only seat of orthodox dogma. Given these conflicting attitudes, the growing Sino-Soviet split of the 1960s was inevitable —though no one could have foreseen then that it would lead to a Chinese-American rapprochement as early as 1971, with an American President visiting China, which his country did not even recognise diplomatically, in the following year.

If China seemed lost to Russia, this had important implications for Soviet policy in the West. One of the reasons for Soviet intransigence at the height of the Cold War in the 1950s was undoubtedly the confident belief that China would continue to develop as a Russian fiefdom, eventually extending Russian influence by proxy throughout the whole of South East Asia, and thus bringing the entire Eastern part of the Eurasian land mass under Moscow's control. With such an ally at their backs, the Russians could afford to defy the Western powers in Europe, and even begin political and diplomatic adventures with the Leaders of new Third World countries—whom Stalin would have dismissed as unreliable bourgeois elements. Khrushchev's ebullient personality, and his naive faith in the economic superiority of Communism, contributed to the self-confidence of this period. True, the advent of the missile age made détente a necessity for sheer survival; but the trend of events in places like Indonesia and Ghana, the establishment of a

Communist state, Cuba, in the Caribbean, and the inexorable turning of the Arab states against the Western oil powers, seemed to point to just that growing World Revolution on which Marxists pinned their faith. If America and Western Europe persisted in their foolish commitment to capitalism, they would eventually be out-flanked and surrounded by the forces of the World Proletariat under Russia's direction.

The schism with China put an end to these hopes for the fore-seeable future. It restored Russia's traditional sense of geographical insecurity; and it split the 'revolutionary forces' not only in the Third World, but in the capitalist states themselves. China cast increasing aspersions on the sincerity of the Soviet leaders, and on their fitness to command the World Revolution—an unheard-of impertinence from the Russian point of view. On top of it all loomed the possibility, even if only a remote one, that chronic instability on the Chinese border could lead to one or other degree of protracted and exhausting warfare. The clashes in 1969 were an incarnation on a small scale of Russia's worst fears about the way her relations with China might develop.

The reaction on Moscow's part was a diplomatic offensive aimed at convincing the Chinese of Russian good intentions, at solving the troublesome border disputes left over from the 19th century Russian advance into Central and North East Asia, and at restoring amicable if not close relations. This was the origin of the talks begun between Soviet and Chinese delegations in October 1969, in Peking. Three years later these negotiations showed no sign of having made any substantial progress on any questions other than a formal re-exchanging of Ambassadors, and a modest increase in trade. China showed not the slightest interest in renewing its once close relationship with Moscow, and its eyes, instead, were turned towards building up a fresh relationship with the Western powers, including the United States. The Chinese decision to buy the Anglo-French Concorde, to which the Soviet TU–144 was a competitor, was a perfect symbol of Peking's attitude by this time.

China's challenge to Russia coincided with the tremendous setbacks to the Soviet image in Europe following the invasion of Czechoslovakia. Clearly it was time for Soviet diplomacy to regain some of the initiative, while still harassing Western interests wherever possible in such places as the Middle East.

Moscow's main answer to its changed circumstances was the

drive for a European Security Conference, a process which involved the solving of territorial and political differences with West Germany. This answered a number of requirements. It encouraged the Western European powers to look towards Moscow as a partner in the search for lasting peace in Europe, just at a time when the United States, the mainstay of the Atlantic concept, had entered a deep political and social crisis and seemed in danger of retreating from further overseas commitments through sheer disillusionment. France's rejection of N.A.T.O. had been a hopeful sign for Moscow. But the Soviet Leaders were incapable of comprehending the nature of disturbances caused by the radical left in Western Europe, and had little sympathy with its leaders. Their policy continued to be two-pronged: attempting to develop contacts with West European governments, and to encourage moderate shifts to the left in the political life of those countries; while at the same time doing everything possible to maintain influence with the larger Western Communist Parties, particularly in France and Italy. With great satisfaction, the Russians saw Britain, the American 'Trojan Horse' in Europe, tortured by the growing strife in Northern Ireland; though this was only partial comfort after President de Gaulle's death brought a change of French heart on the question of British membership of the E.E.C. Russia could have welcomed the expanded E.E.C., as a factor splitting Western Europe from America. She chose instead to view it with alarm, as the start of a new and powerful capitalist block which would one day have serious strategic significance. China, on the other hand, welcomed the E.E.C. as making Europe more independent of both the Super-Powers.

Western Governments were mostly apathetic or suspicious about the Soviet call for a European Security Conference. But they began to change their attitude when the Russians signed their treaty of goodwill with West Germany in 1970 (ratification did not take place until 1972), and held out the possibility of shelving the dangerous West Berlin issue indefinitely. In addition, the idea of a Conference seemed popular in Eastern Europe, where it awakened hopes of more autonomy from Moscow, though this can hardly have been the Soviet intention.

With various gradations, the eventual attitude of the Western powers—including the United States and Canada, which were to be invited to attend—was that a Conference on European Security and Co-operation could do no great harm. At worst it was likely to be a waste of time. Early attempts to link the Conference to prior discussions on Mutual Balanced Force Reductions among the N.A.T.O. and Warsaw Pact powers became bogged down in Soviet resistance, and then in French unwillingness to negotiate in conjunction with the full-time N.A.T.O. countries.

Since France was one of the 'occupying powers' in West Germany, this was a serious difficulty. The question of ground forces in N.A.T.O. was somewhat overshadowed by the partial agreement on limiting the nuclear arms race, which was reached between the United States and the Soviet Union in 1972. Paradoxically, this agreement was likely in its early stages to increase arms expenditure by the two Super-Powers; but it held out the hope of a more comprehensive agreement at a later date.

There was clearly a basic difference of purpose and interpretation in Europe. The Russians attached great importance to a European Conference which the Western powers considered largely irrelevant. On the face of it, this was an ideal situation, because the West could get a Berlin settlement in exchange for little more than a recognition of existing frontiers and a fortnight's propaganda exchanges at a massive jamboree in Helsinki. But it was natural that suspicions should linger about Russia's true intentions for the Conference, linked to anxieties that she might revert to a harder diplomatic stance if the meeting did not live up to her hopes.

The only plausible explanation was that the Russians were still prisoners of their own propaganda with regard to Western Europe. For decades, they had predicted the impending collapse of the capitalist system. They had a well-elaborated system of political thought which enabled them to interpret any event at all as a stage further on this road. Though individual Soviet diplomats or Leaders may have their misgivings, it would be risky to state them openly at policy-forming meetings in Moscow. For all practical purposes, the Soviet Union is still committed to the idea of a Communist Western Europe under its own tutelage.

There is no need to strain Soviet official pronouncements in order to derive this interpretation from them. Any orthodox Soviet Communist should agree if it were suggested to him that there was a good chance of pro-Moscow Communist Governments in Paris, Bonn and Rome by the end of the twentieth century. (It would be almost treasonable pessimism to suggest the opposite.) London is a more dubious proposition, because of Britain's 'Trojan Horse' status and the well-known 'perfidy' of the Anglo-Saxons. But Continental Europe properly belongs within Moscow's sphere of influence—or so the Soviet Leaders seem to believe—and then Britain will be no more than a temporary nuisance.

What scenario do the Russians envisage for this process to take place? A close reading of their propaganda suggests that they favour something like the Chilean model for Europe. They have given massive publicity to the relatively peaceful progress towards governmental Marxism which was taking place in Chile in 1970–72. Such a bloodless Revolution spares them the risks involved in Cuban-type ventures, and shows that, for all their belief in the 'Dictatorship of the Proletariat', their supporters can also work as good parliamentarians when the situation requires it. This makes Communism infinitely more respectable as a political trend in Western democratic societies, in which the use of tanks against Czechoslovakia aroused only revulsion and fear.

A 'solution' for Western Europe might take place, in Soviet theory, something like this. By 1980, economic instability has rocked Western Europe with unemployment, financial crises and strikes. The growth of the E.E.C. has led to insoluble conflicts with the 'monopoly capital' of the United States. Washington withdraws its armed forces from West Germany and other N.A.T.O. countries, because the European governments refuse to contribute sufficient funds to support them. Anti-Americanism grows in Europe and several left-leaning coalition governments come to power. They have initial success in tackling social inequities, and in 'smile diplomacy' with the Soviet Union. Certain social and economic reforms are carried out, which result in a massive flight of capital, and even some capitalists, to the United States. Economic problems increase, and the pro-Moscow Communist Parties acquire control of larger sectors of the masses and of public opinion. Clever parliamentary tactics are used to gain control through minority factions. Right-wing groups attempt to mount desperate military coups.

After this stage the Russians could obviously envisage a situation in which shaky left-wing governments in Western Europe, threatened by coups, might invite Soviet aid. Such a thing is unlikely in a country like Chile, because of the danger of American reaction to interference in the hemisphere. But if Western Europe can be sufficiently embroiled in quarrels with the United States, there need be no reason why Washington should retaliate for direct

Soviet intervention in French or Italian politics by, say, 1990, when there should be a much stronger Soviet fleet in the Mediterranean.

Such a scenario may seem implausible to those who have become accustomed to the individualism of the French, the chronic volatility of Italian politics, the middle-class ideals of the West Germans, and the British commitment to democratic procedures. But that is no reason why it should seem implausible to the Russians, or why they should not stake much on its implementation. The danger is that they may become over-committed to the scenario, and take desperate measures when it does not work out.

Why should Russia be so anxious to bring Western Europe into its own sphere of influence? There are good reasons why this goes against the country's interests as a whole. For instance, in the past Russia has looked to Western Europe as a source not only of new political and social ideas, but of capital to develop reserves of iron, non-ferrous metals, timber, natural gas, and so on, for which its own investment resources are inadequate. It has frequently invited European 'monopoly capital' to contribute technology in which it lags—nowadays, for instance, in motor vehicles and computers. The extension of the inefficient Soviet economic system to Western Europe would largely dry up this source of investment and new technology.

The answer can only be understood as a reflection of the interests of the Soviet Leadership, not of the nation as a whole. The entire Soviet people stand to gain from a reduction of arms expenditure, which means loosening Russia's grip on Eastern Europe and easing the confrontation with N.A.T.O. But all the Kremlin seems interested in is avoiding the most drastic increases of expenditure in the nuclear arms race with America. Russia is already deeply committed to heavy expenditure on such conventional weapons as tanks, and the build-up of an entirely new Navy of imperial proportions.

The Leaders, like a Western business company, appear to believe that survival lies in expansion. Only by spreading their concepts and their system of government to embrace other countries can they make them really convincing at home. Only by holding up the perpetual threat of 'monopoly capital' and 'imperialism', and linking them to historical fears of foreign domination in the Russian people, can they maintain their dominant position in Russia itself.

Khrushchev went too far in permitting *both* internal relaxation *and* attempts at East-West détente. This threatened the entire system of internal control through police methods and intensive propaganda which has been so laboriously and painfully built up since the Revolution, and which has been taken over by the Brezhnev-Kosygin Leadership.

There are signs that Soviet foreign policy will come to concentrate more on the central issues of relations with China and the West, as it matures and develops. The main question is whether it will seek domestic stability through international tension or through détente. Both are viable means towards it, though obviously the latter is preferable from the World's point of view.

Japan, too, is becoming a major concern of the Soviet Union, since through a geographical and political paradox she is reckoned part of the developed 'West'. The Russians are accustomed to the idea that Western Europe and America should outstrip them for the time being in sophistication of living standards, and in managerial efficiency. They have elaborate theories to explain why this is so. But Japan has once again been a shock to them, just as she was when she sank their Navy in the Russo-Japanese War. From being a military threat, Japan has become a powerhouse of production and technology, despite her small territory and lack of natural resources. And she has done so through a total commitment to the capitalist system. In their more optimistic moments, Russians simply call the Japanese *molodtsy*—'fine fellows', or 'grand workers'. But in a more reflective mood, they question the nature of the Japanese 'economic miracle'. 'Is this a Miracle?' was the title of a programme on Soviet television. The idea was to explain Japan's successes as a result of social regimentation and exploitation of the workers. But the criticism of regimentation comes dangerously close to home, so Japan remains a riddle and a worry for the Russians. She will be still more so as she gradually solves her political differences with China, and extends her influence throughout South East Asia and other countries of the underdeveloped world.

Excessive Soviet involvement in the politics of the so-called Third World has been partly the result of an inferiority complex, a sense that Russia had to catch up with the maritime powers of the 19th century in spreading her influence in such places as Africa and South East Asia. The imperial expansion of the Russian State had been checked by British rule in India, by Chinese hegemony in parts of Central Asia, by the short-lived Japanese Empire, and, finally, by American involvement in Asia. African governments, though initially favourable to a colonial power of which they had no direct experience, proved difficult clients. A massive and expensive setback was suffered in Indonesia, even after the expulsion of the Dutch from West Irian, and the end-result of Soviet adventures with Sukarno was a rupture of friendly relations with the Indonesians, and a partial restoration of Western capital interests there. Not even the disruption of post-British Malaysia was achieved (despite the failure of the union with Singapore). The Vietnam war, though it has had almost disastrous consequences for the United States, was expensive for Russia and a bone of contention with China. It has begun to seem increasingly irrelevant to Russia's real security interests, which are in Europe, the Middle East, and Central and North East Asia, not in South East Asia. The denunciations of Soviet policy made by Prince Sihanouk of Cambodia, from his exile in Peking, have underlined the difficulties of trying to deal with Asians as pawns in a Russian grand strategy.

Moscow scored certain diplomatic successes in backing India in the 1971 Indo-Pakistani war. But it could not relish the thought of being asked to take any large measure of financial responsibility for Bangla Desh, the result of that war. And the abandonment of Indian non-alignment seemed to arouse serious misgivings in India, once the pleasure of victory had passed off. Indian politics afford Russia little chance of decisive influence, or even naval bases, in the near future.

The most significant event in Soviet foreign relations in 1972 was the Egyptian decision politely to expel Soviet 'military advisers'. The Middle East adventure had been Russia's most costly attempt to buy Third World support since pouring money into Indonesia. From the point of view of naval power, Russia clearly has as much right as America to keep bases in the Mediterranean. In geopolitical terms, she ought to be more entitled than the United States to exercise an influence on politics in the states of the area. After all, her southern 'lake', the Black Sea, directly adjoins the Mediterranean and she is short of other warm-water outlets.

Similarly, Russia's interest in the politics of the Middle East and South Central Asia is as legitimate, from the point of view of her security, as the interest of the United States in Latin America. Turkey and Iran adjoin her borders. She has millions of Moslems on her territory, and yet her enemies have used neighbouring Moslem states to forge a system of alliances against her. She has a totally reasonable motive in keeping Afghanistan friendly or neutral.

Despite all this, Russia seemed to go too far in her intervention in the Middle East situation, in the 1960s and early '70s, particularly in the Arab-Israeli conflict. Some Western powers may also have been over-committed, but they were still working off historical relationships which had been established in the era of colonial expansion and two world wars, and continued through the oil link. Russian commitment was a new, dangerous and disturbing factor in the Middle East. It inevitably awakened Western fears that oil supplies might be disrupted; and this could do the Arab oil-producing states no good in the long run, because it helped to lead to the exploration and development of other oil fields in areas less susceptible to political pressure, if less convenient to exploit.

The trouble with Soviet Middle East policy was that its aims were ill-defined, whereas the aims of its Arab 'allies' were fairly clearly defined: to rid themselves of European domination, regain Palestine, and achieve greater prosperity and cohesion. The arrival of Soviet 'advisers' in large numbers in Egypt, though welcomed at first, was eventually seen to be fulfilling none of these overall aims. For the Egyptians, the Russians were merely an instrument, and an ineffective one. So when the relationship began to become edgy, Moscow may not have been completely unhappy to save itself many millions of pounds worth of aid by withdrawing under cover of friendly pronouncements.

By then it was clear that the Arabs were too disunited to be reliable allies in the near future, and the Israelis had played havoc with Russia's internal stability by their encouragement of the Jewish Emigration Movement. The commitment of Russia to an anti-Israeli cause was also unhelpful to her relations with the United States and the Western European countries, where there were large Jewish and Zionist minorities.

Jews

SHEREMETYEVO Two is the name given to a small departure lounge on the far side of Moscow's big international airport. It is used mainly by Austrian Airlines.

By 1972, hundreds of Jews were leaving the Soviet Union every week by this 'back door'. In Vienna, where most of them go from Moscow, they are met and looked after before being sent on to Israel.

But in mid-1971 there was still only a trickle, though a growing one, of people being allowed to emigrate in the interests of 're-uniting families' (the only reason officially recognised by the Soviet authorities for the granting of one-way exist visas to Jews).

Two days before the May Day Parade that year, a burly, middle-aged Jew from Saratov, with a drooping moustache, entered the Austrian Airlines lunch-time plane and symbolically donned his *yermolka* before taking his place. He was accompanied by his wife, two teenage sons and sixteen-year-old daughter, and they claimed to be the first Jewish family allowed to emigrate from the Volga city.

'Hundreds of others saw us off at the railway station, and ran after the train crying and weeping,' the Jew said, when he had been assured that the plane had already crossed the Soviet frontier.

On entering the aircraft, he had declared, to the mystification of others aboard the flight who could understand Russian: 'That was the last humiliation in this country.' Clearly something had happened at the airport.

As the plane neared Vienna, he confided that his daughter had been given a compulsory gynaecological inspection before leaving. 'They looked in her gates,' (vagina) he whispered angrily. Ostensibly, this had been to ensure that she was not smuggling anything out, but probably it was just a form of final harassment.

Those were early days in the Emigration Movement, and Westerners came down the aisle of the plane to wish the Jews good fortune, or give them a miniature of cognac as a souvenir. A British woman sitting behind them broke into tears. It all seemed so implausible.

Each person had been allowed to take out only one hundred dollars in foreign exchange—and no Soviet currency, which is almost worthless outside Russia in any case. There was also a basic allowance of jewellery and other valuables, but any amount of furniture or other personal effects was allowed out.

To get rid of their last Rouble savings, they had bought watches and bottles of drink—anything that could be brought out of Russia. A Jewish couple from Riga pressed a bottle of Latvia's famous Black Balsam (a bitter spirit drunk with vodka) on a pair of foreigners and complete strangers, and were only reluctantly persuaded to accept a bottle of Scotch in return.

The Jew from Saratov was inclined to talk freely about his experiences, though his wife kept jogging his elbow to remind him to be discreet (a habit she might not lose for some time after leaving Russia). 'I had a good job down there,' he said. 'I was in charge of a whole workshop at a factory. The manager was one of my best friends. After he heard about my application to leave, he would barely speak to me.'

How were living conditions on the Volga—meat supply, for instance? 'Oh,' (a wink) 'we used to manage, you know . . . the back door of the factory canteen, if you knew the right person. I was all right, personally speaking. I had my own house, larger than most, my children might have done all right . . . I just wanted them to be brought up in their own country.'

The young people looked calm, unconcerned, as though returning to boarding school after a summer holiday, rather than an ancestral absence of a millennium or two.

'You know,' said the Jew from Saratov, 'in all the troubles I went through down there to get my exit visa, the most humane and intelligent person I met was the head of the local K.G.B. He told me: "We're going to let you go, only it'll take time".'

He concluded: 'The Russian's not a bad sort. You can't really call him anti-Semitic. It's just that he doesn't understand that you have your own feelings.

'There are others, though. There was some brute at the Party Committee of the place where my eldest son was, and they called him in and this fellow said to him: "So you're tired of seducing Russian girls, now you want to rape Arab maidens as well?"

'I went straight down there and told him: "My son barely knows the facts of life. If you ever say anything like that to him again, I'll kill you, and to hang with the consequences." That shut him up.'

The dozen or so Jews from the plane were last seen herded together at the spick-and-span Vienna Airport, for all the world like an early-season tour group. A small, pinch-faced old courier from the Israeli mission was ticking off their names on a clipboard.

As anyone who has tried writing about it knows, there is barely a subject that arouses a worse hornet's nest of controversy and ill-feeling than the question of Zionism and anti-Semitism. The entire Western world, from San Francisco to the Eastern Mediterranean, to say nothing of the Middle East proper, is deeply affected by Jewish questions, Jewish feelings and Jewish opinions. In the Soviet Union a tiny part of the 'Jewish question' (which is claimed not to exist there at all in the form of a problem) has even been transplanted artificially, halfway round the world, to a point north of China, Birobidjan.

Russian Jews themselves tell the 'joke' that during the war the Japanese Government asked Hitler: 'Is it true that you are annihilating Jews?'—'Certainly,' said Hitler, 'but please don't talk about it too much.' The Japanese said: 'Couldn't you let us have 50,000 or so?'—'Why,' asked the astonished Hitler. 'We have until now no anti-Semitism in Japan,' was the reply. 'We feel we should acquire some.'

In Britain and Western Europe generally, the majority of people simply do not take into account whether they are pro- or anti-Semitic. The whole subject is generally considered bad form, except by minority factions on both sides of the fence. But it is impossible to live in Russia and have contact with Russians without breathing the Jewish question in, with the very air. The words 'Jew' and 'Jewish' are much more commonly used and more emotionally charged. The whole thing is a live issue.

For the record, the author wishes to state that he is not, as far as he knows, Jewish, could have some Jewish ancestry of which he is unaware, and cares nothing either way. His involvement with Jewish questions was purely a product of his work in Russia. But his Christian name, so widespread in Britain, often led him to be tacitly considered a Jew in Russia, especially since his wife's name is Judith.

This was, if anything, helpful in investigating the Jewish Emigration Movement, but was never used by the authorities as a source of such insinuations as were made publicly about an American correspondent. He was libelled by a weekly magazine published by *Izvestia*, the Soviet Government newspaper, which said that he was trying to 'subvert' Soviet Jews *because* he was himself a Jew. The correspondent asserted that he was, in fact, a Roman Catholic, with a name of German origin.

Russia is one country where it can be, in practice, slanderous or libellous to call a person a Jew (though there could be no redress through the courts). It was reported through seemingly reliable channels that the Professor of Philosophy at Moscow University had been forced to write to the Head of the Academy of Sciences in 1970, privately repudiating rumours that he was 'a Polish Jew', since they might affect his chances of election to the Academy. Thus it can even be a disadvantage to know the Polish language, as this is sometimes associated with Jewish origins.

On one occasion, an official Soviet press agency lured a large number of Western correspondents to the Moscow synagogue, where of course it is obligatory to wear the *yermolkas* handed out at the door. It had been suggested that some rabbis were going to hold a 'protest meeting'. Soviet rabbis being what they are, it was a 'protest' *against* Zionism. But the press agency carefully photographed the rows of Western correspondents—including even the woman correspondent of the Christian Science Monitor—wearing *yermolkas*. What was this photograph for? Certainly it was never published in the central press. But one could well see it being passed round, with clucking of tongues and shaking of heads, at Party Committee meetings, particularly in the provinces: 'You see, Sergey Ivanovich, who all those bourgeois slanderers, who call themselves correspondents, in Moscow, really are?' But this is no more than a speculation.

There were few or no Jews in Russia proper until the partition of Poland in the late eighteenth century. Until the 1917 Revolution and subsequent Civil War, they mostly continued living in the western parts of the country, including the Ukraine, where they had originally been settled. There were, however, more ancient Jewish settlements, in Georgia and Bukhara, for instance, which came under Russian rule in the nineteenth century.

In the early twentieth century, the reaction to the presence of large numbers of Jews in the Russian Empire took its most extreme form in the Black Hundreds Movement and the pogroms. On the other hand, Jewish socialists organised themselves into a significant political force, the Bund, which was eventually dissolved after the Revolution.

Jews had been active in all levels of the Bolshevik and other revolutionary movements (Trotsky being an outstanding example), and it was only Stalin's purges in the late 1930s which removed the majority of them from the upper reaches of Soviet political life. They had come to play a valuable role in the arts, sciences, and learned professions, though many also took lowlier work in factories, in schools, on farms, and so on.

Unhappily for the Jews, the majority of them still lived in those areas which Hitler's armies invaded and occupied in 1941–43, and this led to the extermination of much of Jewry both in parts of the Soviet Union proper, and in areas (like the Baltic States) which the Soviet Union acquired in the territorial upheavals at the beginning of the War. Sometimes liquidation of Jews took place with the tacit or active assistance of elements of the local population who considered them an alien and disturbing element. Sometimes, too, they were considered representative of unpopular aspects of Soviet power, and even of russification.

The Baby Yar case—where Ukrainians helped the Nazis to track down and murder Soviet Jews—is symbolic of this period. Many thousands of Jews fought in the Red Army, some becoming Heroes of the Soviet Union and even acquiring the rank of General. (One of these, General David Dragunsky, was brought out at the famous 'press conference' in Moscow in March 1970, to join in the general condemnation of Israel.)

By the time war came to Russia, Stalin, his political hands completely freed by the recent purges, mass murders and deportations, was turning towards a less internationalist and more essentially Russian type of ideology, emphasising the concepts of Motherland and Patriotism, and to some extent resuscitating the persecuted Orthodox Church. This may have been done out of the sheer need to rally the Russian people; or it may be that Stalin really dreamed of himself as the post-war dictator of a Eurasian empire dominated by Russian culture. (This empire has, to a limited extent, come about.)

The decline of internationalism, the purging of many Jewish

figures among others in public life, and the suspicion of many older people among the masses that Jews were behind the sufferings caused them and the Church by the Revolution, laid the ground for an anti-Semitic campaign, which Stalin may have planned to use as an internal political lever. This would be persecution of Jews *as such* and not simply as part of the generalised persecutions of the past decade or two. (Lithuanians, Armenians, Ukrainians and others had so far suffered as much as Jews from persecutions carried out *by Stalin himself* rather than by the Nazis in the wartime occupied areas.) At any rate, in the last years of his life Stalin appeared to be heading towards a complete purge of all Jewish elements in Soviet society, and only his death arrested (or delayed?) the process. Many Jews were convinced at the time that their fate had already been decided.

Stalin's death in 1953 may have put a stop to the frame-up of the 'Doctor's Plot' and the press campaign against 'cosmopolitan' intellectuals. But anti-Semitism as a secret element of the Soviet state ideology seemed to be to some extent institutionalised. Jews were rarely admitted to positions of great trust or political seniority under Khrushchev or his successors.

As they have done in many countries, Jews in general learned to live with this covert discrimination, and concentrate on those areas of activity where they could be most successful, prosperous and respected. Russian anti-Semitism seemed to have settled down into a mixture of personal prejudice, a system of 'numerus clausus' at institutions of higher education, exclusion of Jews from the most senior political posts, and a variety of jokes—many of them familiar in New York City. Khrushchev closed some synagogues, but he closed many churches, too. The majority of Soviet Jews by the 1960s did not practise their religion, could not speak much Yiddish, let alone Hebrew, and were generally glad to be considered Russian when the authorities allowed them to forget their origins. The situation was no worse and in some ways better than that endured from time to time by Chinese in parts of South East Asia. It would be wrong to talk about persecution of the Jews as an aspect of Soviet state policy in the 1960s, even though there may have been especially anti-Semitic factions in the leadership. On the contrary, the State was anxious to use Jewish talents as much as possible, and encourage the gradual integration of the Jewish population. Russification as a policy went right across the board.

What changed this imperfect but apparently tolerable state of affairs?—seeming likely to bring about a twenty-fold increase in emigration to Israel within two years, with still more pressure for emigration building up behind? Previously, only a thousand or two 'special cases' had been allowed to emigrate each year.

There were two factors. One was the high proportion of Jews among the intelligentsia, a factor which it has always been hard to reconcile with the reports of restricted entry for Jews to institutes of higher learning. The only explanation seems to be that Jews *do* include a higher proportion of intellectually talented people, or of those with the ability to seize the opportunity, when it offers itself, for advancement in fields permitted to them. Intellectual traditions in many Jewish families may also make Jewish students more successful as a group at the universities and institutes, despite the 'numerus clausus' for entry and the difficulty a Jew would experience in actually becoming the Head of an institute himself. The same applies in other cultural spheres. The most famous Soviet violinist, ballerina and comedian are all Jewish.

Active Jewish participation in Soviet Russia's intellectual life led to a preponderance of Jews in the intellectual dissent movement. This may have had a snowball effect, too: the Powers, or the authorities in a given institution, might become more distrustful of Jews in general, if one of them turned out to be a 'dissident'. There can be little doubt that the increase in emigration in the early 1970s will have a very adverse effect on the career prospects of those Jews who choose to remain in Russia.

The real catalyst was the six-day war in 1967, which shook Soviet Jews into the realisation that they really did have a 'home-land', a powerful modern state associated with the West against the Arabs, whom Jews and Russians despise alike (whatever the Soviet press says about Soviet-Arab friendship). Not only Jews in Russia tell the following anecdote: 'The Egyptians learnt their military tactics from Russia. They studied history, and saw how the Russians let Napoleon come on, and come on, until the snow fell, and he was defeated. Then they saw how Hitler was allowed to advance, and advance, almost to the gates of Moscow, till the winter came, the snow fell, and he too was defeated. So now they have let the Israelis advance, and advance, and advance, and they are just waiting for the snow.'

The attitude symbolised by this anecdote is a far cry from Russia's view of the small Jewish state for whose creation she voted at the United Nations. It is a still farther cry from the 'Soviet Israel', the Jewish Autonomous Region in North East Asia, which Stalin set up in an offhand attempt to 'solve' the Jewish question years before the Second World War, and which has been an almost total failure.

At the same time, the six-day war brought Russia into the Middle East still more decisively on the Arab side, and this was a further factor alienating Soviet Jews from their environment. It was inevitable that they should take a secret pride in what their 'kith and kin' had accomplished, and equally natural, that they should be tacitly regarded as a potential 'fifth column' in Soviet Society, however loudly the Soviet press proclaimed the loyalty and anti-Zionism of Soviet Jews. The Soviet Leaders must have remembered that Golda Meir, when she was the Israeli State's first Ambassador to the Soviet Union, was boisterously welcomed during a visit to the Moscow Synagogue, and this probably heightened their suspicions about the loyalties of Soviet Jews.

By the late 1960s, there were already reports of Jews, mainly young people, embarrassing the police by gathering to sing and dance outside synagogues in Moscow and Leningrad on Jewish festivals. (After all, it is supposed to be the right of all Soviet nationalities to observe their own culture and customs, but this had political overtones, and the police broke such gatherings up with much ill-feeling on both sides.)

At the same time, Israel began to step up its campaign to persuade Soviet Jews to apply for emigration. 'Invitations from relatives' were sent to any Jew who, through whatever channels he or she had, let the Israeli authorities know that he or she wished to emigrate. Some of the 're-uniting of families', of course, was perfectly genuine. But the Soviet authorities cannot have been slow to suspect that this was an officially sponsored campaign by the Israelis to disrupt the Soviet State, in revenge for Soviet support of the Arabs.

A good source reported that the 'Voice of Israel' was never jammed in Russia—though the B.B.C. frequently attracted jamming when it broadcast in Russian, to say nothing of such an American-backed station as 'Radio Liberty'.

Why was this? One can only speculate that the Soviet authorities wanted to see what effects the Voice of Israel's campaign would have on Soviet Jews, and thus whether Jews could really be counted on as a 'reliable' element in the future development of the state. The answer—in the form of massive applications to go to Israel—was a clear 'no', and this will obviously have its further effects on Soviet official policies towards Jews who remain. There is also a danger that press attacks on Jews in the provinces who have applied to emigrate will lead to violent anti-Semitic incidents.

The 'Press Conference' of March 1970, as was later disclosed privately by some of those who took part, was not, as it was supposed to appear, a spontaneous manifestation of anti-Zionism on the part of leading Soviet Jews. It was organised by the authorities, and the 'declaration' which they put their names to was simply sent to them for signature without consultation. However, it marked the beginning of the official campaign to dissuade Soviet Jews from leaving, and this led to an airing of the entire issue, in which the authorities were virtually forced to abandon their position that there *was* no 'Jewish problem' in the Soviet Union.

The Policy spelt out at the 'Press Conference' was that Jews did not have the automatic right of emigration, just because of their origins. This has been elaborated into an entire theory of the 'myth' of Jewishness and the 'imperialist-capitalist plot' behind the Zionist movement. Official publications have used expressions and made insinuations which are so anti-Zionist as to be virtually indistinguishable from some of the pronouncements of the early theorists of anti-Semitism in Western Europe. Fortunately, however, the vast mass of Russians shy away from any issues which smack of politics or foreign affairs, and they are also a relatively easy-going and good-natured people, if often rude, and undoubtedly prone to anti-Semitism. Nor does the Arab cause arouse any enthusiasm, since it is associated in the popular mind with such other costly and disastrous ventures as Soviet aid to Indonesia and China. Thus life for Soviet Jews continued, in general, to be as tolerable as for other Soviet citizens, except in a smallish number of cases where the individual's confrontation with authority had become acute. However, emotional pressures were clearly building up in 1972. Roman Rutman, one of the most intelligent and unflappable activists in the Emigration Movement, reported in April 1972 that on a suburban electric train he had heard Russian youths singing an anti-Semitic 'humorous' song to the strumming of a guitar.

The issue of Soviet Jewry had taken on world importance by

Christmas 1970, when two death sentences, later commuted, were imposed in the first Leningrad trial of Jews accused of attempted hijacking. The very timing of this trial showed the authorities' incomprehension (then) of the intensity of feeling in the outside world.

It was in 1971 that the activists really got under way. They had built up good contacts with the Western press, partly through the dissident movements, and partly on their own account. It was enough for a correspondent to show up outside the Moscow court-house where the appeal in the Leningrad case was being heard, and talk to the Jews waiting on the pavement for the verdict, in order to make contacts on the spot. The police confined their intervention to moving people on occasionally so that the pavement should not be blocked, although at one stage they did haul a Jewish woman off, shouting and screaming, and gave her a lecture at a police station.

With hijacking obviously too risky, the activists took to badgering the Supreme Soviet (the country's theoretical parliament) and the Central Committee of the Party (the real government of the country) with mass applications and petitions. They carried out several sit-in protests and hunger strikes at the Supreme Soviet Reception Centre and the Moscow Central Telegraph Office, but were deterred from doing the same at the Central Committee, though one or two delegations were eventually admitted there.

The second sit-in at the Supreme Soviet Reception Centre was a strange scene. There was none of the boisterousness associated with a similar protest in the West. The Jews—about a hundred of them—were deadly serious, frightened but determined. There had been nothing quite like it in Soviet history for decades: this number of people publicly registering their protest, in the centre of Moscow, for hours at a time, with the police apparently shy of intervening.

In fact the police were simply biding their time. During the day, a single militiaman and probably some plain clothes agents kept watch at the door of the Reception Centre, where normal business proceeded despite the large groups of Jews from Moscow, Riga, Vilnius and elsewhere, sitting and standing silently along the walls. Some correspondents were even allowed to go in and talk to the Jews, each of whom was eager that his own case should be broadcast. The atmosphere was extremely tense, because everyone concerned was treading unknown ground and was uncertain how it would all end.

A small group of correspondents returned in the evening to see how the police would cope with the demonstrators when the Reception Centre's closing time came round. They were first photographed from all angles by a particularly unpleasant K.G.B. official, then shooed away angrily by him, with the aid of some uniformed militia.

One thing that the K.G.B. man said revealed just how the authorities felt about their 'non-existent' Jewish problem: 'Get away from here. Occupy yourself with your own business as correspondents. You've gone altogether too far (*raspustilis*).' It was characteristic of official attitudes that the Powers did not consider it to be part of a foreign correspondent's functions to report on a sit-in protest of international concern. The overall attitude towards the press, and foreign journalists in particular, can be dimly discerned in such statements.

So there were no correspondents on hand to report what happened. But they had spotted the lorry-loads of police waiting round the corner in a courtyard behind the Reception Centre, and Jews who were present gave a full account later. One said: 'A senior police officer arrived and told us we must leave. No one budged. The police were moved up in force, but still there was no violence. Some of the older people began to get nervous. Then a squad of special guards—K.G.B. Kremlin guards, or something—arrived at the goose-step, did a parade-ground turn, and halted smartly in the middle of the Reception Centre, just to scare us. The man in charge said he was giving us five minutes to make up our minds. He counted off the minutes. Some people began edging towards the exit. As the time-limit ran out, dozens of police rushed in and started pushing and shoving so that in the end we were all ejected into the street. They dispersed us and told us not to come back.'

Some of the Jews who had come specially from the Baltic states to make their protest were put on trains and sent home under supervision. But most of them received their exit visas within a few weeks, and left. Two of them were actually on the Austrian Airlines plane for Vienna, with the Jew from Saratov and his family.

More remarkable still, in Soviet terms, was the tale of the Georgian Jews who came up to Moscow to make a protest to the authorities, and had to content themselves with a hunger-strike at the Telegraph Office. They were arrested, and put under guard on a train to Tbilisi. But one of them escaped by jumping out of the window, hitch-hiked back to Moscow, and told Jews there what was happening. A long-distance telephone call was made to Georgia, and by the time the train arrived in Tbilisi, a crowd of Jewish demonstrators had gathered to meet it.

The Georgian Jews, by and large, were the most determined group, actually mounting large protest demonstrations outside the Republican Central Committee building in Tbilisi. They won their case. In late 1971 the authorities let them set up a special committee to decide the order of departure of those wishing to leave, and they began to arrive by the thousand in Israel.

Thanks largely to the Georgian emigration, the situation by mid-1972 was that Soviet Jews were being allowed to leave at a rate which might even top 30,000 by the end of the year. This seemed to be the result of a change of policy on the authorities' part, taken after some hesitation and experimenting, towards the end of 1971. Perhaps this was a direct result of the visit by Premier Kosygin to Canada, in addition to Party Chief Brezhnev's visit to France shortly afterwards. These two top men must have had it brought home to them, in the West, just how high feelings were running over the issue of Soviet Jewry, and how strong the support for the Emigration Movement was.

Unfortunately, this increase in emigration gave rise to widespread misunderstandings in the West. Firstly, it was thought that the problem had been solved—'Thank God, they're being let go,' was a general reaction, after which people tended to lose interest in the whole question.

Seondly, it was believed that a freer emigration policy, once begun, was pretty sure to continue.

Thirdly, the idea got around that Israel would soon reach saturation point as far as Soviet Jews were concerned, and that the Jews themselves would soon become disillusioned with their 'land of milk and honey'—which is, according to many reports, a place of rising social discontent and political conflict, and considerable inequities in opportunity and standard of living. Further, it is a mainly capitalist society, to which many Soviet Jews would find it hard to adjust immediately; but excessive attention was given to the small numbers of people—mainly Georgian Jews—who decided to return to their original homes, even if it meant public grovelling before the Soviet authorities.

Let us examine these concepts: Firstly, not all Jews who wanted to go to Israel were being allowed to do so by 1972—far from it, in fact. The bulk of the 30,000 or so originally expected to emigrate in the course of the year were Georgian Jews, and inhabitants of an area of the Ukraine near the Rumanian border who went to Vienna directly by train, with little publicity. It was still difficult, though not impossible, to obtain an exit visa from the cities of Russia, Byelorussia, the Ukraine, the Baltic States and Moldavia, partly because the city applicants tended to be more highly qualified. The authorities did not want to lose such people, handing their qualifications to Israel on a plate. The introduction of a heavy exit tax in mid-1972, allegedly to compensate the Soviet State for their education, underlined this attitude.

In some cases there may have been a genuine fear that technological or other secrets might be betrayed to the West. However, this was also used simply as an excuse for making the application process long and difficult. Some Jews were counting on waiting for two years after their first application, and if they had just served in the Armed Forces, they could expect to wait three, if they were to be allowed to leave at all. There have been some well-publicised cases of city Jews who got out, either through dissident activity which made them a liability to the authorities, or through making a fuss in the Western press. There have also been a good few cases of people who did *not* get out even after making a fuss and having their cases taken up abroad. Boris Kogan, a Jew and Moscow lawyer who had devoted himself to giving consultations to Jews wishing to renounce Soviet citizenship, said in 1972 that the position in the city was still extremely difficult. He himself had been allowed to pay the high fee to renounce his citizenship, then refused the exit visa, as a form of K.G.B. revenge for his previous activity. He is a quiet, civilised and coherent young man, and there seemed to be no reason to doubt his word.

Secondly, the 1971–72 policy may have been a pure experiment, or a 'top of the bottle' campaign to get rid of the most active protesters, and then clamp down again. It is *totally impossible* to estimate how many Soviet Jews 'want' to go to Israel, because their wanting or not wanting depends on how easy it is. If an application to the O.V.I.R. (visa office) means loss of one's job on the spot, and expulsion of one's teenage children from their institutes, with no guarantee that a visa will be granted, then the actual applications will continue to be measured in tens of thousands rather than hundreds of thousands. The Jewish population is probably around three million, though assimilation and integration have made it hard to give accurate estimates. The drop in the figures for Jewish population in the last census, which seemed so mystifying since all other population groups were increasing, may have been explained by Jews claiming Russian nationality, or even using their German-sounding names to call themselves 'Soviet Germans' (formerly settled on the Volga and elsewhere, but deported by Stalin and now scattered across Siberia and Central Asia). More recently, there has been an opposite tendency: some Georgians were reported to be offering as much as 500 Roubles for a false internal 'passport' showing them as Jewish—just in order to get out. The price probably rose higher as time went on, for Georgians, through their black market activities, tend to have a surfeit of Roubles. Previously, many Jews would have paid almost any amount to get the stigma *off* their 'passport' (which is not valid for foreign travel, and therefore grossly misnamed).

Thirdly, the Georgian Jews were mainly small artisans and traders, who were going for religious reasons or through herd instinct, and may have been disillusioned in some cases by the difficulty of finding scope for economic speculation, by the secularity of the Israeli State, by the difficulty of living together as Georgian-speaking communities, and by the tougher life in some of the areas they were assigned to. It was rare indeed to hear of a Moscow or Leningrad Jew who wanted to return—even though he might find the bus fares higher in Israel. Most reports from Israel emphasised that the authorities there were confident they could cope with many more Soviet Jews. (It is in the nature of K.G.B. misinformation techniques that at least some of those who applied for repatriation to the Soviet Union must have been sent deliberately in order to do so and make a great fuss about it.)

The Emigration Movement produced some strange anomalies and humorous situations, as well as much heartache and frustration. The K.G.B. put a woman named 'Izraelova' in charge of Jewish Emigration at the O.V.I.R.; apparently she was not Jewish herself— it is said to be a surname found in the Caucasus. A well-known dissident, the son of a famous Soviet poet, was called in one day by the K.G.B. and told that he could leave. He still had to fill in the O.V.I.R. application form, however. So at the point where the questionnaire asked: 'Why do you wish to leave the Soviet Union?'

—he wrote: 'In connexion with the fact that it has become possible.'

The dissident 'leader' who has been called Pavel in this book disclaimed any intention of wanting to leave Russia, and in his case this was not an easy decision, for he is a Jew and a 'trouble-maker' and could probably obtain an exit visa easily. 'What can a person brought up in Russia do in the West?' he once asked. 'He can beat his breast, and say: they did such and such to me, this is what happened to me. Then he can give a little information about how things had been going so badly on his collective farm, and so on. And then people will say: yes, what else? or: so what?'

It was certainly true that the increasing chances of emigration for people of Jewish descent made others think more soberly about the real prospects that would await them if they found some way to get out of the Soviet Union. Ever since the Terror of the 1930s and the War, there have been millions of Russians, Latvians, Armenians and others who have dreamed of escaping from the Soviet Union to what they regarded (quite rightly) as the freer West. Not all of them would necessarily have made good in the West, however, just as many refugees from China perish through drug addiction in Hong Kong. The West is a rough-and-tumble society. In the Soviet Union, a person may be poorly off economically, and very poorly off in terms of personal freedom, but if he keeps his political nose clean and stays clear of the law, he can claim a reasonable measure of security without even working very hard for it. It is impossible to state how many people of Russian and other non-Jewish nationalities would 'vote with their feet' if the Soviet authorities threw the frontiers open tomorrow. That mere fact would imply such drastic changes in Soviet domestic policy that individual mentalities, and attitudes towards the dream of emigration, would also change almost overnight. The fact remains that the labour camps and 'special psychiatric hospitals' contain many cases of people who have tried to escape Russia by walking across the frontier. But there are few places to go: Iran and Turkey are almost the only feasible outlets, even if a person can escape the border guards and tracker dogs, which is rare. The attitude of the Finnish authorities towards Soviet defectors could hardly be favourable, in view of Finland's delicate political situation vis-à-vis Moscow.

So the Jewish Emigration Movement represents a sort of vicarious wish-fulfilment for people of other nationalities, who may previously have longed to depart from the Soviet Union. Television interviews with people who come back from the 'free world', complaining of its iniquities, inevitably make a great impression, however sceptical the more intelligent Soviet citizen may be. It is in the nature of the medium.

On the other hand, the Jews succeeded in showing that neither the Party nor the K.G.B. was omnipotent, and that determination could overcome mountains. The unrest in Lithuania in 1972, ostensibly linked to the persecution of the Roman Catholic Church there, may have been fuelled by the successes of Lithuanian Jews whose persistence won them exit visas. A country with as many national minorities as Russia must be wary of any movement which suggests that particular groups can claim special privileges for themselves because of their nationality. This is especially true when the second largest group, the Ukrainians, represent a powerful industrial and agricultural state, with a historical and cultural tradition of their own, and certain russophobe tendencies. The arrests of Ukrainian nationalists and dissidents in 1972 were probably one of the most serious problems which the Soviet leadership had to face in that year, apart from the running sore of economic difficulties; and the Jewish issue may have helped to irritate Ukrainian feelings.

What about the 'Soviet Israel', the Jewish Autonomous Region on the Chinese river frontier, with its capital, Birobidjan, which the Soviet authorities began frantically propagating early in 1970 as part of their anti-Zionist campaign? (They even flew some local Jewish worthies all the way from Birobidjan to take part in the Moscow 'Press Conference', and subsequently sent them abroad to make publicity for the J.A.R. and for the happy state of Soviet Jewry in general.')

Birobidjan, though it attracted some Jews in the late nineteen twenties and in the 'thirties, was an obvious failure, because by the 1960s even the official census admitted that only nine per cent of its population were, in fact, Jews. There were more Jews in Moscow, or in Leningrad, Kishinev, Odessa, Bukhara and probably a dozen other cities than in Birobidjan. None the less, in this dull little town in South-East Siberia, the street signs are still doggedly reproduced in Yiddish as well as Russian. It is a real Jewish comedy, explained, for no obvious reason, by a young engineer who befriended a couple of foreigners at a loose end there one day in 1970.

Naum Chakovsky, as he may as well be called, worked as a technical supervisor at a light industrial plant in Birobidjan. His great ambition was to be a writer—but a Russian writer. He could also write Yiddish, which is becoming increasingly rare in Russia, so he was able to contribute to the J.A.R.s Yiddish-language newspaper (mostly a straight translation of the more widely circulated Russian newspaper published at the same office in Birobidjan).

Having completed the requisite period of years at his factory, he and his wife had acquired that most sought-after possession for any Soviet family: a two-room flat within walking distance of work. There was no light on the concrete-walled staircase, and the flat was almost bare of furniture. The floorboards and wallpaper were crude, and the kitchen stove tiny. They had an infant daughter, who slept in the living-room so that the parents could have privacy in their bedroom. Naum ate at the factory canteen most days, and in the evening his wife just opened a can of Bulgarian tomatoes and served them cold with some home-pickled gherkin and a hunk of bread. The child was put to bed between eight and nine, and any guests had to leave then so that she could sleep.

Naum regarded the Jewish Autonomous Region as a bit of a joke, although despite his fair hair and Russian looks, he was a Jew and was anti-Zionist. He explained that Yiddish culture had been on the wane, even in Birobidjan, until the Jewish Emigration Movement got under way and began attracting attention in the outside world. (The local Party bosses had been Russian or Ukrainian—not Jewish—as long as anyone could remember. None the less, shortly after the Moscow 'Press Conference', a Jewish First Secretary was put in, with much publicity in the official media.) Attempts were being made to revive the local Yiddish drama troupe and increase the frequency of publication of the newspaper. The bright, modern hotel may have been meant to receive admiring delegations from abroad. But after the author had been allowed (with some hesitation on the part of the Foreign Ministry and the Visa Office) to visit Birobidjan and report on it at first hand, the authorities never permitted another Western correspondent to go there, though they continued to give it occasional publicity. The irrelevance of the whole place to the question of Soviet Jewry was too evident.

Naum's wry picture of the J.A.R. was not the one given the next day by the handful of Jewish worthies who were brought out for official interviews. One was Vladimir Peller, Chairman of the

Waldheim Collective Farm, who has subsequently even been sent to Western Europe in the Birobidjan public relations campaign. Peller applied the well-known tactic (thoroughly rehearsed in Gogol's play *The Inspector General*) for dealing with awkward visitors from the big city: show them a few charitable institutions, and get them drunk. This may seem a mean way to return Mrs Peller's hospitality in cooking lunch, but it was all so palpably *laid on* that the visitor's intelligence was insulted, especially when he was told: 'We eat like this all the time.' Grapes, brandy, canned shrimps and fresh meat were obviously brought in specially, or supplied from some private store for senior Party officials, because grapes and shrimps are rarities even in Moscow shops, and brandy and meat are still rarer luxuries in Eastern Siberia. (Naum had disclosed that the local shops even ran out of cigarettes from time to time.)

To the delight of the other collective farm administrators, Peller pushed the brandy toasts hard and fast at the lunch, evidently following Gogol's recipe for a quiet life. This merely led to one of those acrimonious arguments which most Westerners have from time to time with orthodox-minded people in the Soviet Union. It also resulted in some aggressive interviewing in the afternoon, which confirmed what Naum had said the previous day: Jewish culture was merely a notion in Birobidjan. The Yiddish language was not taught in the schools, nor was the history of the Jewish people. There were a few books in Yiddish in the library, and still fewer in the local bookshop; there was virtually nothing in Hebrew. The single synagogue was obviously neglected, and was in an area of new development which seemed to make it inevitable that it would soon be pulled down. It was reported that the original building had been burnt down some months before, and that 'only a few old people' went there anyway. The 'Jewishness' of Birobidjan is simply a front for the gullible.

While Peller was trying to convince a foreign journalist that Soviet Jews were perfectly happy as they were, Jews in Moscow, Riga, Kishinev and many other cities were cranking up their campaign to obtain exit visas—and even, if the results of the Leningrad trial were to be believed, being investigated for attempting to hijack an aircraft, as the sole means of escape from Russia. This was in late 1970. By mid-1971, the Jewish publicity campaign was so successful that the K.G.B., in desperation, were hauling off Jews in broad daylight when they met foreign correspondents on the street, holding them on non-existent charges, then releasing them with 'warnings'. One Jew in Moscow was thus detained several times in a week.

In the spring of 1972, a talented Moscow artist named Kupperman obtained an exit visa for Israel. So did his wife, a tall Russian blonde who looked every bit the fashion model that she was. While they were completing their departure arrangements, the print shop on Gorky Street continued to sell a lithograph of which Kupperman had made fifty copies.

The picture is a subdued composition in washy grey shading into a mauvish pink. Pinocchio, the wooden puppet with jointed limbs, walks stiffly by a sea-shore, waving to a small, storm-tossed ship in the middle distance.

Pinocchio's problem was how to become a real boy. Was this the meaning of Kupperman's symbolism?

Fat Sasha and the Urban Guerilla

KOSTYA Markman was the closest thing imaginable to a professional dissident. He would call at any time of the day, any day of the week. If he had other work, he never talked about it. His pockets were usually stuffed with protest documents, his diary full of telephone numbers. When he asked to be taken into a foreigners' block, he temporarily confided the diary to a foreigner, in case the police should detain him on the way out and confiscate the precious phone numbers. His information was usually good, though not always as important as he made out. He worked and worried, and he never gave up.

Kostya was not beautiful. He squinted slightly, and was normally unshaven. One of his front teeth was in an advanced stage of decay.

He could also be a nuisance. He would demand a rendezvous for 'something important' which turned out to be less than what it was billed as. He would spring meetings with strangers, and demand rides into obscure parts of Moscow. He was a hopeless guide, because he did not understand the traffic rules, and always called for right turns when the car was irrevocably committed to a left-hand lane.

None the less, Kostya was a fine contact, and a loyal friend of the young dissident who had just been given a long jail sentence for talking to foreigners about the 'special psychiatric hospitals' where he and others had been incarcerated and maltreated. Kostya spent weeks trying to obtain a picture of his friend, which had been published in a West German magazine, and which he desperately wanted to give to the prisoner's mother for Woman's Day. (Her son was already in Vladimir jail, the most feared of all punishment centres.) The picture turned out to be much smaller than he had been told, and it reached him too late for the proposed act of charity to be carried out. But when he got it in his hands, he gave it a look of misty devotion as though the wretched prisoner were his own son—though he can only have been a year or two older himself. They had met in a 'psychiatric hospital'.

Some people who knew Kostya believed that he was indeed a

little 'touched', because he was so reckless. Once he started talking about the state of affairs in Russia, his voice would rise and rise, even on the street where passers-by could hear him, perhaps denounce him. For a foreigner in Moscow, this was an agonising style of conversation. But Kostya didn't care. 'The K.G.B. know everything I think,' he used to say. 'I've told it all to them plenty times already. Why should I make a secret of it?'

Being a Jew, Kostya had been told by the K.G.B.—with whom he was almost on first-name terms—that he had better leave for Israel soon. 'Otherwise,' he quoted an officer as saying, 'we'll put you in another clinic, and return you to society as a totally healthy person' (as though that were a decision for a police force). Kostya said: 'I know very well what they mean by that. But I'm not going till I see our friend's appeal through, and then I want to go riding in the Caucasus one last time. I expect I'll leave in the autumn.' The prisoner's mother needed help and advice, and Kostya kept getting involved in all sorts of other cases, concerned with the Human Rights situation in general, and more often with the Jewish Emigration Movement. He knew practically every activist in the city, and some as far away as the Urals.

Why did the K.G.B. let Kostya continue his activity? Perhaps because he was so reckless and open about it that they found him a convenient means of observing the overall trends in the Movement, and keeping track of the correspondents who were reporting it. Perhaps because they were building up a dossier in order to make a really tough charge stick on him, without resorting to the feeble excuse for a trial which was exposed in the Western press after his friend's imprisonment. In fact, though he gave the appearance of recklessness, he knew the precise points about which to be careful— for instance, his diary. And he never handed documents over openly on the street. He always slipped them across in a car, or inside a building.

Kostya, who seemed to be about thirty, had a 'pad' in outer Moscow, from which, by obscure means, the authorities managed to have him ejected. But he also had access to a room in a communal apartment in central Moscow, where he would occasionally invite his acquaintances for brief periods.

It was the typical communal apartment: in an old building, with a dark and filthy staircase, and rickety front-door onto the street. The apartment was on the first floor. Kostya always gestured for silence when he opened the door and ushered anyone into the almost totally dark and winding corridor of what had once been a fashionable and spacious home. Now it was split up into a series of cave like bed-sitting rooms, opening off the corridor at unexpected points and suddenly throwing a little light in from the street when a door was opened. The room was usually in a mess. Once there was a mysterious blonde woman there, dressing. Kostya mumbled something about it belonging to his mother, but she was never in evidence.

The first encounter with Kostya took place outside a courthouse, where he was volunteering information about the proceedings inside, having just talked to the relative of a political prisoner on trial there. (Only a very few relatives, and no friends of the accused, were admitted to such trials. Others with an interest in the case, including correspondents, simply stood around on the pavement outside, waiting for news. In the winter, this was no joke.)

Telephone numbers had been exchanged, and a week or two later there was a call, and a voice which was to become very familiar in the future said: '*Zdravstvuyte*, this is Markman speaking.'

'Who?' (It could be a provocateur.)

'Markman. You remember, we met a week or two ago.'

Light gleamed.

'Yes. What can I do for you?'

'I'm calling from the phone box across the street from your building next to the bookshop. Maybe you can see me from the window.'

'Wait a minute.'

A glance through the window, on the side of the block facing the street, showed a figure in a raincoat in the telephone booth, and another younger man in a green windcheater standing outside it.

'I can see you.'

'Can you come down now and meet me? I want to introduce you to someone, and I have something important to tell you.'

'All right.'

Friends in the flat could watch the scene from the window, and report if the K.G.B. intervened to break up the meeting, as they had done several times that summer. But no agents were in evidence.

Kostya introduced his friend: 'This is Boris. You'll be seeing more of him.'

Boris was in his early twenties. Apart from the green windcheater of rather military cut, he had a straggling, fair beard, and a generally knowing look, which led another foreign acquaintance to christen him 'The Urban Guerilla'.

'We shouldn't talk here,' said Kostya, with a caution not typical of his future behaviour. 'I've been scouting around your block, and I see there's a piece of wasteland round the back. Let's go and talk there.'

There was, indeed, a winding and narrow path, usually deep in snow or mud, which led round the back fence of the foreigner's compound and was bounded closely on its other side by the fence of an adjacent building. It was just out of view of the militia post at the entrance to the compound.

This path led across one patch of waste ground, a back-street and a sort of gap between the courtyard of two buildings, also out of view of the militia spy-post.

'This is a good spot,' said Kostya, though residents of the Russian housing blocks came through the gap from time to time and looked suspiciously at the group standing there. Normally such a group of three would suggest drinkers, with a bottle of vodka to split.

'I wanted to give you this,' he said, passing over a piece of folded typescript. 'Pass it on to the others, if you can. Try and use it in full.' Like all dissidents, Kostya always wanted his protest materials used in full, preferably on the front page, immediately. This was by no means always justified by their content, though there *were* occasions when it was, in the judgement of Editors.

'In future, when I call and say let's meet at, for instance, seven o'clock, that means here, at six. Always one hour ahead of time. We can fix another meeting place next time.' There were handshakes, and the group broke up.

These complicated timing arrangements never worked, and were always abandoned after a while in favour of a more open approach. Neither side could ever be sure whether the other had understood or remembered the 'code' correctly, or whether it was being used at all. After a few meetings in the backyard, Kostya took to a permanent rendezvous on a busy street corner just beside the place where he had access to the room in the 'communal apartment'. The K.G.B. never interfered.

From time to time, the Urban Guerilla would show up, too, but he became increasingly involved in his own attempts to obtain permission to leave the country, and seemed to fade from the scene fairly early on.

Not so Kostya. He called in bursts, concentrating now on one correspondent, now on another, accepting it regretfully when a meeting was not convenient, but gently insisting that something be arranged 'later in the week—because the sooner this gets out the better'.

He was not the only person who had taken to calling regularly on the telephone. There was also Fat Sasha.

Fat Sasha was so nicknamed in order to distinguish him from another acquaintance called Young Sasha. Sasha (short for Alexander) is such a common name in Russia that a dozen male acquaintances are pretty sure to yield at least one.

Fat Sasha was not a dissident. He was, to all appearances, a kind of Soviet journalist who lived on the fringe of the foreign community. He was an Arabist, and he showed up at diplomatic receptions from time to time, where he could engage Arab diplomats in fluent conversation in several types of Arabic. He liked to be invited for *cous-cous*, as he had served in North Africa in a Soviet diplomatic mission.

Fat Sasha was not like other Soviet journalists, who will graciously accept the odd invitation to lunch by a Western colleague, turning up or not as the mood takes them, with or without warning. Or they will come to Embassy receptions, gather impressions, spread the odd rumour, deliver harangues and drink a good deal. But they will hardly ever reciprocate Western hospitality in their own country. An invitation to a Pravda man's home, or to lunch at his expense, or to a reception at the paper's, is a rarity even for those Foreign Correspondents who cultivate them carefully. It is *they* who expect to be entertained. Or they may just be afraid of being 'compromised'.

What made Fat Sasha different was the fact that he was prepared to invite foreigners to his own home, entertain them quite lavishly, and come to their home reliably and punctually, sometimes bringing female members of his small family. He was amiable, amusing and just a little bit informative about everyday matters. He was thoroughly at ease in the company of foreigners, and he devoured English paperbacks.

He took to ringing frequently, in order to ask for help with odd points in his English translations. But since he had a native English-speaker in his office, this could hardly have been his real motive. It seemed he just wanted to keep the acquaintanceship going, and was intelligent enough to realise that English-speaking people like to be asked questions about their own language.

'Soon my wife is coming home,' he would say on the telephone, 'and you must bring your wife to my place for some fresh *pirozhki* (a cross between doughnuts and sausage rolls). But please, if you do not mind, bring some gin and a bottle of lime juice or some tonic, as my wife is very partial to it and she cannot get it in the shops. And please remember, if you have some paperbacks, which you no longer need, to bring them too.'

'Unfortunately, Sasha, most of the paperbacks we have finished with have some sort of anti-Soviet content. So it would be wrong of me to distribute them.'

'I would of course denounce you immediately for doing so,' Fat Sasha would reply with mock offence. *He* knew very well what limits a foreigner had to impose on himself in handing out books in Russia.

'I shall give you a copy of our journal,' he would say. 'It has a very anti-Syrian article in it. I am sure you can make use of an anti-Syrian article from the Soviet press.'

Or he would say: 'Here is a good story for you, but if you print it in your newspaper, please do not say that Sasha told it to you. In Leningrad recently, there was a big queue for those large cans of salted herring which come on the market occasionally. People were being allowed to buy one can each. But one woman in the queue said she had not enough money for a whole can, and would the shop assistant mind opening it and giving her half the contents. Then all the other people in the queue began shouting her down, saying they had no time to waste, and if she did not have enough money for a whole can, then she should leave the queue. But another woman said that she also did not have enough money, and would share a can with the first woman. So the shop assistant, over the protests of the majority in the queue, opened a can—and discovered that it was full of black caviar, which has been unavailable in the shops for several years, except for foreign currency. They checked some of the other cans, and found the same thing. A mistake had been made with the labelling. All the people in the queue knew about it, and they wanted to get a can before the mistake was discovered. The two women were the only ones who did not know.'

It was hardly a story to set the Thames on fire, and it was simply a rumour heard from a single person. But such titbits made Sasha interesting company. For instance, one could ring him up and ask what system exactly prevailed in the issue of bus season-tickets. His answers usually strayed towards optimism, but at least he could be asked and would give a reply without first clearing it through the Foreign Ministry, as would be the case with a normal Soviet bureaucrat—if he were contactable at all.

Sasha made it clear quite early on that he was a member of the Party and strictly loyal to the overall lines of the Communist system. But he was careful to avoid sharp arguments, which a better-known and still more highly westernised Soviet journalist used to provoke, apparently just for the fun of watching foreigners get angry.

'Well, well,' Fat Sasha commented, after hearing a journalist's tale of woe about working conditions in the Soviet Union. 'When they make me Head of the Press Department of the Foreign Ministry, I shall bear all your complaints in mind.' There was not the remotest chance of his receiving this job, of course, but since he was, if anything, on the official side of the fence, there seemed to be no harm in dropping a word in his ear and hoping it would be passed on.

Then he would be after things again. 'Please, when you go on leave, remember my request to bring back some more paperbacks. And if you have some books in German, I have a young cousin who is ill and is learning the language. And if I may make one last request, could you spare a small bottle of gin and some tonic or lime juice?'

Sasha was careful not to commit his free-and-easy relationship with foreigners to paper. When asked to send a postcard to an elderly Australian couple, whom he had entertained handsomely in his home a few months before, he dictated some dreadful twaddle about 'strengthening the friendship and understanding between our two great countries'. But then he had been helping himself to vodka and brandy from 1.30 p.m. till nearly 6 p.m. (his idea of going out to lunch).

Oddly enough, the telephone calls from Sasha and Kostya, usually so different in tone and content, coincided once in their subject matter. The journal *Novy Mir*, formerly a stronghold of relatively liberal opinions—until the ouster and subsequent death of its long-time Editor, Tvardovsky—had dropped a monstrous brick. It had printed a longish poem by a little-known writer called Markin, ostensibly describing a lonely buoy-keeper who has been betrayed by his wife. But all sorts of internal and circumstantial evidence made it plain that this was an allegory in which Markin regretted having been forced to vote for the expulsion of the novelist Solzhenitsyn from the Ryazan branch of the Writers' Union some two years before.

Kostya was most helpful when asked for a little background to this story. He checked around, and rang back in half an hour with the whole, dramatic tale. The hardest thing to understand was how the allegory had escaped the attention of the new Editor of *Novy Mir*, a Party-controlled bureaucrat, and of the entire censorship apparatus. Perhaps they just assumed that the 'Novy Mir problem' had been solved by the change of Editors, and henceforth no one would try to use it as a vehicle for liberal views.

Sasha also phoned a day or two later, apparently puzzled about the whole business. 'What is this I hear about a poem by this *Jew*, Markin?' he asked. He obviously linked Markin's Jewishness with the fact that the writer had attempted to make a gesture of atonement for his betrayal of Solzhenitsyn. Sasha was not above telling the odd anti-Semitic joke, but generally he steered clear of the subject because he understood the sensitivities it aroused.

From time to time, mainly through Kostya, one would hear progress reports on the Urban Guerilla. 'They picked him up again yesterday and held him for four hours for questioning'—or: 'He tried to get into the Central Committee with the last delegation, but they turned him out'—or: 'He has been refused his exit visa for the ninth time.'

Kostya had very definite views on the situation in the Soviet Union, which seemed extreme even to representatives of the 'bourgeois' West, although they were all based on sound premises. 'You must never underrate the tricks that this bunch (the security police) will get up to,' he said one day. 'This is a *gryaznaya razvyedka* (an intelligence service using dirty methods). They will use any lie, or blackmail, or provocation, to get people into their power. They are totally without morals.' He was not interested in being told that amorality was a frequent characteristic of intelligence services, not only in Russia.

'The last time they hauled me in,' he said, 'they told me they had conducted a sociological survey of dissidents and protesters, and found they fell into three groups: children of former "repressees" (i.e. victims of Stalin's purges); Jews seeking to emigrate; and psychiatrically ill people. There was some sort of small, fourth category, into which they put people like P. (a friend of Pavel's) who simply dream of overthrowing Soviet Power.

'The way Western governments toady to this leadership is a scandal. The only thing our leaders understand is force. By entering into agreements with them, and flirting with them, the West is simply playing their game and helping to keep them in power.

'Now our press has been making all this fuss about Angela Davies, the Black Communist in America. And her sister has come here and been shown on television, and there are protest meetings all over the country. Well, Angela Davies calls herself a Communist, but just let her come here for a few months, and try getting a flat or buying some trousers in the shops, and see how she feels about it then.

'I know you don't like it when I talk like this.—Don't worry about him, he's just an old boy, he's not listening.—But you can't understand what it is like to be Soviet unless you have climbed into our skins. This is a doomed order.' He kept repeating that phrase—in Russian, *obrechonnyi stroy*.

Fat Sasha did not think the Soviet Order was doomed at all, though he was rarely profound on the matter. He used to complain about all sorts of things, such as shortages, or administrative red-tape, or some Governmental official. But he would never directly criticise the Leadership or the Party. He did not try to stop his wife when she launched into her fanatical pro-Stalinist tirades.

He seemed a little scared of his wife, in fact. She was a tough customer, who had fought in the war and looked back to it with nostalgia. 'We worshipped Stalin and I carried his portrait all through the war,' she used to proclaim. 'Why should I change now?'

On Woman's Day, someone asked jokingly: 'There is supposed to be equality of the sexes in the Soviet Union, so why is there not a Man's Day as well?'

Fat Sasha said: 'Oh, but there is. Armed Forces Day is Man's Day in the Soviet Union.'

'What do you mean?' bellowed his wife, who was older than he. 'I served right through the war! When were you at the front?'

'Well,' Fat Sasha rejoined lamely, 'I did my service, too, and furthermore, I was an officer.' His wife snorted.

Another example of the toughness of Fat Sasha's wife came when they told what happened in the case of a woman who occupied another room in their communal apartment, and was a total alcoholic. 'She is very bad,' Sasha said. 'She has so much of it in her system, that one drink renders her almost unconscious. Usually she barely eats anything. But the other night my wife heard a noise in the kitchen, so she went in and found our neighbour raiding our food-cupboard—simply eating out of it on the spot.'

Sasha's wife took over the anecdote at this point. 'I gave her one wallop in the face, and as she fell I gave her another and left her lying on the floor.'

Sasha concluded: 'She disappeared for a few days after that, but lately she has been round here again, drunk as ever.'

It became more and more obvious that Fat Sasha had some special kind of licence to mix with certain foreigners, and that to cadge things from them was one of the perks of his job. But it was not clear what exactly his job was. For he never tried to mount a provocation, to subvert or to blackmail. His role, apparently, was just to sooth feelings, watch for weaknesses—and win confidence.

In the end, all Fat Sasha's cultivation of the acquaintanceship, pleasant though it was in itself, was wasted. And anyway his cover had been blown some time since. He was, in fact, a K.G.B. agent known to people who took an interest in these matters.

The progress reports on the Urban Guerilla became fewer as time went on, until one day Kostya was asked what had become of him. 'Oh, they got him good and proper,' Kostya said with his nervous giggle. 'They slapped him in the Army for two years, so they'll have him for another three after he gets out, for having had "access to military secrets".' The Urban Guerilla would by then have spent most of his twenties in attempts to leave the Soviet Union by legal channels.

Five Roubles to One

WHAT did Kostya mean when he passed scathing remarks about Angela Davies, the American black Communist? Did he believe that blacks and poor people in the United States had no genuine grievances, or was he just under-rating them? How well did he understand the comparison in living standards between Russia and America?

Economic standards of living are usually measured in terms of money. So in Russia they have to be measured in terms of Roubles. The exchange rate of the Rouble is the subject of more misunderstandings about Soviet society and standards of living than almost any other single factor. It needs to be spelt out exactly.

The Rouble is not an international currency. It is forbidden either to import or export it. Although the Soviet Union prints its foreign trade statistics in Roubles for prestige reasons, all payments are carried out either on a barter basis, or in gold, or in the hard currencies of the capitalist world. The so-called 'Transferable Rouble', supposed to be the unit of exchange for trading purposes with East European countries, and eventually with other countries as well, remains a very shadowy concept, actually a disguised form of barter trade.

Importing and exporting is in the hands of the State, so with rare exceptions the ordinary citizen has no justification for holding unchanged foreign currency. If he is permitted to travel abroad, he will be given an allowance of it by the State. If he receives foreign currency remittances from, say, relatives abroad, the State changes them into Rouble 'certificates' at a rate highly advantageous to itself, and allows the citizen to use special shops where goods are cheaper or where things can be bought that are simply not obtainable in the ordinary shops.

All this means that the Soviet authorities can fix the value of the Rouble at virtually any rate they please in terms of foreign currencies—it makes little difference to their exchange position. Tourists, who bring foreign currency into Russia, live mainly in an artificial world of special vouchers, hotels, restaurants, bars and shops, where prices are fixed at something approximating to normal international standards, despite poor service.

By fixing the Rouble at a realistic rate (say, about nine or ten to the pound), the Soviet authorities could stamp out most black-marketeering in foreign currency, and do away with the embarrassing comparison between the high prices of goods in Soviet shops, and those in the West. For instance, a can of fruit juice, which is now seen to cost 46 pence, would then appear to a British tourist to cost only about 10 pence, i.e. it would seem that the cost of living in Russia was low or at least very reasonable, but it would also show how very low wages are. As it is, any foreigner walking around the shops, and making price conversions at the official rate, should find the cost of living incredibly high if his mental arithmetic is correct.

The exchange rate against Sterling in 1972 was around 2.17 Roubles to the Pound. This means, if one takes the exchange rate literally, that a new compact saloon car, modelled on the Fiat 124, costs nearly £3,500 for the Soviet citizen with only Roubles and no foreign currency to spend. He will also have to go through the troublesome process of getting his name down on a waiting list and then waiting months or years for his car. The Soviet authorities sell the car readily, however, to foreigners, at the equivalent of £484 in hard currency. They will even buy it back second-hand with only a nominal reduction in price—but they will pay in 'soft' Roubles. If they give 1,030 Roubles or £475 for a slightly used car, they can resell it to a Soviet citizen at, say, 5,000 Roubles, with a clear profit of 3,970 to the State. It is all the same to the foreigner, who is obliged by the law to accept the official exchange rate—unless, as in the case of a number of Embassies, he has illegal access to 'cheap' Roubles purchased outside the country and smuggled in through the Diplomatic Bag.

All these calculations about exchange rates and cars would be meaningless, if one did not take into account the earnings of Soviet citizens in Roubles, and the prices of other goods and services. After all, the authorities make no bones about it: their automobile industry is under-developed, because other priorities have been attended to first. Well and good. Perhaps the West should have done the same.

As it happens, however, the high *cost* of living in the Soviet Union is not matched by an appropriately high level of average wage *earnings*, as the case is, say, in the United States. An average industrial wage in Russia would be between 100 and 200 Roubles (£46 and £92) per month, or about £11–£22 a week at the official rate of exchange. The minimum wage for industrial workers is now fixed at 70 Roubles a month (£7.50 a week). Collective farmers may earn less wages, but they have access to cheap food and can sell their surpluses.

Since most Soviet wives work, a family income of 300 Roubles a month (£32 a week at the official rate) would not be unduly difficult to achieve in a city. There is minimal income tax, and many people are in subsidised flats costing only a pound or two a month with hot water and central heating included. Public transport is extremely cheap, though overcrowded. Health services are free, except for medicines. Education is free, except for text-books. Books and records are cheap, though of low quality and narrow choice. Holidays are frequently subsidised by trade unions. Domestic air travel is cheap, though with a scramble for tickets. So that £32 a week ought to go a fairly long way, even for a married couple with two children (the normal maximum size of family in the northern parts of the country where most of the population live).

This, indeed, is the picture which Soviet propaganda consistently puts abroad: workers enjoying most of the essentials of life free, or at heavily subsidised prices, and spending most of their earnings on the beautification of their socialist existences.

The real picture is very different. The reason is simple: high prices in the shops, low quality of goods, shortages, and primitive service industries. Since the State owns the shops and service industries, and fixes the prices, it makes up for subsidised housing and other benefits with a truly *massive* purchase tax. Only the name is missing.

The disguised purchase tax hits the lowest paid worker worst, because it affects prices of food and other basic essentials almost as much as consumer durables and luxury goods (when they are obtainable). In fact, the food supply situation in the cities is so inadequate that the Soviet authorities are forced to this day to retain a remnant of free enterprise, in order to maintain a minimum dietary standard. This is the 'collective farm market' or food market, where peasants from the surrounding countryside are allowed to sell off production which they have withheld from the State. (Many country people themselves pay train and bus fares to come into the city and shop at the market, in order to obtain simple foodstuffs which may not be available in their particular village.) The prices are extremely high for most market foodstuffs at most times of the year, though they fluctuate widely. Without markets, people would have a diet so starchy and monotonous that malnutrition would be a still more common complaint. At present, it is reflected in widespread hypochondria, poor resistance to infections, and bad female figures.

What does one mean by high food prices? Say, 58 pence a lb. for chickens or leeks at the market, with tomatoes going up as high as two or even more pounds sterling a lb. in the winter. In the shops, prices are regulated but still high, for instance: milk, 20 p. a pint; butter, 82 p. a lb.; margarine, 32 p. a lb.; eggs, 5 p. each; cheese, 60 p. a lb.; flour, 9 p. a lb.; white bread, 6 p. a lb.; rice, 18 p. a lb.; chocolate bars, £2.44 a lb.; cocoa, £1.06 a lb.; tea, from £1.17 to £2.17 a lb.; low-grade coffee beans, 85 p. a lb.; sugar, 20 p. a lb. These sterling prices are calculated at the official rate of exchange, and they give a realistic idea of food prices in the sense that the official rate makes wage levels roughly equivalent to those in a rather depressed Western economy. So the cost of the family food basket each week is really very high, and it more than makes up for the various State subsidies on housing and social services. All the more so because the quality and packaging of the Soviet products is generally poor, and consumer durables are similarly expensive.

Then there are the great inequities in living conditions in different parts of the country. It is not surprising if Moscow and Leningrad have the best-stocked shops and the finest theatres and cinemas. They ought to, as major cities. But settlement in such large cities is strictly regulated: Russians say that almost the only way for a non-professional person to get permission to settle in them nowadays is by taking a job as a caretaker at a block of flats (for which accommodation is provided automatically), or as a policeman. The police prefer to recruit in the provinces so that their members will not have local loyalties. Outside Moscow, the standard of living declines sharply, the smaller the town and the farther East one goes. In northern regions and in Siberia, special allowances are paid to entice workers, but these are wiped out by supplements on the prices of consumer goods, by poorer services, and by the still greater demand for spirits, from which the Government takes a huge excise tax. Only in the South are certain aspects of food-supply easier than in Moscow or other big cities of the North-West, because fruit and vegetables grow more easily locally, and because sheep are widely reared for meat. In the Baltic States, the 'bourgeois' traditions of the pre-war period have left their mark in better city planning and a more cultured approach to living. But the general rule for a rewarding life in the Soviet Union is: the bigger the city, the better; and the closer to Moscow, the better.

The domestic situation in Russia affects the world evaluation of its currency, which is still traded in West European banks, despite the official ban on its import and export. Certain foreigners, who earn their incomes in hard currency, clearly have an interest in buying Roubles cheaply outside the country, and smuggling them in. This tends to devalue the currency domestically, and is therefore a crime. But foreigners have no interest in smuggling Roubles out— they could only lose in the process. A foreigner who purchased 2.17 Roubles for £1 in Moscow, and took them out of the country in his hip pocket through carelessness, would find that he could not unload them to a Western bank except at a rate of about 7 or 8 pence per Rouble. The people who illegally take Roubles out of Russia are Soviet citizens, who are being sent abroad on one kind of assignment or another. Say a Russian attends a conference in Geneva, and manages to smuggle out 1,000 Roubles in notes. He can take them discreetly to a Swiss bank, and get perhaps the equivalent of between £50 and £100 for them, as opposed to their official value of about £460. The bank will off-load them at a profit to some risk-taking foreigner on his way to Moscow. The Russian will instantly visit Swiss shops and buy up woollen knitwear or Beatles records with his hard currency, though it might amount to more than four months' worth of his earnings at home. Provided he gets them past the Customs in Moscow, he can probably make a net profit by selling his purchases again privately for Roubles. Or he could bring his family and friends valuable and much sought-after gifts.

Of course, the free market rate for Roubles will be depressed by the risks involved in shipping them in and out of the country. But all things taken into account, it seems that the present official selling rate for the Rouble is somewhere around four or five times its true value. It has to be borne in mind that the value of a country's currency reflects more than its economic performance. It also reflects the general judgement on the desirability of living there, or purchasing things there. In such a calculation, the lack of personal and political freedom in Russia obviously helps to debase its currency, since it makes fewer people inclined to go there. And its consumer goods are unattractive as purchases, except for a few souvenir-type items such as vodka or wooden dolls.

Forgetting about the official exchange rate, and the question of the real value of the Rouble, Western economists have done studies which show average prices of a wide range of commodities in various countries, measured in terms of the average number of minutes which people in different professions have to work in order to buy them. The studies show that Soviet prices are nearly all twice, three times or even more than those prevailing in Western Europe and the United States, in terms of the shoppers' working time and real wages. This does not take into account the lower quality of the Soviet goods, or the amount of time wasted in queueing or trying to discover where a scarce article is on sale. And it effectively wipes out the benefits from various subsidised services.

What about the housing situation? Subsidised housing, even when it is crude and cramped, is undoubtedly a great blessing, and something which most Soviet families set their hearts on unless they are ambitious enough to put up the money for a co-operative flat, which they can then own. Friends are liable to rally round with loans. The prices of such flats are certainly low by, say, London standards, but it has to be borne in mind that accommodation acquires value from the facilities available to the resident in the surrounding area, as well as the property itself. Considering the extremely poor public facilities—cafés, shops, laundries and so on— in a Soviet suburb, the prices of co-operative flats there are not cheap. They would not stand up for a week in a British suburb, because most people would simply refuse to live in such poorly-serviced areas.

Nor is subsidised accommodation as widely available as the Soviet authorities like to make out. The Soviet family of four dreams of a small, rented, two-room flat, with its own plumbing and kitchen. This is their escape from the proximity of in-laws, or the squalor of a communal flat where it is impossible to use the lavatory with proper privacy, and where food has to be locked up in individual cupboards in the kitchen. Or it may mean release from a picturesque but decrepit wooden house, without running water, and full of cockroaches.

How does the family go about getting itself improved accommodation? It may be lucky, if it lives in a particularly old-fashioned area due for redevelopment. Its housing will then be pulled down and the rubble burned: a new housing block will be put up, and the family assigned a flat in it. *Krokodil*, the official humorous magazine, pointed to some snags, in a cartoon: the demolition squad is waiting to tear down a wooden house, but an old woman refuses to budge from it in order to take up her new quarters in the modern block nearby. 'I can't live there,' she says. 'I've got used to having some water and heating.' In other words, the installation of basic facilities in the new housing blocks frequently leaves a lot to be desired. This is due to the haste with which they are thrown up, and the bureaucracy involved in getting dozens of different organisations to deliver the correct parts at the right time. The fabric of the buildings is crude, and so is the finish.

A common way of finding a new flat is through one's place of work. Most sizeable industrial enterprises operate their own housing schemes, as do many other organisations. If a person works there for a few years, he or she will expect to be given a flat. If it is a completely new town being built round a big industrial project accommodation *may* be available within the first few years. Otherwise, the workers live in hostels without their families. Recently, there has been pressure on industrial enterprises to take the work-performance and social behaviour of their employees into account in allocating places in the housing queue: if a man is frequently drunk or absent from work, he may be passed over for a new flat. In general, Soviet industrial managers and 'trade unions' stray towards leniency over such offences. The restrictions on individual movements, and the bottlenecks in planning, create artificial labour shortages in many industrial areas, so that managers will seek means to over-pay their workers and overlook their peccadillos. Otherwise they cannot fulfil their Plan, which means that they will earn no bonuses for themselves or their workers, and may even be penalised financially. (Russia has no trade unions in the Western sense of the word, a fact recognised by the use of the English word to describe the British type of trade union in Russian. The Soviet variety are called *profsoyuzy* or 'professional unions'. They have no role in organising labour against management. There are no strikes, because they would be treated as serious crimes. The *profsoyuzy* are totally subservient to the Party, which makes them collaborate with management in almost everything except individual cases of wrongful dismissal, in which they might make representations if the Party approved. Their chief role is as organisers of workers' benefits, and as propaganda organs, for instance in the implementation of new economic schemes or experiments.)

A problem faced by the industrial enterprises is that they cannot automatically evict a tenant from their accommodation if he leaves their employment in order to seek a job elsewhere. Thus the factory's flats may gradually drift away from their owners. But they will revert if the tenant decides to move away. The ban on free trading of property naturally makes people reluctant to spend much on improving or maintaining the premises in which they live. This, combined with low building standards, leads to rapid obsolescence of new housing.

Moving house is a complicated business, because it often entails a swap with another family. There is a special system of advertising for this, e.g.: 'Will exchange one-room flat, 15 minutes Yugo-Zapad Metro Station, for similar in Avtozavodskaya area. Ring 154-28-82.' Apart from factory flats, there are quantities of housing owned by local authorities, and allocated on a basis similar to the Council House system in Britain.

But take the case of Viktor N., a man of about 30 who was encountered by chance in the town of Yaroslavl, north-east of Moscow. Viktor was an industrial draughtsman, but he had itchy feet and rarely stayed long at one place of work. So he never qualified for subsidised accommodation. He lived at home, sharing a single room with his mother. His sleeping space, beside the only door, was separated off by a small partition. He had been married twice, and brought his brides home, but Mama was jealous, and the cramped living quarters made it virtually impossible to consummate the marriages. Both wives had left Viktor within a short space of time. In order to rent a room privately, he would have had to pay about a third of his salary. He did not have enough savings to put his name down for ownership of a co-operative flat. So he continued living at home with his mother, and conducting desultory love-affairs with the wives of his friends. Yet he did not consider himself badly off.

Had he obtained a flat, and then wanted to change it, there was a simple method which he made a point of showing: on a particular street corner in Yaroslavl, at particular times of the week, there is always a crowd of people, standing around and haggling. This is the 'housing market', where people come to offer exchanges of accommodation. Why was it on that particular street, Viktor was asked? 'Oh,' he said, 'the city housing bureau used to be here, until it was moved away to another part of the town, but many people have got used to coming to this spot, so they keep on doing so.'

Given reasonable industriousness and economy, a Soviet working family can purchase most of the consumer durables which it is feasible to obtain, within about seven years of setting up house. These will include a refrigerator, a television set, rugs and a suite of furniture. (The furniture may prove the most difficult.) If the head of the family is particularly ambitious or energetic, he may put his name down for a car, and eventually obtain one. But then it is likely to become an obsession. The neighbours will complain if he tries to build himself a garage. So he will have to lay the car up for the winter, unless he lives in the South. If anything goes wrong, he will have a devil of a job finding spare parts and getting servicing. If he has an accident and smashes the car up, he will not get a new one out of the insurance company (yes, there is insurance in Russia). So most people simply do not bother as yet, though motoring is sure to become an increasingly popular pastime.

Beyond this point, there is liable to be an end to acquisitiveness. 'Keeping up with the Joneses' does exist, but it is less of a mania than in the West, because over a certain limit it becomes so extremely difficult and expensive to lay one's hands on novel consumer goods. There is no chance of buying a bigger car, because there are no bigger cars on the market. Nor is it possible to blow some money on a holiday in Spain or the Caribbean: ordinary citizens will rarely be allowed to leave the country except on delegations, or on 'trade-union'-sponsored group visits to other Communist countries. A few weeks in a rest-home on the Soviet Black Sea coast will cost little: it is mainly a question of finding some means to get a sponsorship from one's place of work.

The ways Soviet people spend their leisure are essentially no different from those favoured by people in the West, except that in Russia leisure activities are more strictly regulated by the State and it is more difficult to gain access to the basic facilities. The narrow confines within which most Soviet existences are led, combined with a well-known Russian tradition, lead to what is probably the world's worst alcoholism problem. On many public holidays in Moscow, the street scenes by early evening are as bacchanalian as a Scottish New Year. No one who has not lived in Russia can conceive what mass social alcoholism means. Russians may not drink every day, as the French do, but when they drink they have a tendency to drink methodically, with the aim of blotting themselves out for twelve hours. In the towns, no one even turns a head at the sight of a drunk unconscious on the pavement. Eventually a van will pick him up, if he stays there long enough, and take him to a sobering-up station for treatment and a 15-Rouble fine, which at least will deprive him of his next two bottles of vodka. But the shame and stigma of the process—which may be reported to his place of work—may drive a man to go out and get drunk again. The Russians distinguish between someone who is dead drunk and someone who is only staggering drunk—'just tipsy', as they put it. The popular definition of a real drunk is someone who needs 'one friend to take each arm, and a third one behind to move his feet.' Pay-day at factories gives rise to so many carouses that the authorities have mounted an experiment with payment of wages through savings banks.

A man who does not have enough money for a whole bottle of vodka goes into a store and discreetly wags two fingers. Another joins him, and they wag one finger till a third man turns up. Then they go off and finish the bottle somewhere with a crust of bread or a bit of preserved fish (to drink without eating is considered unhealthy). There is a joke about a three-man Western spy ring which is being tracked down by the Soviet authorities. Two of its members have already been caught, but the third is more elusive. He is captured one day, because someone comes up to him in a grocery store and says: 'Would you be the third?'—and he surrenders.

The other great release from boredom in Russia is meddling in other people's business, and this is one of the most important support systems which the country's political structure relies on. When people live at close quarters in cramped housing blocks, with thin walls, they tend to know more about each other than is considered healthy in the West, where privacy is regarded as a basic liberty. They are constantly lectured by their press and Leaders on the need for active participation in social improvement campaigns, so that they moralise excessively about their neighbours' behaviour. The mass of people in a housing block or a factory are supposed to take responsibility for the social behaviour of individual members. There are so-called 'comradely courts', at which a drunk or a presumed petty thief may be hauled up and given a dressing-down before his workmates or neighbours, before he 'gets so bad' that he has to be turned over to the police. (A scene observed on a train from Novgorod to Leningrad illustrates the submissiveness of most Russians to hectoring. The conductress addresses a coach-load of grown-up passengers: 'Now, I'm going to let you travel on your own today, but you must behave yourselves, not get up and walk around, and not get the coach dirty.' No one seemed to find it humiliating or irritating to be addressed in this way.)

In theory, this may be a good thing: a necessary stage on the road towards the formation of 'socialist man', whoever *he* is. In practice it leads to officially guided mob decisions, and systematised gossip as a means of political control. An able Party worker knows how to use the usual quota of meddlesome old women in a housing block, in order to keep the bulk of the residents in line. The moral and social ideals proclaimed by the Party are essentially those associated with late middle-age and elderliness: they are anti-dissent, anti-sex, anti-innovation. There is no youth in the age group 15–25 so inarticulate as the youth of Russia. The weight of social conformism bears down on young people until they either conform, turn delinquent, or, in rare cases, opt for free thinking and political dissent.

At the Moscow Watch Factory, in 1972, 'activists' pinned up a satirical rhyme and an insulting caricature of a young male worker who had not had his hair cut for a while. The most hopeful sign was that the boy had still not gone to have it cut.

The Young Ones

IT IS a terrible thing to be envious of one's wife, especially if one is jealous of her at the same time. Zhenya was around thirty, and he was plagued by the fact that people kept referring to him as 'the guy with the beard whose wife got put away'. He shaved off the beard but later he let it grow again.

Zhenya's wife was a strikingly attractive though not actually beautiful girl, with bright blonde hair which was (in fact) brown at the roots. She was always stylishly and tastefully dressed, and Zhenya loved her painfully. She had an odd, nasal voice, and her attractiveness was a presence rather than anything one could define.

She had also done a year or two in labour camp for activities connected with the Democratic Movement. When she came out, she was more married to the Movement than to Zhenya, and she seemed to be in love with another, younger man, who had done a similar stretch for making a political demonstration. Zhenya kept hoping it would work out somehow, and she would come back to him. Permanently broke himself, he borrowed some money so that she could go off to Siberia and meet a prominent dissident who was coming out of exile. He hoped that this might 'get it out of her system'. But she just came back and stuck with the other man, and Zhenya seemed almost to want to go to prison camp, just to compete.

He apparently had no fixed residence. He had started a physics degree years ago, and his career had been chopped off for the usual political reasons. He lived with different friends, sometimes sleeping in different places on consecutive nights. He drank heavily when he had drink, and to people he trusted he poured out his heart about his wife. She, busy with the Movement, started asking people not to give him drink.

Zhenya was also active in the Movement—too weak, perhaps, for his wife, but strong enough to stand up to the K.G.B. His father was fairly senior in the Party or Government, though ignorant of or shocked by his son's activity. Zhenya would not reveal who his father was, but perhaps the relationship afforded him a marginal protection.

Zhenya is an unusually charming person. He has soft eyes, a broad smile, and a general easiness about his manner which makes him instantly attractive to all who meet him. His favourite hobbies are drinking a pint of beer in three seconds (he usually spills a good deal of it), and composing palindromes (phrases which read exactly the same from back to front). The masterpiece consists of a 42-letter sentence, which is rather indecent.

After visiting a foreigner's flat one night, Zhenya walked to the Metro Station to go home, went down the escalator and onto the platform. Instantly two or three K.G.B. men began pushing him towards the edge of the platform. A train was coming. At the last moment, they pulled him back, shouting: 'He wanted to do away with himself!' What happened then is not quite clear, but Zhenya said later: 'There were some good lads around who got me away and put me on a train by myself.'

Determined not to be intimidated, Zhenya refused all offers of accompaniment and went to the same Metro Station after visiting the same foreigner on another occasion. This time, the same K.G.B. men picked him up on the grounds that he had been drinking, had him taken to a police station, and searched. But actually he had won, because he had refused to be frightened.

One day Zhenya proposed going to supper with some friends who lived a few Metro stations away, behind Komsomolskaya Square. The hosts were a young married couple, but their parents and in-laws and some younger acquaintances came along too. Very soon the questions started coming: 'What do people in the West think of Russia?' . . . 'What is the meaning of the Soviet Union's Middle East policy?' . . . 'What is the real origin of the Vietnam situation?' . . . 'Is it true that only the children of the rich can go to university in your country?' Often, one does not know the answer to such questions, or they are too complicated to explain, particularly in Russian. But a willingness to give honestly of what one knows, or what one knows how to express, is reciprocated in the end.

The host, Volodya Simonov, was particularly interested in Canada, as a democratic society not afflicted by as many ills of excessive freedom as the United States. But Zhenya said: 'Is it true that the Canadian native people have been badly treated? If so I reject Canadian democracy too.' (He meant, 'As well as Soviet Socialism'.)

Simonov retorted 'I've met some of our fliers who go up to the

Arctic regions, and they say local people up there are shockingly exploited by the Russians, their furs are bought at cheap rates for vodka, and their way of life is ruined.' This would be a striking contrast to the pictures of happy reindeer-herders in the Soviet press.

The meal progressed in the slow, random way Russians favour. A few *zakuski* are brought on (canned herring when it is in the shops, sliced cheese, a little salted salmon, chopped salads, hard boiled eggs and plenty black bread). If anyone has been thoughtful or extravagant enough to bring vodka, this is drunk throughout the meal, but preferably in chorus, with a toast each time.

The correct way to drink vodka, as it is explained by Russians, is to breathe out, swallow an entire, small glassful at a gulp, wait a few seconds till the raw spirit hits the stomach, munch some *zakuski*—and only then breathe in. Afterwards, some people breathe heavily on the back of their hand, or sniff a piece of black bread.

This ritual is explained as a custom developed by the Russian aristocracy, who considered vodka to be a foul-tasting, peasant concoction, but one which they found much cheaper for getting drunk on than the wines they imported. Vodka should be served cold—preferably below zero centigrade—but this is rarely the case nowadays, even in the 'best' Soviet restaurants. A real vodka drinker can put down half a tumblerful without pausing for breath, just as a starter. But not many people can afford to do that often, for spirits are even dearer than in Britain.

Simonov's wife Lyubov disappeared into the kitchen to cope with the carp. It had been bought live, at a special shop, because fresh fish is a rare commodity in Moscow—mostly it is crudely frozen and quite unpalatable. There was a big fuss when the carp, which had been put in the refrigerator to 'go to sleep' and gently die from cold, woke up on being taken out, and started flapping around so that someone had to bludgeon it. The detailed reports of this episode from the kitchen took the edge off some of the guests' appetite, but Lyubov did a splendid job of braising the carp.

Russians toy endlessly with the main course—having eaten many *zakuski* and got tipsy already—waiting until it is cold. Later there is tea or coffee, and a freshly made cake for a special occasion. It all takes a lot of effort and expense, particularly in a communal kitchen, and proper appreciation ought to be shown.

When even the *portveiny* (sweet wines from the Black Sea) begin to run out, the guests take their leave, sometimes singing, arm in arm in perhaps minus 25 degrees centigrade, accompanying each other insistently to the Metro station, or the nearest point where a taxi or other passing car can be persuaded to take a fare home in the snow. There may be a good deal of hugging and kissing among men as well as women, while the driver waits impatiently with his engine running.

Lyubov took to dieting a bit to get her weight down, although plumpness suited her. 'I'm just longing for a slice of bread,' she announced one day. 'If it weren't for the potatoes, I don't know how I'd manage.' She was utterly despondent when told that potatoes were every bit as fattening as bread.

The Simonovs were sociable people, who liked doing things together with friends; and he, for his part, had an insatiable curiosity about the outside world. But although he tried to follow foreign affairs closely, he refused to read the Soviet press, saying that it nauseated him too much.

He got hold of a copy of Orwell's '1984' and read it with great excitement. He could hardly believe that the author was English, or that his name was not just a pseudonym for a Soviet underground author. 'I can't imagine that anybody but a Russian could have written it,' he said. 'It is so accurate.'

There were joint excursions to the theatre, the cinema, the countryside, and several of the long, random meals with ample conversation. One night they arranged a visit to the *Dom Kino* ('House of Cinema'), a very modern and sumptuous building which shows the latest films to selected audiences of film-workers and other intellectuals, in order to gauge their reaction for censorship purposes. On the night in question, the films were preceded by an almost hour-long lecture on 'The Role of the Hero in the Soviet Cinema'. It seemed awful, and one girl in the audience openly read a book throughout. But Volodya Simonov whispered that the lecturer was not too bad by current standards, and was making a few interesting points.

The first film was an abomination—over an hour, mostly close-ups of a famous surgeon, explaining why he was a famous surgeon: a magazine interview on film. The Simonovs were unnecessarily embarrassed. In the interval the men went up to the restaurant—one of the best and most modern in Moscow—and shared a flask of Caucasian brandy. Zhenya stayed behind to go to the lavatory, and arrived after the start of the second feature, in the dim light from the screen. He started pushing past a row of other spectators, with the elaborate politeness of someone who knows he is already half drunk. He got about five places along—then discovered he was in the wrong row. His friends had been watching this scene with gaiety from the row behind, where his place was, and no one took offence when he came shuffling back.

The second film was a gem—very *nouvelle vague,* and produced by a woman. It dealt sensitively and subtly with the relationship between a middle-aged woman and her teenage son. The woman in the film worked for Intourist, and kept trying to imitate foreigners by keeping up a show of sophistication, difficult enough in a country where even hair-dye seems to come in only one or two colours. Her son just wanted to get *with it* in some way. He stuck up posters and writhed on his bed reciting poems. Cynics and careerists drove Volga cars and ate huge meals at country villas. There was a scene of corruption at a Soviet post-office.

A few weeks later the word got around that this film was definitely not coming out on release—though it would probably have won prizes and earned considerable amounts of foreign exchange and artistic prestige for the Soviet Union in France, Italy or the United States. At the same time it was reported that Tarkovsky, producer of the superb and long-censored historical epic 'Andrey Rublyov', was being told to remake substantially his latest effort, based on a book by a futuristic Polish writer. A good film is a painful birth in Russia.

One weekend, a picnic with the Simonovs was arranged at Fili, on the Moscow River, where there are some shaded woody spots. After the thaw, few Russians would venture into the woods before May, and Volodya had to be coaxed, because he said it would be too muddy. It was early spring, though a warm day, and some men were still sitting on upturned buckets on the crumbling ice, fishing.

The male excursionists left the women to set up the picnic table, and went off to look for a place to relieve themselves. Volodya said: 'Did I tell you the story about the Siberian toilet?'

A leaf bent under the pressure of liquid. 'No.'

'It seems that in Paris or somewhere they had an international exhibition of sanitary ware. The Russian exhibit aroused great enthusiasm, because it was totally modernistic. It consisted of two sharpened, iron spikes. Everyone wanted to know how it was used, but there was only a Siberian *muzhik* looking after the stand. So they got a Russian émigré in Paris to come and interrogate him, and the answer came out as follows: "You stick the first spike in the ground, and hang your trousers on it. Then you use the second one to fight off the bears." '

It was a most pleasant picnic, with a walk around the woods. On the way, Volodya said: 'They have been asking about you again.'

'Who?'

'*They*, of course. I told you the last time.'

'Yes, of course.' Volodya had revealed before that the K.G.B. were taking a 'soft line' with him, and had assigned an outwardly agreeable fellow of his own age, who simply phoned occasionally and asked to meet him on the street. It was not a formal interrogation, which requires a written, stamped and signed demand for the person concerned to present himself at the interrogation centre.

'Don't tell my wife,' Volodya mumbled. 'I don't want to worry her.'

'Are they threatening you?'

'Not in the least; he's quite a pleasant young chap. He just wants to know where you get your information, and on what you base your "slanderous inventions" about the Soviet Union. I pointed out to him that if they were based on information, they weren't inventions. We agreed to differ on a number of points. Anyway, I told him that one of your stories had come from me and he didn't seem to care. I said I knew that you always tried very hard to check the accuracy of your information, but didn't know who your sources were. That was all there was to it.'

At supper at Volodya's one evening, he said: 'I don't think we'll be seeing each other again.' (He was going on a walking tour of the Urals the next day, and would not be back for a few weeks.) In the event he was right.

Volodya was keen on yoga, mostly *hatha* yoga. There is a minor fad for it among the younger generation in Moscow. At his house on the first evening there was a very correct and pedantic Jewish intellectual, a youngish dissident who was said to be an adept at yoga. He sat very straight and would drink nothing but plain water, and he did not approve of the Soviet Human Rights Committee, because he thought its doings were unreal. Later he went off to sing in the Russian Orthodox choir at the Novodevichy Monastery—a hobby of his. Later still, he succeeded in getting to Israel. There had been trouble with his wife's parents, who had refused to acknowledge her desire to leave: they were forced, in the end, to accept a registered-delivery letter declaring her desire to do so. She was Russian, not Jewish, but she wanted to go, parents or no.

Volodya is probably still toying with yoga and dreaming of Canada, where he has a distant cousin. He never did anything to warrant arrest or serious interrogation, but if the moment of choice came he might take the hard way. Lyubov—good-natured, fond of a glass of vodka, and a good cook—would accept whatever he did. They have a small circle of friends with whom he discusses everything that needs discussing in Russia, but they prefer not to get directly involved in the 'Movements' (apart from their personal friendships with Zhenya and other active Democrats). They are not unhappy, and would probably be misguided to try and find some way to emigrate. They do not take their jobs too seriously, but they find their work interesting enough, and they like to spend hours in Moscow beer-cellars, gossiping with friends.

Lyubov said on Woman's Day: 'They put an extra armed guard on the door of our institute yesterday. That was because they knew anyone who went out that day, on any excuse at all, would be going for vodka.'

Volodya said: 'At our place there is a whole group which has been drinking in the office for days, because of Woman's Day.' Some aspects of life in Russia are surprisingly lenient.

The Simonovs' friend, Zhenya, was sometimes a little too free and easy for comfort. One night we succeeded in getting four tickets for the theatre; foreigners could usually get a couple without difficulty, but four were harder. The Simonovs were keen to see a Shakespeare play which was being done in Russian, and it was arranged that they would come back to the foreigners' block for supper afterwards. During the performance, Volodya said: 'I hope you don't mind. I've asked Zhenya to meet us after the theatre and come along too. He wanted to see you.' —'Why not?'

The Shakespeare was not very good, and it was cold outside the theatre at the end of the performance. Zhenya was nowhere to be seen. Volodya strolled around the theatre arcade, whistling softly in a special call which he and Zhenya used to each other. Still Zhenya did not appear. Everyone was shivering, so it was decided to give up and drive home for supper.

Just as the stew was being served, Zhenya rang. 'We're coming in half an hour,' he said. (It was then about 11.30).

'Won't that be a bit late?'

'We're coming.'

He rang off, without saying who 'we' were. Volodya and Lyubov exchanged embarrassed glances. A party of unspecified numbers were arriving at midnight, in the middle of a meal which would now have to be hurried; the fresh guests would have to be brought in past the militiaman, brought out again in the small hours, and found transport home. The Simonovs felt responsible for spoiling the evening, and were apologetic. They were very nice people.

In due course Zhenya arrived with Pavel, and a political exile who spent most of his life in Siberia, and was just snatching a few months in Moscow between stretches. They were served drinks, and then began helping themselves, though they had obviously had a few already.

Zhenya was in a very bad way over his wife. He sat on the sofa confiding his troubles to Lyubov, who was an old friend of his and who cuddled him a little to make him feel better. The political exile kept playing record after record on the gramophone—he was a starved jazz enthusiast—and drinking whisky too fast, as though he would not have the chance again for years, which was pretty near the truth. He went through the bookshelves with a hungry eye. He could read English. As he got drunker, he insisted on dancing with one of the women, though the flat was much too small. Then Zhenya wanted to dance, too, fell over a coffee table, and would have hurt himself badly had he not been lucky. Lyubov dragged him off to the kitchen and made him eat raw eggs. This seemed to calm him down, and he just sat on the sofa grinning to himself, wanting to dance every now and then, and having to be restrained.

Through it all, Pavel kept up a long and serious harangue on the help dissidents needed, and the mistakes that correspondents made about them. The exile began dropping broad hints about needing books.

Finally Volodya and Lyubov realised it was getting late, and began pushing the party to leave. The political exile seemed to have made up his mind to stay the night—which would have certainly got him arrested the next day—and was only with difficulty persuaded to go with the others. Pavel was by now morose and resentful, as always happened when he drank. Outside, it was snowing and about minus sixteen centigrade. The whole party had to walk half a mile to find a taxi on Gorky Street. They all piled in cheerfully. It was well after 3 a.m., the end of a quiet evening at the theatre.

A Scandinavian correspondent who used to have similar gatherings at his flat from time to time called them his 'Dostoyevsky evenings'.

Later Zhenya seemed to reconcile himself to his broken marriage, and began appearing with another girl, a pretty, doe-eyed creature who soon announced that she was pregnant, and tried to make Zhenya settle down a bit. She would forbid him to drink too much in company, so that he waited until she was out of the room and then sneaked a quick one behind her back, assuming a look of great innocence when she reappeared. They were living somewhere on the edge of town, and she would weep if he tried to stay too late so that they missed their electric train.

Staying late is a Russian vice which every foreigner must accustom himself to if he wants to have Russian friends. They always seem surprised when foreign guests in *their* homes start looking at their watches well before midnight. They care little about the Metro and the buses, because they have an extraordinary confidence in their ability to find some means of transport home at any time. In the end, they are usually right, because even if there are no taxis, there are inevitably some free-lance drivers prowling the streets until dawn. They make a big profit, and perhaps the watchman at the garage where they get their vehicle has a rake-off too. Most such free-lance taxis seem to be cars owned by one government organisation or another. In the daytime, it is enough to flag down a few passing cars, and eventually one will stop and take a fare to most destinations within Moscow for a rouble, or at most two. Little irregularities like that make the Soviet system workable, because empty taxis refuse to stop more often than not.

Ion and Alina were not connected with Zhenya, Pavel or the Simonovs. They kept to their own circle of friends and steered well clear of the Movements, though they were far from satisfied with the state of affairs in their country. It was not clear why they liked to cultivate the odd foreigner or two. They never wanted to widen their circle of foreign friends, and they hardly ever tried to introduce foreigners to any of their Soviet friends. In fact they avoided doing so. It was an acquaintanceship in a box, consisting entirely of discreet exchanges of visits for supper.

Ion and Alina were much more typical of their generation than the others. Despite the title of this chapter, most of the people in it are a year or two on either side of 30. People younger than 25 are almost impossible to get to know, unless one is a student or manages to do some teaching at the University. They are too cowed, and too anxious to pass their exams, to mix with dangerous foreigners. While receiving higher education, they are under the overall disciplinary supervision of the so-called 'Military Faculty', a sort of glorified cadet corps which tells them how to cut their hair, and so on. To qualify at all, they have to memorise chapters of Marxist-Leninist classics, and parrot them in routine examinations which only a few prigs take seriously. Only when they have graduated do they begin to allow themselves the luxury of a little more independent thinking. There are exceptions, of course, like Vladimir Bukovsky, who was a dissident from the moment he grew up. But these are rarely allowed to finish their studies, and so they are a warning to the others.

Ion and Alina were post-graduates. She worked in an academic institute, and he taught Latin American Literature at the University. As students, they had experienced the excitement of the Khrushchev period, and their minds were still humming from it. But they were gradually running down, as they battled with the problems of living in a communal flat, shopping, and getting medical attention for their child. Like the majority of Soviet children, the child had been over-swaddled when young, and his diet was too monotonous because of the shortages of fresh fruit and vegetables and modern medicines. So he was perpetually ailing with sniffles and sore throats, real or imagined, which just meant more swaddling. On a bright summer's day in the country, he had to have a kerchief tied round his head to be taken for a walk, so it was not surprising if he sweated too much and caught summer colds. But he was a nice little fellow, and used to say 'good day' instead of 'good night' when he went for his afternoon nap. His father was allowed to go to Mexico for a year to further his studies, and the child insisted that he had gone to 'Meñinco'.

Before Ion's Mexican trip, he had to visit the Central Committee building to be given a lecture by an official who knew much less about Mexico than he did himself. This is standard procedure for people being allowed out of the country. They are expected to know the Soviet Union's policy towards that country, and the way they should behave there. People who do not pay due attention will simply not be allowed abroad again.

Ion and his wife had built a private world for themselves in Moscow. The walls of their two rooms were lined from floor to ceiling with books and curios, old music sheets, records, family albums and small archaeological finds. They collected pictures and icons, and their bookshelves bore a liberal collection in several languages which could put many Western post-graduates of their age to shame. They had access to a small cottage in the country for the summer months, where Alina baked Ukrainian cherry dumplings and they picked their own mushrooms nearby, eating at an old table under a tree. Still they were not happy.

Alina did most of the talking, and seemed to be the driving force behind the acquaintanceship with foreigners. She was a bright and humorous creature, with a liking for bawdy jokes; but her whole being was poisoned by anti-Semitism. After a few drinks, she would start talking about the 'Chews', and that would be the end of a pleasant evening. She had all the popular myths at her fingertips. 'Chews' were running all the institutes, so no one else could get ahead. They only helped each other. They were all well off. They could get out when they pleased. They got higher marks at school. They did not care what happened to Russia. She told endless anti-Semitic jokes.

Only for a week or two, at the height of the Jewish Emigration Movement in 1971, she changed her tune. 'Now I admire those people,' she announced one evening. 'They have got what they wanted, just by persistence.' But at the next meeting her face was twisted with hatred again, when she spoke of some Jew in her institute who was getting out of the country.

Ion kept trying to silence her, but she paid no attention. So he just lapsed into a moody silence, drank a good deal, and then put on tape recordings of unofficial songs. These used to cheer him up, and he would grin and lift his forefinger when the punchiest couplets came round. But Alina would berate him: 'What are you putting that on for? You are just boring people. Put on something else.'

They were at their best when Alina could be steered off the Jewish question, and they would swap ordinary jokes. For instance: 'What is alcoholism? Answer: an intermediate stage between Socialism and Communism.'

Or the following: 'A schoolteacher distributes portraits of Lenin, and tells her children to hang them on the wall at home. Next day one little boy is crying, because he was unable to comply. "Please, miss," he says, "our family lives in the middle of the room".'

Another favourite: 'A plane full of Soviet aid officials crashes in the African jungle. A tribe of cannibals capture the survivors and begin preparing them for the pot. But their chieftain says: "Spare that one over there. He was my room-mate at the Patrice Lumumba Friendship University in Moscow".'

And a joke about jokes: 'Three people of different nationalities were arguing about who was the bravest. The Englishman said: "We are, because one in every ten of us is drowned at sea." The German said: "No, we are, because one in every six of us is killed in battle." The Russian said: "We are the bravest, because every second Russian is an informer, and yet we still tell each other political anecdotes".'

Alina had no time for most of the active dissidents and protesters. 'Those people are just a snobbish clique,' she said once. 'They don't want to have anything to do with people outside their own circle.' But she kept some respect for Pavel, whom she knew of by hearsay. 'Oh, yes, Pavel, of course, well he's something different . . . But the people around him . . .'.

Ion was thrilled at the chance of going to Mexico. He had never been out of the Soviet Union before. Russians are supposed to visit East European countries on probation before being permitted to go to the West, and a trip he had once planned to East Europe had fallen through because of some international crisis. Now this requirement was being waived, because he had kept himself to himself and worked hard at his teaching and research. In the year of the Lenin Centenary, he ran himself into a state of nervous exhaustion by undertaking organisational work for the celebrations, which of course were of a highly political and propagandistic nature. A year later Ion went off to Mexico, grinning like a nervous schoolboy.

Then his letters started coming. He was unhappy. It was natural at first. He had to settle in, and make friends, before he could feel at home. He was missing Moscow and missing his family. It would get better. But it didn't. He was quartered in a hostel too far from the University. The other students didn't want to mix with Russians. He was anxious to come home. At the end of the year, he did.

Alina once said proudly: 'We Russians know how to suffer. If there is another war, we will live on bread and potatoes again and be happy.' Nothing any foreigner said or thought about Russia could possibly be right, because only a Russian could understand it. 'It is very bad,' she would say, 'but it is not the way you have put it. You don't understand.'

They both wanted to help a foreigner to understand, but they despaired at his obtuseness. They wanted the world to see Russia suffer, to admire and wonder at her, but not to dig too deeply into her motives. The idea of action to make things better reduced them to hopeless gloom. They resisted any attempt to make comparisons between conditions in the Soviet Union and in other countries. Russia and Russians must be unique, incapable of comparison.

In the end, the relationship with Ion and Alina petered out. It was hard to say what had gone wrong with it, for they were good people despite the racist poison in Alina. She was not, alas, unusual in this.

The Dear Departing

KOSTYA was the origin of this chain of incidents.

He called early one afternoon and said: 'Come to Sokol Metro Station at four o'clock. I'll meet you. You won't regret it.'

'Note the location,' he said after the meeting outside the Metro station. 'You might want to come back here. No. 82, Block 2, Entrance 4, fifth floor, flat 291. All right? Take it down.'

The occupant of flat 291 was a middle-aged woman, pinched and stern, but courteous. A teenage boy sat on a bed, smiling slightly. After pleasantries, she said: 'I want to play you the tape of my interview with the Party Committee at my Institute. Listen.'

Her son made a gesture of amusement and slight surprise. 'I'm sorry,' she said in French. 'I didn't explain. I was summoned after I asked for a character reference in order to obtain the exit visas. I put the recorder in my handbag, and this is the . . .'.

'*La pellicule,*' said the boy.

'He is going to a special French language school,' said the woman. 'I teach French. *Votre femme préfère parler russe? Nous pouvons parler français, mais comme vous voulez. Je ne parle pas anglais.*'

She switched on the recorder, and it was necessary to strain to catch anything of the hencoop barny which ensued in Russian. The woman—who will be referred to as Agnes—claimed to have demanded that at the meeting the question should not be raised of her other son, who, she claimed, was murdered by being thrown down a stairwell by an anti-Semitic drunk some years before. The mere raising of this subject reduced her almost (though not quite) to speechlessness. According to her, the Soviet police had failed to trace the murderer.

It appeared that someone at the meeting, because of this warning, had been deliberately briefed to raise the subject and thus throw her off balance: it was a woman. One of the characteristics of the system of Soviet state control is that it often chooses women to do the most psychologically sadistic things (e.g. the prosecution and judge at the trial of Vladimir Bukovsky were both women). There seems to be some lingering belief that the act will be harder to criticise if performed by the member of a sex traditionally supposed to be gentle.

The topic was raised almost immediately, and Agnes, predictably, began to 'blow her stack'. This was probably the idea—to make her put up such a disgraceful show of petulance and hysteria that her application could be dismissed as irresponsible and she could be refused the 'character reference'. The Committee had reckoned without her fierce temperament. Every time someone tried to get a word in, she began shouting them down. At one point she criticized 'Soviet Justice', and someone was bold enough to say: 'Now don't say anything about Soviet Justice, Agnes Ivanovna, I have worked in Soviet Justice, and I know what it is . . .' Agnes never let him get any further.

The whole thing lasted about 40 minutes, so it was either a long-play cassette, or there was an interval for visits to the toilet with the tape-recorder in Agnes' handbag.

About the same time, other Jews were actually smuggling tape-recorders into interviews at the Central Committee, and recording the voices and arguments of senior Party officials explaining why Jews did not have the right to go to Israel. The cassette recorder was a piece of equipment which the Soviet authorities were unable to render ineffective, although by 1969 they were carefully registering every one brought into the country by foreigners. But they were for sale in the foreign currency stores, and many fell into Russian hands. At some stage, too, the domestic industry had to start turning them out as a mere matter of prestige.

After the tape had been played, Agnes suggested an introduction to a person whom she described as a student of Chinese. This sounded interesting.

A week or so later, the 'person' rang. The telephone conversation proved that he could, indeed, speak some Chinese. So there was another car-ride to the block of flats where Agnes lived.

He turned out to be a lecturer in other Oriental languages, expelled from the University and now more or less a 'full-time dissident' and activist in the Emigration and Democratic Movements. Chairs were produced, and an interview was begun.

'Are more Jews getting out just now, or is the situation just as bad as it was?'

The Orientalist, who may as well be called Ilya Gorbachov, spread his arms from the shoulder. 'We, like you, have no figures.

In some places, it is easier now. I am convinced that in the end the Soviet authorities will let the Jews go.'

This was still a novel concept in mid-1971. It seemed to go completely against the grain and temper of all Soviet policy-making to that date. Gorbachov was more interested in the matter from its historical and even spiritual aspects, than as a question of numbers.

'You must understand the relationship between Russian and Jew,' he said. 'The Russian is a soil worshipper, and a mother worshipper. He is fundamentally religious. He worships the earth, not heaven, but he does so in a religious way. He reveres the mother, while the Jew reveres his father.'

'Why a soil worshipper?'

'The cult of the sacred earth, the *Rodina* (Motherland) ...' Gorbachov spoke at length, confusing his monologue with long digressions into Oriental mythologies which had nothing to do with either Jews or Russians.

The conversation was interrupted by the arrival of two young Jewish boys—they looked about 18, and were virtually twins—from Odessa. They had light travel goods with them, and were on their way back to the Black Sea port to await the decision of the Soviet authorities on their application to emigrate to Israel.

Ilya Gorbachov kissed them both. The elder (or it could have been the younger) said with the determination of very early youth: 'See you in Israel.'

They left, calm and confident. Gorbachov sighed. 'I am afraid for them. Both are artists, exceptionally talented boys. They are determined to go. But Odessa is not Moscow. They have no access to foreign correspondents.'

A scene flashed from the memory: a train from Odessa to Moscow. The Ticket Collector, in a cap two sizes too large, is a student on holiday work. 'Where are you from?' he asks, sitting down in the compartment to take a rest—or more likely out of curiosity. 'Moscow, British, oh, oh?'—'And you, what nationality are you?' A momentary hesitation, during which the light blue eyes become still more striking in the Jewish face. 'Russian'.

The other couple in the compartment—plain Russian mechanic and his wife, who live on former Tartar lands in the Crimea—stiffen slightly (or is it only imagination?) They know. An Odessa Jew, of course. But the young Ticket Collector persists. 'Shall we meet in Moscow?'— 'Certainly. Here is our address.'

He never turned up, and quite possibly was denounced by the couple opposite for trying to associate with foreigners, and sent back to Odessa in disgrace. Or perhaps he carried on working, but felt he had gone far enough already with the contact.

A further meeting with Gorbachov was arranged, this time at his flat, for which he drew elaborate directions. Finding individual flats in Moscow is almost as difficult as in Tokyo, for the numbering system goes through a whole diapason of street numbers, block numbers, entrance numbers, floor numbers and flat numbers; the city is growing and changing constantly, and the only adequate city map is printed by the American Embassy for its own use, out of date, and in very limited supply. There is no public directory of personal telephone numbers or addresses.

It was a long drive the next week down the highway in south-eastern Moscow, which, like a person, obtained its own nickname: 'Information Alley'. The nicknames were partly no more than a way of putting humour into situations which were sometimes painfully lacking in that quality: more often, a way of talking at home, to confuse electronic eavesdroppers. Dissidents became known variously as 'Beard', 'Wall Eye', or 'Mutton Chops' (side-whiskers). It may not have confused the K.G.B. for long; but at least it made their job more difficult.

There is always a feeling of guilt in parking a car with a white (i.e. foreign) registration plate near a non-official Russian block, and going to pay a visit. Russians have black plates with white numbers. Even infants know to recognise the white number plate as that of an *inostranets* (foreigner). The 'K' in the registration identifies a journalist, and there is no knowing what the neighbours think, let alone the Block Committee.

It was muddy, and the access road was deeply rutted. The entrance hall—prototypal Soviet down to the numbering on the mail boxes—smelt of kennels. Gorbachov lived on the ground floor.

'Come in. I am delighted to welcome you to my home. Please forgive the mess, but you understand ... This is my wife, my daughter, my sons ... Oh, you need not have bothered. We shall taste it in a minute. Tanya, make some tea.'

It seemed to be a three or four roomed, fully self-contained flat, a 'co-operative'. That is, Gorbachov put his name down on a list some years back, a committee had been formed, and everyone had put up his money. If the committee turned out to be honest and competent, a building organisation eventually constructed the block and everyone on the list had a flat which could be willed to an heir or re-sold at the same price (but only to the 'co-operative' itself). There were repeated scandals of committees diverting the funds, or getting into insoluble administrative tangles, or breaking the law in some way, or failing to get the builders moving, and the prospective tenant simply having to start all over again on a new list, perhaps losing his money. But Gorbachov and his family seemed to have had a smooth passage, if only in the 'co-operative'.

Gorbachov conducted his *salons* in his study, which was also the living room. Today there was only one other guest, an elderly man, who beamed at meeting foreigners, and instantly started engaging them in Russian conversation, until he was cut off by the host.

'He does not speak English,' Gorbachov explained in English. 'And you must not let him run on, or we shall never be able to talk.'

At this point Gorbachov's wife broke in with irritation in Russian: 'T. has done more in his lifetime than the whole bunch of you will ever do.' She seemed to have a protective instinct towards the old man. It turned out that he was a poet who had continued to publish relatively independent and sensitive verses at some of the darkest times, and still defied the Writers' Union when its bureaucrats tried to intimidate him.

Gorbachov's young wife, Tanya, was also a scholar; a historian, and still a junior lecturer at the University. She complained that her students were totally unqualified and uninterested in what she taught, with few exceptions; they were being earmarked to associate in the future with foreigners, and therefore must know something about their countries. She had an oddly irritating manner of insulting people in the third person, and expecting the person addressed to laugh. For instance, she would gesture towards her husband's friends and say sarcastically: 'Look at them, these *hawks*' (a term of high praise in Russian). This was usually just when the conversation was at some particularly interesting stage.

But she was hospitable, and invariably brought in slices of bread with sausage and cheese, tea, apples or biscuits. A bottle of Grand Marnier, brought as a gift, was wantonly poured into the tea, thus ruining both. Russians do not generally understand liqueurs.

Tanya, who seemed at least ten years younger than Gorbachov, was his second wife, and appeared to get on well with his daughter by the first marriage. The daughter was just grown up and her dark, Jewish looks contrasted sharply with Tanya's blonde, unkempt hair and fair colouring.

Sometimes they would sit on the divan bed, listening and giggling when Gorbachov talked with wide and narrow gesticulations. Once they were encouraging his younger son to imitate him, cheekily. 'Not just now, Venyamin,' he said with commendable patience. 'Later you can imitate me.' The women just laughed, and Gorbachov said with a smile of genuine amusement: 'They are my two witches.'

Those informal *salons* at Gorbachov's place were invariably a source of information and insight, although, as one of his acquaintances once unkindly commented: 'He is an excellent conversationalist—you never need to say anything at all.'

This was not entirely true, because Gorbachov had questions to which he wanted specific answers, and he listened to the answers with attention and respect. But he was perpetually trying to organise random Russian discussions into strict, round-table forums, at which one person got so many minutes, then surrendered the floor to another. The trouble was that, as Chairman, he tended to take over completely when any other speaker surrendered his position. And the poet called T. would also run on endlessly as soon as he got started, and refuse to stop until Gorbachov simply cut him off in mid-sentence.

There were others—a bearded young philosopher, and a mysterious man with a type of beard which made him look like a minor character from Gogol. This man seemed disturbed and irritated by the lack of clarity in all the proceedings.

There was also a tortoise, which the family for some reason insisted had belonged to Napoleon, and which noisily munched apples and dragged itself raspingly from one corner of the room to another.

One thing that disturbed them all, except the tortoise, was the state of Western youth. The Soviet press fed them daily with the worst horror stories about the excesses of hippies, Beatles, long hair, the Manson family and all the rest of it. All the Soviet correspondents abroad had to do was copy items from the Western press, and do what many Western news media are almost equally guilty of—turn small-group activities or flashes-in-the-pan into mass youth trends, allegedly revolutionising an entire generation and leading it headlong into unspeakable corruption. Anyone who knows, say, suburban Britain, is aware how superficial these movements often are, and to what extent they are simply absorbed into the fabric of the society. But the growth of short-wave radio listening in the Soviet Union means that current Western fads become known of and adopted there more quickly: the hottest item among Moscow University students in early 1972 was 'Jesus Christ Superstar'.

It was difficult enough explaining that many serious sociologists in the West regarded the various youth movements as often leading society, and setting a more general trend for the future. More acceptable to Russians is the explanation that the Western 'generation gap' has been exaggerated deliberately by their own press, and that it is simply a freer and more widely publicised expression of urges almost as evident in Soviet youth.

The guitar-strumming teenager, drunk at night with his friends on the street, may annoy the middle-aged just as much in Moscow as in Manchester. A Soviet father feels more horror at his son's slightly uncut hair (and calls him a 'hippy' because of it), than the average British father seems to feel nowadays about shoulder-length hair. If the 'crazy' Western teenager buys himself a motor-bike, the Soviet kid cannot afford to, and anyway the thing would be unusable for half the year because of the cold, and there would be no room to keep it. The typical outburst of frustration in Soviet youth consists of crashing a stolen car or knifing someone in a drunken fight. Then there will be a long, moralising article in the press, blaming the boy's personality and associates, but carefully avoiding any suggestion that *overall* social conditions might have had anything to do with it.

Gorbachov's type of friends tended to be slightly prudish, and were shocked by the tales of the 'sex wave' in the West. The old poet T. said: 'The West has lost all spirituality, hasn't it?' Sex is almost a taboo subject in the Soviet periodical press, though it is handled a little more freely in literature. Those who eventually left the Soviet Union, and saw the sex shops in the West, would understand the apathy about this subject which clinical commercialism engenders. But some of them, after all, were people to whom even 'modern ballroom dancing' was a forbidden fruit when they were teenagers, because it was officially considered lewd and decadent.

The odd thing about this type of people is that in some current Soviet slang they are called 'leftist'—because they oppose the domestic establishment. In Western terms they would be reckoned conservatives, even 'hard-line anti-Reds'. Having had the Vietnam question rammed down their throats for so many years, they refuse to believe that the American role there is as evil as many of their intellectual counterparts in the West suppose automatically. (The apathy about Vietnam in Russia is such that when a 'prize-winning' Vietcong film is shown at a festival, claques have to be organised in the audience to applaud key scenes.) Such people feel that Soviet foreign policy is imperialist to its core, and tend to blame Russia for international crises, even when Moscow may not have been the only one to blame.

The scepticism is not confined to a minute handful, either. Even in the depths of the provinces, anyone of average intelligence, who reads the foreign reports in the Soviet press daily and observantly, can deduce *by logic alone* that he is not being told the truth or the whole truth. The extent of the deception is confirmed by the Western short-wave broadcasts. An event like the withdrawal of Soviet military advisers from Egypt throws the entire propaganda machine—from editorials in *Pravda* down to small-group lectures on the factory shop-floor—into the most acrobatic contortions of explanation and cover-up. Only the unusually stupid or cynical, or those who deliberately close their minds to foreign affairs, can fail to get at least a general idea that they are being misled.

The 'leftists' long for aspects of Russian culture set aside or stifled by the Revolution. When the song-writer and dramatist, Alexander Galich, the idol of discontented intellectual youth, was expelled from his two professional unions and thus deprived of his livelihood, Gorbachov said: 'Ah, you should meet Galich. Such a Russian *barin* (gentleman). There is not a thing about Russian culture that he does not know. You should see his flat, so elegant, such good taste. He used to write such delightful little plays.' Both Gorbachov and Galich were Jews, but they considered themselves Russian intellectuals first.

The main point over which these 'leftists' actually agreed with the Soviet official view was in their rejection of Maoism and the Chinese Cultural Revolution, which they found quite incomprehensible. There is a general distaste for China in Moscow. The eyes of all but a tiny handful of the Russian intelligentsia are trained on the West. 'Spiritual' Oriental culture and Maoism leave them equally cold, although there are, of course, professional Orientalists like

Gorbachov, and a few yoga enthusiasts. A Soviet Maoist has yet to be encountered.

Gorbachov himself kept coming back to the same question, on which the future happiness of himself and his entire brood depended: 'Should we emigrate?' It was just the period, in early 1972, when exit visas for Israel were being handed out at a rate approximately twenty times faster than anything experienced before, and although most of those departing were from Georgia and the former Bukovina, there was a fair trickle from the northern cities, and certain active dissidents (including non-Jews) were actually being *encouraged* to go, sometimes threatened with imprisonment if they did not!

Gorbachov kept framing his questions in impossible ways: 'How will people receive us in the West?'—for instance.

It was typical of his Soviet training that he thought of countries as places where certain policies are pursued, at the personal as well as the official level, towards people from other countries, with a well defined system of discrimination. In other words, if 'The West' was accepting Soviet Jewry, what did it intend to do with it? (His intention of not going to Israel itself was pretty thinly masked.)

'Will *they* just think of us as spies and Communists?' he asked.

How to reply? Firstly, no unofficial foreigner should give a Soviet citizen advice on these matters. Russians usually have much better channels of information than any foreigner, about the opportunities open to them, and about their chances for a successful or disastrous emigration. Secondly, it is impossible to reply to such a question without defining the word 'they'. The only answer is that it depends what circle of friends an émigré chooses, what job he obtains, how hard he works, and—in the end—on pure chance. That is the essence of the West as it has to be explained to Russians. It is a concept quite alien to most of them.

Then Ilya would ask: 'Is it not true that the West has become atheist, whereas in Russia people are still religious?' Of course the answer was 'No!'—but how to explain about the Ecumenical Movement, the Church attendance situation, or the 'new' religions of the youth?

Eventually he got the idea, and seemed to lose interest. He would have to make up his own mind. About ten of these meetings took place: Gorbachov sawing the air with his karate-postured hand to make a point, the others straining to get their word in, the foreigner trying to maintain an attitude of neutrality and general good-will.

After the wave of searches in January 1972 Ilya was conducting one of his *salons* in an atmosphere slightly tenser than usual. Pavel had been searched a week or two before, and thousands of documents taken from his flat, where he had defiantly kept them, knowing that this could happen at any time.

'Did you know,' said Ilya, 'that Pavel struck the K.G.B. Colonel in the face?'

A silence fell, while those present rolled this information round their mental palates.

Ilya said: 'It happened this way. When the Colonel decided that too many of Pavel's friends had come to witness the search, he telephoned for a squad of uniformed militia. After all, things have changed. Previously, if there was a search, everyone remotely connected with the victim would run away, hoping nothing would happen to them. Now, when the word gets round that a search is on, the person's friends start arriving and wanting to know what has happened. That was what happened at Pavel's place. They all started coming, and watching.

'When the militia arrived, the Colonel pointed to the Zhukovs, Kostya Markman and Yelena Gips, and said: "Take them away." Now these were all people who had histories of confinement in mental asylums for protests, and it seemed they were to be victimised by being sent to clinics again. At this, Pavel erupted with fury, screamed like a wild creature, and hit the Colonel full in the face. Everyone was waiting to see what would happen. He could have been shot down on the spot. But the Colonel just paused for a moment, then told the militia to leave. The Zhukovs, Markman, and Gips were left alone.'

There was a pause, and Tanya nodded, then shook her head: 'Yes, Pavel . . . he is a saint, there is no doubt.'

An earlier scene came suddenly to mind. The day after the big search, when the others were gathered at Pavel's flat, with that strange look of serenity and not-being-of-this-world, grouped standing and sitting around the room like a modern Last Supper. Pavel sat at the central table with some of those closest to him. The walls were still lined with books and papers, despite the K.G.B. search. He had started telling what happened when the militia were summoned. Then he grinned and checked himself.

The others also laughed a little and exchanged glances. Obviously there was something they were not telling. Pavel said: 'You know, it was what we used to do in the camps. When you had no other way left, you just went screaming mad at the guards, and sometimes it did the trick.'

The old man called T. had so much to say, and wanted to say it so fast before Gorbachov interrupted him, that he was almost totally incoherent. But one thing he succeeded in saying stuck in the memory: 'Everything in this country is *lumpen*: we have a *lumpen*-government, a *lumpen*-Army—you can't call it an Army, it's just a lot of soldiers and technology—and *lumpen*-writers, including *lumpen*-poets . . . well, no, not *exactly*. You can still write poetry, in a way.'

Gorbachov broke in: 'T. is not prepared to admit that his own profession is *lumpen*.'

T. shrugged, and Tanya looked angry.

Another person encountered at Gorbachov's was a physicist who sometimes associated himself with the Human Rights Committee. He seemed to spend a lot of time explaining that he was half Moldavian, half Turk, otherwise people kept asking him for expert opinions on the Jewish question. Once he was asked how the political atmosphere was, in the very specialised institute where he worked: 'Pretty good,' he said. 'Most of the people there are highly qualified, so I can talk to them just as I talk to you.' (Gorbachov once said: 'I can talk to the K.G.B. more freely than I can to my mother-in-law.')

'What about the students?'

'Oh, there are no ideas *there*! They just want to cram, pass an examination, and get a well-paid job as a *Kandidat* or Doctor of Sciences. They would run a mile rather than express a political opinion other than what they are told to say.'

This man appeared to be in his late thirties. So the generation gap in Russia seems to work the opposite way round from the gap in the West, in the political sense . . .

Gorbachov was a kind host, not only in the personal but also the professional sense. There was a drawer in the table at which he sat: it came to be known as 'Pandora's box'. At some point or other, he would reach into it with a quizzical smile and say, for example: 'Would you like to see the letter written by the son of Bill-Byelotserkovsky to the First Secretary of the Writers' Union?' (Bill-Byelotserkovsky was a Soviet Jew who had lived a long time in

America, and who wrote the play 'Storm', nowadays still recognised as the first 'correct' dramatic portrayal of the Bolshevik role in the Revolution. He is sometimes called the 'father of Soviet drama'. His son had decided to leave for Israel, and had been abused on the telephone by Sergey Mikhalkov, a power at the Union. He was now circulating his reply.)

Or Gorbachov might reach in the drawer and say: 'Would you like to have Solzhenitsyn's open letter to the Patriarch of Moscow? Tanya or Lyenochka, go and type a copy out.' Or he would simply lace his conversation with anecdotes about the latest scandal at the Writers' Union.

He was particularly worried about the fortunes of a remarkable but as yet little known Soviet author, whose *chef d'oeuvre* was due to come out in the West in 1973 (through what channels, one did not enquire). 'This is a marvellous work,' Gorbachov said. 'Some people are calling him another Solzhenitsyn. But to me there are aspects which put him above even Solzhenitsyn. He approaches Soviet society not just with an eye on its past, but with a spiritual feel for its present and future. He is so terribly subtle. For instance, in this book there is the person who describes the courtyard of the block of flats where he was brought up: all the human catastrophes and twisted lives, the general madness of society. Then he is put into a psychiatric asylum, and he finds it full of the most intelligent, normal people, who can sit and talk all day about literature or philosophy. The only true madman there is one who spends all day reading *Pravda* and shouting "Hurra, our lads have won," or "Hurra, they have completed construction of a new power station".'

Together with a gentle and attractive woman (an expert on Oriental art) Gorbachov arranged an expedition to meet this author. He had had one or two things published in the Soviet Union officially. One had been translated and brought out in the West; but the 'blurb' described it in terms which can have done the author no good. He came even closer to the pale when one of his short stories, unpublished in the Soviet Union, was brought out by an émigré publishing house in the West. The publication of his major novel in the coming year was seen as a challenge which the authorities would not ignore.

There was a sense of intrusion in visiting this man. His father was put away under Stalin. He became a wandering urchin and borstalled juvenile delinquent. He acquired a deformed hand, and he had drinking bouts when he would drain the furniture polish if nothing else was to hand. But in his good periods he could take a glass of wine, and sparkle with earthy Russian wit and common sense, so that people listened to him almost breathlessly.

It was no place for a foreigner, except that the support of the outside world might be useful to him one day, and he never showed that he considered anyone unwelcome. Quite the opposite. Unfortunately, one of his drinking bouts had landed him in a mental hospital for a while, and from then on the authorities had a hold on him for ever; he was on the so-called 'dispensary list'. The resident psychiatrist at the Writers' Union summoned him for re-examination, but he simply did not go. How it would develop was uncertain.

It is not only Gorbachov who cultivated this writer. Zhukov, the painter, and his wife Dusya, went to see him from time to time, as they liked to stay in touch with anyone connected with opposition movements, right up till the moment when they finally heeded the K.G.B. warnings and left the country for good. They also had been in 'clinics' for political reasons.

They lived near a foreigners' block, and Dusya would sometimes just pop in past the policeman to see a West German correspondent with whom she was friendly. She was always tickled about the ease with which this was possible. Probably the policeman at the gate took her for a Bulgarian or an Arab woman, and was shy of challenging her in case she turned out to be a genuine foreigner, living in the block. She had very dark looks.

Zhukov, the painter, and his wife, were both up at the German correspondent's flat one evening with some other foreigners, having a drink at his private bar (one of the sights of Moscow). Suddenly she said: 'Let's go and see that author.' She had been complaining bitterly how Solzhenitsyn had cold-shouldered her and others when they went to congratulate him on his Nobel prize, and she wanted to retain other literary friends. A bottle of vodka was fetched as a courtesy, and a long taxi ride brought a straggling group of foreigners and Russians to the author's flat. He was not in the least put out, only he asked to be excused from drinking vodka, as he had recently had a 'bout' and could only take a little wine. He laid on a cold supper.

Afterwards, Dusya Zhukov suggested going back to her own flat —a grimy, gloomy cave in an ancient wooden house near Mayakovsky Square—for instant coffee (which she had demanded from one of her present guests a week or so before). She was a pushing woman, but had every right to be so, because her husband, the painter, was barely of this world. The most animation he would show, not connected with his work, was when he argued with Pavel about which of them had been the first to start the Democratic Movement. Pavel was very rude to him.

They had received their exit visas for Israel—indeed, had them urged on them by the K.G.B.—and complications concerning their daughter had been sorted out. Now it was a sheer question of money: how to raise the 1,000 or so Roubles (about £460 at the official rate) which each person in the family needed to pay for renunciation of Soviet citizenship, buy an airline ticket and meet other expenses? Should Zhukov sell some of his paintings in Moscow before leaving, and would he find a buyer? Dusya said: 'Why should we sell them now for forty Roubles each, when we could get hundreds of dollars for them outside?' She was probably being sanguine about his prospects in the Western 'art world', but he *had* had some paintings exhibited and reproduced abroad, and *might* just touch a particular chord in the 'art world' at the right political, aesthetic and commercial moment.

It was all highly dubious. But at least they would be free of the white-coated female 'dispenser' who used to come to their house from the mental clinic to dissuade them from going out, at any time when there was the prospect of a protest demonstration. The 'dispenser' had the right to bring a uniformed policeman with her, to demand entry and examination of the person on the 'list'. It is one of the most horrific methods of thought control yet invented, but often it is possible to break through its net by stubbornness or bluff.

Then Gorbachov also got his exit visa. Tanya claimed to have been weeping for weeks at the thought of leaving Russia, and to be nervous that her academic qualifications had been blunted by the stultifying nature of her work. Gorbachov commented ironically: 'They are expecting the great authority Professor Gorbachov, and all they are going to get is this young girl who has forgotten half of what she knew.' Some of Tanya's friends said that in fact she had reconciled herself and was quite keen to go. Lyenochka, Gorbachov's daughter by his first marriage, was anxious to go with him, but in despair about her own mother, who would be left behind. She also loved the kitchen of their flat, where she had entertained her friends and taken part in family meals for several years.

The books began to disappear, and the dust to appear, on the shelves in Gorbachov's study, as the move gathered momentum. The Block Committee expressed dumb horror at having harboured a traitor in its respectable midst all these years (though they must have known all along that Gorbachov was a dissident).

The hardest moment was telling Tanya's mother. She had never been informed that Gorbachov had lost his job in 1968, and that he was regarded as a political outcast, even a candidate for jail. Then, one fine day, her daughter suddenly told her the lot, adding that they were off in a few weeks and might never see each other again. The sobs from the corridor shook the flat.

At the last moment, Gorbachov showed his hand. He had not the slightest intention of going to Israel and working in a Kibbutz or even a University there. The West was his spiritual home. He knew from friends, who had already tried it, that it was possible to go to Rome and be looked after by an American-backed organisation, which would then obtain speedy entry visas and American citizenship for Jewish emigrants. Anyway, he said, it was impossible to book a flight to Vienna, the normal route to Israel, before the exit visa ran out, because of the number of Georgian Jews going.

In an understandable panic, he demanded to know whether the British Government would let him in at short notice (he had an invitation, and total three-month sponsorship, from a British scholar of Soviet literature; but it was not clear whether this person knew that Gorbachov might bring with him four women and children).

The American Consul warned him informally that if the Soviet authorities saw any Jew trying to hive off to the West instead of going to Israel, they might dock his exit visa, and make him go through the application process all over again. There had, apparently, been such cases. But in general the authorities had by now accepted that anyone with an Israeli visa was already beyond the pale, and could go to Rome or London or Paris, if he wished to and could get the entry visa.

The British Embassy was asked to make rapid enquiries in London, but did nothing. Apparently the British Government, besieged by immigration problems already, had decided to discourage Soviet Jews from going to Britain as a first stop, since they already had a 'homeland' of their own.

Gorbachov walked, astonishingly, into the Italian Embassy,

straight past the Soviet militiaman who would normally have
grabbed him by the coat collar. He obtained Italian visas for himself and his family, and was in Rome within ten days. A few of his
friends did the same thing.

Gorbachov had regarded himself as a kind of founding member
of the Democratic Movement, though by 1972 he was prepared to
joke that it was not, as the Soviet-style abbreviation had it, the
Demdvizheniye, but the *Dymdvizheniye* ('Smoke Movement', or
'illusory movement'). This was typical of the disillusionment
which many dissidents were feeling at the Movement's prospects of
bringing about change, or even acquiring sympathy among the
masses.

Gorbachov had once said, with simple sincerity: 'I love Russia,
though I am leaving her'—as if he were leaving a wife. Indeed, he
compared the Russian intelligentsia to a man who beats his wife all
day, and throws buckets of ordure on her—then creeps into bed to
make love to her at night.

He had decided to make a grand gesture before departing, although there may also have been the hind-thought that this would
speed the granting of the exit visa. He and four other protesters
communicated a letter to a well-known British newspaper, correctly
predicting the arrest of Pavel, deploring the other oppressive
campaigns, and declaring that they left behind them, with their
friends, 'a part of their hearts'.

The letter was moving to an outsider, and Gorbachov was a
sincere if sometimes devious man. The others signed each for reasons
of their own. By mid-summer, all but one of them had obtained his
visa, and left. None went to Israel. Gorbachov and two others took
the by now familiar route to Rome. Another landed up as the guest
of a Sovietologist in Greece. The fifth was a 'hard case' who had
somehow offended the K.G.B. so much that they kept him and his
wife and young daughter in Russia indefinitely, apparently out of
sheer vindictiveness. (There are a dozen or two such cases in
Moscow alone.)

But the letter provoked a wide range of reactions among those
left behind—mostly hostile. The bearded man who looked like a
character from Gogol said: 'Jews in general are angry at those five
people. The Jews have always tried to avoid identifying themselves
as a *group* with the dissident movement, and the signatories were
mostly Jewish.' (This, however, was a case of bolting the stable door

after the horse had fled: the Democratic Movement is at least half Jewish in any case.)

Chalidze said: 'If they want to leave, very well, let them leave. But why should they try to justify themselves, and suggest that the entire Movement will be finished once they go? They are giving up. But why make such a fuss about it?'

Kostya Markman said: *Bog s nimi* (literally, 'God be with them', but in current parlance, 'who cares about them?'). These reactions were typical of the jealousies within the Movement, one of the reasons for its lack of progress.

What about Agnes, who had effected the first introduction to some of this disparate group? She suffered a mild heart attack, apparently as a result of over-excitement, and was last seen lying on the divan bed in her flat, taking pills, but still totally sanguine about the whole affair. Her surviving son had got himself to Paris already. But the term of her own exit visa was running out because of her illness, and would have to be renewed.

One could visualise her son, *le jeune russe*, toast of the discothèques with a surfeit of slim admirers.

Agnes herself recovered, made a surprise marriage, and left from Sheremetyevo Airport a week or two later, carrying the ashes of the other son in an urn. Someone pointed out to her that the Customs might demand to stir around the ashes to discover whether she was smuggling anything out in them, and this almost gave her a new heart attack.

But the Customs and the K.G.B. have done worse things than that. When Zhukov, the artist, left shortly after, they sprayed dozens of his paintings with acid, so that all that remained of them were a few tatters hanging from the frames. In Rome, he set about painting them all afresh. They consisted mainly of tortured Christs.

The Systems Analyst

'SOVIET propaganda is very well thought out,' said the man with the bear d which made him look like a minor character from Gogol. 'It is wrong to underrate it.'

He had called on the telephone after a chance meeting at Gorbachov's place, and suggested a further acquaintanceship. He lived in another district of Moscow, but almost equally far from the centre.

'See the position of our block,' he said, when escorting a foreign visitor back to his car. 'We live in one made up entirely of cooperative flats. They are inhabited mainly by members of the intelligentsia. Around us—over there, and there—are blocks of workers' flats. You can see the difference very clearly in the mornings. The lights in the workers' flats go on at seven, or earlier. In the cooperative flats, they may not be lit until eight or nine.'

The man with the beard will be called the Systems Analyst. This suits both his training and his hobby. He made a living as an electro-chemist and an industrial consultant, but his passions were Soviet sociology and Soviet history. By his family background, he was well qualified to understand both.

The Systems Analyst's Ukrainian father, like the parents of many dissidents and quasi-dissidents, had been a member of the early 'Soviet aristocracy' purged by Stalin. All things taken into account the Systems Analyst was lucky to have escaped Pavel's fate: half a childhood, and an entire adolescence and early youth spent in labour camp through no fault of his own. The Systems Analyst had only spent some time in Siberian exile with his father, as a child. His father had been allowed to die a natural death, though still exiled.

If Gorbachov was right about people needing minds baked hard by the million-ton pressure of propaganda, this certainly applied to the Systems Analyst. His mathematics had made him analytical, and his personal history had made him sceptical. So he brought to Soviet history a mind which saw it in a light too sharp and bright for most of his contemporaries.

'To understand the modern history of this country,' he said, 'it is necessary to remember the minutest details which are now forgotten or covered up. And it is particularly important to keep the nationalities question, and the question of religion, always in view. Both are of great significance in the development of the Soviet State.

'It is often a question of the smallest things. How many people nowadays remember that, after the signing of the Molotov-Ribbentrop Pact, Stalin ordered a special performance of Wagner's "Ring" in the Bolshoi Theatre in honour of Germany and the Nazis? Incidentally, have you noticed how seldom our press uses the term "National Socialist?" This is because they dislike to see the term "Socialism" linked with a former enemy. They usually prefer to call the Nazis simply "fascists".'

The Systems Analyst spent most of his time at home, apparently comfortably off through consultancies. His wife, who had a professional qualification, had given up her job to devote all her time to their children. Like so many Soviet women, she pampered her small son and kept him away from school at the slightest sniffle or complaint. This was quickly turning the child into a hypochondriac. When he was perfectly healthy, you might ask him how he was feeling, and he would wrinkle his brow anxiously, like a little old man with pains in his bones. Given a felt-pen and asked to draw a picture, he would take fright and say: 'Oh, no thank you, I don't know how to draw.' But he loved to be brought some foreign stamps or coins, and he had a passion for chewing gum, which he probably shared out sparingly among his very best friends at school.

The Systems Analyst watched benignly as his son was mollycoddled like a little silkworm. He was a good family man, but his real thoughts were elsewhere. His ambition was to write the history of the Soviet Union from the inside, and he was anxious to try his ideas out on foreigners to see what impression they made.

Gorbachov, who knew the Systems Analyst, said he regarded him as faint-hearted, apparently because the latter had refused to commit himself to the Democratic Movement, or sign open protests. But the Systems Analyst was prepared to do something which Gorbachov avoided on principle: visit the home of a foreigner, even bringing some of his family with him. It was a lunchtime invitation.

The entire party arrived by car, and drove past the militia post to the correct entrance nearly a hundred yards away. By the time everybody had got out, and the car had been locked up, the militiaman was standing by the entrance with his legs spread, and a grim look on his face.

This is a standard intimidation technique, used against Russians outside Western Embassies, sometimes even against Westerners themselves. The police pose—legs apart, hands thrust into greatcoat pockets, shoulders hunched—is intended to suggest that it is forbidden to set a foot any further. On this occasion it seemed particularly obnoxious, when used against a party of lunch guests which included an ordinary Russian housewife and a little boy. The silent message passed to them by the militiaman was: 'I can't stop you going in there, since you're accompanied by a foreigner. But you can be sure that you will be identified and checked up on.' The Systems Analyst and his family simply ignored it.

More frequently, there were get-togethers in the Systems Analyst's flat, one of the most comfortable of the modern types of Soviet accommodation, apart from that available to the most privileged. It has three rooms, separate kitchen, bathroom and lavatory. The furniture is up-to-date and everything is always spotless. People take their shoes off at the entrance. The study is lined with old editions of encyclopaedias, science, history and philosophy, representing almost every period of pre- and post-Revolutionary thought. There is barely room for the typewriter on the small table, and the day-bed in the corner.

The Systems Analyst's wife always took care to bake something special when guests were coming. She could make cream puffs to perfection, but since Soviet packeted cream does not whip, she filled them with sweetened condensed milk. They received a quantity of dried mushrooms—which cost the equivalent of about £15 for a four-foot string in the market—from relatives in the country. This was a special treat. She soaked them until they were soft, then chopped them finely and baked them into *pirozhki* with lightly-greased, well-leavened dough.

Her husband is something of a gourmet, too, though he observes moderation in everything. He sometimes had a bottle of Hungarian rum—a harsh spirit for which he apologised—or straight vodka with a fluffy red powder drifting at the bottom. This was an exotic, peppery spice brought all the way from Georgia to sharpen the vodka's flavour without the heart-burning fusol which attends the brewing of vodka with fresh peppers, Ukrainian-style.

Brought some rare Soviet berry liqueur as a present, he said: 'Thank you. Personally I like it. Nowadays it is difficult to get hold of, but I see you have it in the foreigners' shop. In fact, few Russians like these sweeter liqueurs. They consider that there is too little alcohol in them, and it is too difficult to get drunk.'

Introduced to a well-known French liqueur, he picked up his glass, looked into it testingly, then drained it at one swig. 'Very pleasant,' he said.

However excellent the snacks at the Systems Analyst's flat, the real fare there was intellectual. He had thought about everything: history, economics, administration, cybernetics, biology, race. He followed the foreign situation avidly.

'You cannot buy the right kind of short-wave radio here, in order to listen to the B.B.C. and other foreign stations. So people simply get a radio mechanic in, and give him a few roubles to add the missing wave-bands. During the war, all private radio sets were confiscated by the authorities in case people listened to enemy propaganda. They were stored and returned after the German defeat.'

He followed the news so closely that it could be embarrassing. 'What is this I hear about an attempted coup in Cyprus?' he might ask.

'I am not quite sure what interpretation to put on the propaganda in our press, and I have not heard much on the foreign stations.' Sure enough, the next B.B.C. Overseas Service news bulletin carried something on tension in Cyprus.

His greatest interest, on the foreign side, is in Soviet Middle East policy, and he has proved a rare prophet. He foresaw the withdrawal of Soviet military advisers from Egypt months before it happened.

'To understand our foreign policy, you must understand the language of our propaganda,' he said. 'In the Western press, you read an article for its content, and regard the heading merely as a rough guide. In the Soviet press, you can tell the content of an article by reading its title, and noting its position on the page and in the newspaper, and the type of print. Presentation is the key.' This is a truth known to every serious Sovietologist, but few foreigners have reduced it to such a fine art as has the Systems Analyst, who has been reading the Soviet press for over thirty years with minute attention.

He sees the ways in which the Soviet State is bounded by the geopolitical considerations which affected the behaviour of Tsarist Russia. But he also makes allowances for the changed political and ethnic situation since the downfall of Tsarism.

'The Soviet Union is a federation of allegedly self-determining states, whose boundaries have been drawn and fixed,' he said. 'Thus the Ukraine and Byelorussia have even been admitted to the United Nations, and they have been given a national status which they did not possess before the Revolution. This has created a situation in which national aspirations have been given a political framework within which to develop more strongly, and—who knows? —to claim complete autonomy one day. The Ukraine is the biggest problem, because of its industrial power and its nationalist traditions. So when there are sounds of dissent in the smaller republics, like the Baltic States, they may be used as stalking horses for Ukrainian factions which seek more autonomy for themselves. Such factions may exist in the national leadership, with its large proportion of Ukrainians, as well as in the Ukraine itself.

'Russia has taken in too much territory to be a completely governable unit on an efficient basis. Yet the leadership has to apply strict centralisation in order to maintain its own position. So there is a contradiction which helps to explain the inefficiency of the administration.'

The Systems Analyst had an original and consistent explanation of the role of the Communist Party in Soviet society. 'You must understand the system of promotion within the upper ranks of the Communist Party. Once a person's name has been put on the card index of top officials, the so-called *nomenklatura*, it is virtually impossible for him to be expelled from it. If he commits a blunder or a misdemeanour, it will be strictly investigated. The results of the investigation will be made known to him, then the dossier will be put away—and he will be promoted. This means that the higher a man rises, the more dependent he is on his superiors, and the more ready to do anything they wish. The usual punishment for anything at that level is, at worst, removal from one post and re-instatement in another of equivalent seniority. It is a terrible system, because it creates such a dependence on one's bosses.

'At the lower level of the Party, there is also a system of rewards for loyal service. People who are not very efficient at their work are liable to join the Party in order to gain security. The brightest people sometimes deliberately do not join the Party, because it may affect their mobility early in their career: if they are considered Party stalwarts, their superiors may want to keep them indefinitely in the post where they have proved themselves. Those who remain at their posts and do the Party's bidding in everything will eventually be rewarded by being given a simple but well-paid administrative job. For instance, it is common to find the older Party activists appointed as the managers of such institutions as hairdressing salons or cinemas, posts where only a little administrative ability is required, and the work is light.

'The situation in all but the best academic institutes is bad, because of the number of false qualifications obtained through bribery. There are people who make a living by writing 'theses' for people quite incapable of becoming Candidates of Science on their own merits, let alone Doctors. In Georgia and Armenia, for instance, it is quite accepted that an academic qualification can be bought for money. This has led to a glut of Georgians and Armenians presenting theses, something which you can confirm merely by looking at the surnames on the public lists. One of the favourite subjects is local Party history, because it can be written to an entirely set pattern. One merely looks up the most modern version of the history of the Party at the national level, obtains permission to gain access to certain local records, and interprets local history in the light of the national interpretation.

'The purpose of having an academic qualification such as *Kandidat* or Doctor is that it brings the holder prestige and an automatic increase in salary, whatever his job. He does not have to do any teaching or prove his qualification in any way.'

(The Soviet press did in fact publish the scandalous tale of a Southerner who made a living simply by moving from University to University giving hopeless lectures for a year or two until he was exposed, then resigning 'of his own will' and taking an equally well paid post elsewhere. There seemed to be no way of stopping him, other than publishing an article and hoping that all University Rectors would read it.)

'With a higher academic qualification,' the Systems Analyst added, 'you can be very well off in the Soviet Union. You can give private tutorials, without which it is now very hard to gain access to a

University, because of the pressure on places. And you can earn retainers as a consultant.' His own experience proved this to be true, for he was clearly quite well off, though there was no reason to doubt the validity of *his* qualifications.

'Our propaganda boasts that we have a higher proportion of students in institutes of higher education than any other country. But look at what the majority of these people are studying, and you will see the reason. In order to do the simplest jobs, they may go to an institute for a year or two. They are enrolled as students to learn jobs which a normal person could pick up in a few weeks.' (This explains, among other things, the fantastically liberal distribution of the title 'engineer' among people in the Soviet Union who are, in fact, no more than slightly-qualified supervisors—for instance, at garment factories.)

'Although on paper we have the highest proportion of doctors per head of population, our medical services in the polyclinics are quite inadequate, through shortage of doctors. Many people, who qualify as doctors in the provinces, try to enrol on the staff of a Moscow polyclinic or hospital simply in order to get to the big city and have a more interesting life. But to work as a straightforward doctor is not well paid, so many of them abandon or neglect the jobs for which they were given permission to settle in Moscow, and find better paid work, or practice medicine privately on the side for high fees.'

The Systems Analyst was not negative about Soviet society on principle. He had simply made a careful study of a wide range of subjects, and documented the discrepancies between the official claims and the reality. (The sacredness of the official claims often makes it taboo to call for them to be brought more into line with the reality.) He recognized the existence of concealed unemployment in Soviet industry, and confirmed that it was a problem which exercised every economist in the country, although it is discussed only obliquely in the press. But he did not think that the Western system of overt unemployment, as a means of redistributing the labour force, was any better than the chronic over-payment and inefficiency in Soviet industry. 'Each is as bad as the other,' he said.

He did not count himself a member of the Democratic Movement or any other Movement. 'Those people really know no more about democracy than our leaders do,' he said once, in a harsh judgement.

'If they were put in power tomorrow, they would be equally dictatorial, merely in different ways.

'These are not the people our leaders are frightened of. They are too easily identified and dealt with. The thing that frightens the leaders of this country most is the phenomenon of the so-called "honest Communist". That is not the person who is a Communist, but makes it clear, early on, that he genuinely believes in Communist ideals and will try to implement them. He is not much of a danger, because he also can be picked out and made harmless. What they really fear is the person, like Dubček in Czechoslovakia, who manages to gain the trust of those around him, sufficient to win power at the national level, and *then* starts implementing the ideals of truly democratic Socialism. That is the one kind of person they are really worried about.'

After the event described in the next chapter, the Systems Analyst did not make a demonstrative show of solidarity or friendship by coming to our farewell party—as other dissidents did, defying not only the militiaman at the gate, but a squad or two of civilian vigilantes and some plain clothes men who had been watching the block ever since my expulsion order.

He simply called, and said: 'Well, is it true?'

'Yes. I am having a party, but I don't want anyone to come if they feel . . .'.

'I understand. Listen, I have some gramophone records of yours. How can I return them to you?'

'Oh, don't worry about them. Keep them as a souvenir. I also have a book of yours which I shall try to return to you. I have a feeling we shall see each other again somewhere.'

'Yes, yes. Give my best regards to your wife.'

'And to your family.'

'Thank you. *Do svidaniya*.'

Weightlessness

ON THE night of the searches in Moscow in January 1972, our telephone rang most of the night at intervals of an hour or two. One of the dissidents had taken it on himself to find out exactly what was going on, and call at regular intervals.

Before that, Kostya had rung quickly: 'They're at so-and-so's place,' he said. 'I'm going down there. If I don't ring in an hour, you'll know they've picked me up.' He was not heard from again that night, because the K.G.B. officers forbade the use of the telephone from premises being searched.

The other caller remained in the entrance hall of the block where the main search was taking place, occasionally dashing out to a call-box, collating news from friends. 'That makes it eight known, and another two possible,' he said at one stage. 'Here are the names.' Later he would call with corrections or confirmations. The total number of homes searched seemed no more than about a dozen. Every time the caller rang off, he would exclaim: '*Privyet!*' ('greetings'), in a falling intonation, which made him sound as though he were disappearing behind the far side of the Moon.

It was a Friday night. The searches continued into the early hours of Saturday morning. The Western press reported them as the opening phase of a new K.G.B. crack-down on dissidents—correctly, as it turned out. My wife Judy and I skipped a date at a Soviet acquaintance's place that afternoon, although he was not on the telephone and there was no way of telling him we were not coming. He would have heard of the searches, and would understand.

By the Sunday, the wave of searches seemed to be over. Only one or two people had been arrested. I rang one of the best-known people who had been searched, and asked him for the details. He was not charged with any crime. The search was ostensibly carried out in connexion with the prosecution of another, minor dissident. But its aim was clear enough: to provide evidence supporting further arrests later in the year.

Judy and I caught a Metro to the dissident's flat, interviewed him, and were then accompanied down in the lift and shown out of the front door. It was cold, and the dissident was not wearing a jacket or coat. We urged him to go back to his apartment. He consented. There had been men on the stairs, watching. But that seemed to be all.

We turned left along the pavement on the main road towards the Metro station. I looked over my shoulder. Two men were following, about twenty yards behind. It was dusk. We walked on. A car drew up on our right, at the kerbside. One man walked quickly round in front of us. The other flung the car doors open. The first said: 'Come with us.'

I said: 'Who are you?'

He said: 'Criminal Investigation Division,' and started pushing us towards the car.

I said: 'Show me your identification.'

They both started pushing. I started shouting: 'What are you doing? Who are you? I am a foreign correspondent, not a criminal.' Judy was also shouting. There were few people on the street, but one or two young men were approaching along the pavement.

The strangers got Judy by the back of the neck and forced her head into the car door. Then they pushed. I was afraid they might start some really rough stuff. I got in with her, still shouting. The leader of the squad and the other men piled in over me and dragged the door shut. Judy landed up sitting across the seat with her legs over one of them. The policeman said primly: 'Please make yourself comfortable.' One or two young people had gathered on the pavement. The driver let the clutch in. One of the young people bashed the lid of the boot with his fist. Why? We sped off down the street.

It was an illegal detention, because they were not in uniform and had refused to show their identification, even fleetingly. This was almost certainly because they had K.G.B. identification cards, not Criminal Investigation Department cards.

I asked them: 'Are you militia or K.G.B.?'

One of them replied immediately: 'Militia.'

A pause. I asked: 'Why didn't you show us your identification? We would willingly have gone with you then.'

The number two man said: 'It was dark.'

I said: 'This will be an international incident. It will not look good, particularly your treatment of a woman. Why did you arrest us?'

'We didn't arrest you.'

'Then it was simply hooliganism.'

The second man began to say something. The squad leader hushed him up.

Judy said: 'Is that you trembling?' She was sitting on the other side of the squad leader. 'I don't think so,' I said, though I was extremely unnerved by the whole business.

'Then it must be him,' she said.

It was true. The K.G.B. man was shaking bodily from the excitement of the arrest. Probably it was his first foreigner. Perhaps he had not expected to be challenged or physically resisted. Perhaps he was worried at having violated procedure by not showing his identification.

'If he goes on like this,' Judy said, 'he'll have to give this job up, or he'll get a heart attack.'

They got lost. The driver did not know the way to wherever it was we were going. We were nervous, because the incident might mean our expulsion from the Soviet Union, and because there might have been a change of policy at the national level, and they might be planning to make an example by imprisoning a correspondent after a mock trial. All sorts of unlikely possibilities come to mind at a time like that. We exchanged a few phrases in English. I told Judy not to say anything under interrogation until she had spoken to the British Consul. The squad leader mumbled something which showed he knew at least a few words of English.

Eventually they seemed to find the place they were looking for. They drove into a dark courtyard surrounded by a high fence. Our alarm increased. Then we saw a light above a sign saying: 'Moscow Proletarian Region, Militia Division', and that was a slight relief. If they were to continue with the fiction that they were militiamen, there was little they could do, since we had broken no law.

'Wait here,' said the squad leader, getting out of the car. He entered the building. The second man got out and stood guard. The driver remained in the car. Still they had not asked to see our identity papers. It grew cold. We asked the driver to turn on the heater. He did so. We asked him if they had made some mistake, and had really intended to arrest someone else.

He said: 'Everything will be made clear.'

After about ten or fifteen minutes, the squad leader came out of the building and got back in the car. Only then did he check our papers. He said something about not being able to get through on the phone. Then he said: 'I have been told to tell you not to go to that address again, and not to interfere in our internal affairs.'

I said: 'Who says this?'

He gave the name of a Militia Captain of the Proletarian Region of Moscow. I said: 'Is it a crime to visit Soviet acquaintances?' He merely repeated the warning. Then he said: 'You can go now.' Judy insisted that we had no idea where we were, and wanted to be taken back to the Metro station, or the place where we had been detained. After some hesitation, they agreed. It turned out to be just round the corner, though we had taken nearly ten minutes on the drive to the militia station.

We got out. The second man also got out, and stood so that his body covered the car number plate. But as it drove off, we took the number. The car did not have a Moscow city registration. It was a registration normally used for cars from the surrounding *oblast'* (region). It was clearly not a normal city police car.

This incident raised a serious dilemma. Circumstantial evidence was enough to confirm that the men who detained us had some connexion with the police, of whatever ilk, and that they therefore had the right to ban us from visiting a certain address, at least for the time being. But their warning about 'interfering in internal affairs' was not capable of any clear interpretation, and the Soviet authorities never referred to the incident further.

Were we to cease all contacts with Soviet dissidents, on the strength of this vague warning by a stranger who declined to identify himself? We decided to wait for a while and see if there were any further developments. There were not. A Soviet dissident phoned and asked for a meeting. There seemed no valid reason to refuse. That would have been conniving at intimidation which was illegal and irregular even under Soviet Law. What could one have said to Russian acquaintances, who had all this time been sticking their own necks out to pass on information of international concern? We obviously had to continue, though nervously and reluctantly. The first rendezvous after our detention was a tense affair. But the K.G.B. seemed to have decided on a 'hands off' policy for the time being, and gradually things returned to 'normal', whatever that means in Moscow.

Or almost 'normal'. It was just over four months later when Tamara Mikhailovna rang from the Foreign Ministry. She is a middle-aged woman, who deals with British journalists in the Ministry's Press Department. I had last seen her a few weeks ago at a cocktail party, when she had amicably given a warning that foreigners were no longer to be permitted to visit a new restaurant just on the forty-kilometre limit, which is supposed to restrict their movements around the centre of Moscow (actually many areas within the limit are officially banned, too).

We were in the middle of lunch—the last soup Judy was to make with Russian sorrel, one of the tastiest things available at the local market. '*Gospodin* Bonavia,' Tamara Mikhailovna said, her voice only betraying the slightest tension, 'we would like to ask you to come to the Foreign Ministry at 3.00 p.m. today.' It was then 2.10. Such summonses usually meant only one thing.

I was received at the Foreign Ministry by Fyodor Simonov, Deputy Head of the Press Department, who had given me my blue accreditation card three years and one month before. It had been in my pocket ever since, because it is officially considered a gross indiscretion to lose it. Mr Simonov now asked me to surrender it. He recited a short, prepared statement. 'For systematic activity incompatible with your status as a correspondent, you are deprived of your accreditation and it is suggested that you leave the confines of the Soviet Union within a few days.'

We had thought about such a possibility so often, and seen it happen to so many other correspondents, that the event seemed a complete anti-climax. I asked to clarify one or two points. How soon must I leave the Soviet Union? Could I interpret 'a few days' as 'ten days' (a Russian holiday was in the offing, and it would be difficult to pack and make all other final arrangements in time). Mr Simonov replied with a vigorous '*nyet*'. What about six days? He said neither 'no' nor 'yes'. I decided to take a week.

Mr Simonov allowed me to ring Judy from the outer office. In the revolving doors of the Foreign Ministry, I became caught in an elaborate courtesy ritual with a Soviet diplomat who was also leaving the building; neither of us would go first. It was a warm and sunny day. On the way back, the office driver, a Soviet citizen, was more agreeable and human than he had been for months. Then he began to fret, because he would have to look after most of the packing.

An astronaut leaving his native planet sees its colours and con-
tours more brilliantly and with more completeness, as he moves
away from its orbit. To be expelled from a country, with little
chance of returning, conveys a similar feeling of clarity, though
perhaps it is misleading. As we were relieved of the burden of
perpetually having to invent rules to govern our own behaviour,
and to guess at the attitude the authorities were taking at any given
moment, many things about the country seemed to fall into place.
But there was little time to think about them then.

An entire office operation had to be wound up, for the time being,
farewells attended and given, *samizdat* destroyed, files put in order,
furniture and crockery wrapped, magnetic tapes checked for anything which might compromise a contact, endless telephone calls
answered, plane tickets booked, the maid given notice, the cat
given a rabies injection, the samovar evaluated for export duty by
the Tretyakov Gallery, second-hand opera scores checked for
antiquarian interest by the Lenin Library, the Soviet car sold back
to the authorities. Through it all, the driver slogged on, packing
box upon box of books and other possessions, carefully listing their
contents for the Customs. Good friends and semi-strangers rallied
with offers of help.

There were two major problems: one was the question of a farewell party, which has become traditional for foreigners leaving
Moscow, whether voluntarily or otherwise. The other was how to
get rid of the *samizdat*.

Of the two, the *samizdat* was the more troublesome. Much of it
had already been reprinted or reported on in the West. Some of it
was of no particular interest to the K.G.B. But there was the
general problem, described in an earlier chapter, of not giving the
police samples of individual typescripts, or making things too easy
for them. We were clearly going to be given a thorough Customs
inspection on the way out, so we decided to destroy every scrap of
samizdat except one or two topical and unused items, which were
passed on to other correspondents. (I no longer had the right to
transmit news stories.)

Anyone who has tried disposing of a large quantity of paper,
thoroughly, in an apartment without an open-hearth fire, will
understand the difficulty. We tried burning it in the kitchen, and
washing the ash down the sink. But after a page or two had been
burnt, the flat was filled with acrid smoke, and there was a danger

that the neighbours would call the fire brigade. So we decided to shred it minutely and flush it down the lavatory.

Shredding paper small enough not to block Soviet plumbing is a seemingly endless job: first it has to be torn in half, then in quarters, then in eighths: then each of the eight piles of scraps has to be shredded further. It is like the Greek riddle about Achilles and the tortoise. The further one goes, the more work there is.

Then the pipes began to block. The maid complained that ash from the kitchen waste-pipe was floating up into the bath in the adjoining cubby hole where she used to do the laundry. One of the lavatories had become almost completely blocked. We went out to a luncheon invitation, and when we came home, we found that the plumber had come at the maid's invitation, and cleared the blocked pipes in our flat. She would never have taken such an initiative on her own in normal circumstances. But at least there would be no more desperate poking around at midnight with pieces of bent wire; and it was unnecessary to use the powerful, block-busting chemical lent us by a friend as a last resort.

The farewell party seemed to be an intractable problem at first. It would have to be on the last night, so there would be no crockery or cutlery left unpacked. Should Russians be invited, or would that be futilely provocative? We remembered the Praga Hotel, which looks after foreigners' catering from time to time. It seemed impossible that they could cope at such short notice. But on the last evening, after barely more than a conversation and the payment of a quantity of ten-rouble notes, a team of three waiters arrived with a ready-made Russian buffet supper, and began calmly pouring drinks.

The only remaining worry was whether any Russian friends would try to come, and whether it would cause unpleasantness.

The day before, I had gone for a stroll in the courtyard, when Judy shouted from the balcony: 'Pop across the street and buy a couple of packets of cream.' Only then, I realised that I had not been outside the block unaccompanied since the expulsion order. I was curious, and not a little nervous, to see what the K.G.B. men, who must be watching the flat, would do.

They did not show themselves till I was in the shop, waiting in the queue at the cash-desk with the two packets of cream. The shop had recently gone over to self-service, but it was a small one, and there was the usual shortage of change at the cash-desk. There were arguments, with much shouting and ill-feeling. I was standing by the plate-glass window.

He was standing three feet away, on the other side of the window, red-haired, with a cigarette hanging from his lip, staring fixedly just beyond the middle button of my raincoat into the shop. He seemed to have come from nowhere. On the pavement, looking up and down the street, was another one, with a dark raincoat and felt hat, the physique of a professional wrestler, a broken nose. He seemed to be signalling discreetly. A Volga car pulled up; the driver, weasel-faced, peering into the shop.

The K.G.B.—subject of so many dim reports and speculations— are not pretty when seen at close quarters. The nature of their work shows itself clearly in their faces. But their job on this occasion was simply to ensure that I had no more contacts with Russians, and made no calls from public telephone boxes, before leaving the country. I walked out of the shop without looking at them again, and returned to the flat. They melted back to wherever it was they had come from. It was an unpleasant sensation.

Among the dozens of phone calls we received, there were some from dissidents and from plain Russian acquaintances. It seemed wrong not to tell them there was to be a farewell party. They would have to make up their own minds about whether to come or not.

The British Ambassador arrived in the Embassy Rolls with the flag flying, promptly, as the proceedings opened. This may have decided the watchers on the street not to interfere, though civilian vigilantes with red armbands were walking up and down outside the entrance. Whether there was a sudden change of policy at the sight of the Ambassador and other diplomats arriving in the compound, or whether there had already been a decision not to interfere, was unclear. But Russians also began arriving, and reporting that they had not been molested at the entrance.

Academician Sakharov came, apparently the first time he had associated directly with foreign correspondents and diplomats. He was shy, but soon got into a conversation with a Scientific Attaché. Other people who have been referred to under pseudonyms in this book also began arriving, and promptly calling for private conver-sations on the balcony to pass last-minute messages and items of information.

Fat Sasha came, though looking stiff and out of place. Dusya

Zhukov kept running round the flat asking people: 'Who's that *stukach* (informer)? What's he doing here?' Apparently she had already gathered that he was not a dissident. His Stalinist wife seemed decidedly unhappy in the company, and spent most of her time in the kitchen.

The waiters also began to seem unhappy, and the drinks stopped coming round. They had to be chivvied out of the laundry-room, where they had gathered. But they went off quite content before midnight, each carrying two opened bottles of obscure foreign beverages, which were clearly not going to be drunk up that night, in lieu of tips.

Within an hour or two, many people had made new contacts and exchanged telephone numbers. At least it would not all be wasted. The Russians, untrue to their usual form, began leaving fairly early. They had risked enough by coming, and were glad to be offered lifts out of the compound by foreigners.

There was the usual round of kissing among the men. I can still feel stubble and beard-hairs between my front teeth when I recall those farewells.

Roman Rutman, the Jewish activist, decided to walk out past the militia post, with one or two other Russians. The guard stopped them. Rutman put on a foreign accent and said: 'They're with me.' It didn't work. The militiaman asked for their identification. Then he asked by what right they were in a foreigners' compound. Rutman said: 'We were invited to a foreigner's party.' With a curious twist of legalism, the militiaman said: 'Where's your invitation card?' Rutman fished in his wallet, and brought out one of my old visiting cards. The militiaman was not satisfied. 'Well then,' said Rutman, 'do you want me to go back to the flat, and get the host down to explain that we were his guests?'

'Clear off,' said the militiaman.

When everyone had left, one of the best-known dissidents rang from another flat, apparently drunk. 'I'm coming back to your place,' he said.

'Don't do that. It'll just be you and me and the militiaman alone on the pavement. And the K.G.B. are watching. It could lead to trouble.'

'I want to come back.'

'No, let's say goodbye now.'

'Uh-huh, 'Bye.'

A few weeks later, he was searched again and arrested. He had been expecting it for several years.

The final scenario came at Sheremetyevo Airport, where a special plain clothes man had been assigned to go through our luggage. I had told Judy to scream the place down if she was subjected to a gynaecological examination like the girl from Saratov, but they waived this formality.

The British Consul and several senior diplomats watched as the plain clothes man went through our luggage methodically. He opened all files and looked at the papers inside. He apparently understood English. But he only took two things: the Russian original of a letter which had been published in *The Times* weeks before, and an essay on alcoholism in Russia, which a crank had sent to my predecessor, and which had lain around the flat for several years. It had been slipped into a file simply in order to get it out of the way. I still wonder what the K.G.B. made of it.

Where From Here?

IF THERE is anything to be deduced from the Soviet authorities' treatment of dissenters of all kinds, it is that there is little new to be deduced. The Soviet Union is evolving in many directions, but not towards a more tolerant official attitude with regard to political protest or intellectual challenge. Nor is it rushing backwards towards Stalinism: the feeling at the top appears to be that neither Stalin nor Khrushchev provided the right set of answers to this problem, and perhaps that it has not been found even yet. In such a vacuum of policy, the aim of the authorities will be to suppress manifestations of the thing they do not know how to cope with. Possibly, that in itself could be called a policy: it looks more like a series of expedients.

In other words, there is no room for protest in the Soviet system as conceived of by its Leaders. This does not mean that protest will cease to exist. On the contrary, it will continue and probably grow. But it will exist *vis-à-vis* the system, because the system has no nook in which to institutionalise it, as American society has institutionalised many forms of American protest.

This should be constantly borne in mind by people who see Soviet protest as a manifestation of social 'convergence', a proof that we are all becoming more and more like each other. It is the firm determination of the Soviet Leaders *not* to let their people become more like us; and it should equally be the determination of freer peoples not to let themselves be made more like the long-suffering Soviet people. Convergence as an idea looks very neat. As a policy, it has little to recommend it, which is why no government espouses it. The closest that governments get to it is to say that they are prepared to respect each other's systems; there has yet to be found a government which honestly says over a long period of time that it wants to make its system more like someone else's.

It can be argued that the present system suits the Soviet people reasonably well, bearing in mind their checkered political development and their need to concentrate on certain economic priorities before others. In such an argument, the protesters are simply the gadflies of society, products of a law which states that any social system will engender such and such a minimum percentage of malcontents. In that case, the Soviet authorities are perfectly right to suppress protest, and even to treat it as a form of schizophrenia. As social engineers, they are merely clearing a few molehills which impede the construction of a pyramid. When the pyramid is built, there will be no more molehills, because all the moles will come to live in it happily ever afterwards.

To test the validity of this argument—which finds a glad response among all supporters of the Soviet system—it is necessary to return to the most basic judgements about human nature. Eventually it comes down to this: does the system produce the kind of people we like and admire, or does it suppress the qualities which appeal to us in people? Do the protesters strike us as eccentrics and rogues, or do they seem to be holding some flame of human values which the system seeks to extinguish?

No one should glory in the fact that the majority of free-thinking foreigners, who have spent *more than a few weeks* in the Soviet Union, and escaped the deceptions of Intourist or the sponsors of official 'delegations', are eventually repelled by its present social, political and economic system, and by the effect it has on human beings. There are those who come with blind preconceptions of one kind or another, which no amount of reality can shake. But the majority of foreigners who have an opportunity to live in the Soviet Union for a few months or years are not blind. They are ordinary, well-intentioned people, who come to the country with a deep desire to form their own independent judgements about it, whether as students, diplomats, correspondents or businessmen. They feel this the more acutely since nearly all those who have visited the Soviet Union and written about it before seem *parti pris* in one way or another. Every new person who comes to live in Russia for a while believes that he or she will be able to leave the country with a detached and balanced view of it.

The extraordinary thing is that no one does—except for those who isolate themselves so much in the foreign community, or in some kind of illusory world, that they have no significant contact with the country at all (and that is their right). Among those who seek real contact, the final reaction is usually one of disillusionment and bitterness at what it reveals.

Russia does not merit bitterness, but sadness. This very sadness is built into its literature and its history, is an element of the nation's psychology. Everyone has heard of the Russians abroad who weep when they hear their native songs. Are they weeping out of a desire to return there, or out of a deeper sadness which they acquired through living there in the first place?

Russia does funny things to people. Some it unlocks, others it closes up tighter. It arouses disputes and arguments so sharp that people living there temporarily learn to avoid them altogether, for fear of that very sharpness. The people who have to live there all their lives exist at a different level of emotional activity from people in freer societies. Their emotions are stronger, but more carefully suppressed for most of the time. They can live and work in situations which would drive Western people half insane. They acquire obsessions which help to keep them stable, and they fight long social and psychological battles with a single-mindedness which seems to be its own reward. They spend so much energy struggling to make the system workable, that they become built into it. Many of them would go to pieces if suddenly moved into another environment. The sense of being trapped for life, between one's surroundings and one's character, contributes to the overwhelming sadness of Russian society.

On a moral or philosophical level, the sadness is a correct appraisal of what the last fifty years of Russian history have done to humanity, above all in Russia itself. Leaving aside the questions of the Terror and the captive nations of Eastern Europe, no thinking person can become well acquainted with a sizeable number of Soviet citizens who dare to speak their minds to him, without experiencing a sense of loss and wastage. He will mentally contrast the courage, frankness and sincerity of the people whom Soviet society casts aside, with the callousness and instinctive mendacity of those whom it raises up. For many foreigners, it is enough to walk into a Soviet shop or hotel, and experience the rudeness and arrogance of the service staff, to be turned against the system for ever. For others, it is a longer and more painful process: determined to let the system show its best and worst, and to weigh them carefully against each other, they come to witness the fearful and irrational cruelty of the country's social processes. And in the end, they are thrown back once more on the human judgement of good and bad: do I like this person, do I dislike that one? The relatively small number of foreigners who have a chance to meet *both* the dissenters *and* the officials in Russia have an almost unanimous reaction: they like the dissenters, and dislike the officials. If this is a personal judgement, it is also a moral and social one, because it is people who make such judgements and always will be.

Here are samples of two points of view about Russia, and about the author's point of view. The first consists of extracts from an article, written, for his own interest and that of his acquaintances, by a British businessman who happened to be visiting Moscow when the invasion of Czechoslovakia took place in 1968:

'*It is in considering such questions as the efficiency of the Metro, or the power and scope of the electrification programme, or the co-ordinated invasion of Czechoslovakia at a few days' notice, or the inevitable space programme and its achievement, that the central mystery of the Soviet system obtrudes itself. How can an organisation seemingly dedicated to inefficiency at the ordinary level of existence, binding itself hand and foot with red tape and buried under a mountain of forms in triplicate, yet find the inner drive and strength to carry these vast projects through to success? It is not enough to say that the Government allocates huge material and manpower resources selectively and without stint to their projects. This they certainly do, but it is not manpower but men that must finally direct the efficient application of these resources, and nothing in their life or education encourages such men to emerge. Quite the reverse. Every circumstance of his upbringing conditions the Soviet citizen to avoid initiative, responsibility or decision, to suspect objectivity even if he can recognise it, to prefer the mediocre to the exceptional, to fear the highest when he sees it . . .*

'*How, then, does the Soviet Union secure the men it needs? Seven days is not too long a period in which to find an answer. The first easy conclusion is that a great crime has been committed here against the human race—or at least against the Russian people. A little later, after a look around and a brief glance at Russian history, one begins to wonder with von Herberstein, the Emperor Maximilian's Ambassador in Moscow in 1517, whether the (tsarist) autocrat has brutalised the people, or have the brutish people made the autocracy necessary? For centuries the Russians have been ruled as though they were the most dangerous and difficult people in the world to govern. Their rulers, mad or sane, hereditary or imposed, have tortured and slaughtered their way to power. To the outside observer, the people seem docile enough—all too docile perhaps. But the Russians themselves may know better.*

'*At all events, to raise leaders from these oppressed masses, the system must offer rewards of privilege and power to those few who will dare to accept its challenge; and of course it does. Nowhere is there greater disparity between the living standards and power resources of leaders and led; nowhere is it more important to "know someone" if life is to be made tolerable. Even the pathetic merchandise displayed in the lighted windows of Gum, the great department store that stretches ponderously down the length of Red Square opposite the Kremlin, is well beyond the reach of all but a tiny percentage of the population . . .*

'*Those who have the will and the courage to break out of this stultifying and frustrating environment, in science, in the arts, or above all in politics, must be remarkable men and women indeed, needing something almost demoniac in their make-up. And "demoniac" is the adjective that most readily occurs to those who may watch the long black cars streak out from beneath the great floodlit red flag that flies above the Kremlin's Council Chamber, to dive through the Saviour's Gate into the dark town beneath the walls. One might be forgiven, at such moments, for repeating the old Russian proverb, "Light a candle for the Devil too: you never know".*

'*To attempt a rational conclusion would be callow and presumptuous, but the final impression left by such a visit is overwhelming. It is that the new rulers of Russia have discovered in Communism and Marxist economics one more of the many systems that have been designed in the past to keep this vast and varied group of nations under control. The more successful of these systems have depended on strongly centralised power, administered by comparatively few—very few—devoted servants of the State tied by fear and advantage to the central authority, with a population kept in ignorance and subjection or—today's variant —in a state of mental paralysis. Little wonder that the transition of the "new economics" is proving difficult, or that the winds of change blowing from the erstwhile satellites should strike so chill.*

'*The tragedy is that the mechanism sustaining this mediaeval autocracy should be offered to the rest of the world as a viable political and economic system—and accepted as such by so many of that world's innocents. There can be no gradual "coming together" of the Soviet system with that of the world outside Russia. The one is utterly incompatible with and wholly irrelevant to the other. No compromise between them is possible for a "free world" determined to find a way to the good life for mankind.*'

The second view was ascribed by the Moscow *Literary Gazette* to a person indentified as L. Byelyanko, a former worker, living in Minsk. As readers of *The Times* pointed out, it is impossible to obtain copies of that newspaper in Minsk, as in nearly all other Soviet cities. Nevertheless, Byelyanko wrote:

'This scribbler began as early as February, 1971, to exercise his open slander against our Soviet reality. He denigrates Soviet culture and presents facts and events in a distorted form, thus showing his anti-Soviet face. How long can this continue? Why do we tolerate in our own home "guests" who pour filth all over us?

'To me, a former worker, it is not difficult to understand the tendencies of this "specialist" in slander. Evidently Bonavia's bosses are directly interested in spoiling Anglo-Soviet relations. They evidently have no taste for the atmosphere which has developed in Europe, they are disturbed by the successes achieved by the peace-loving states in the cause of strengthening European security. But we Soviet workers do not like the dirty "exercises" of Mr Bonavia. In fact, I think the British people will hardly believe Bonavia's ravings.

'If this journalist thinks he is a great original, then he is mistaken. We are long acquainted with such "compositions"; we also know well that each time their authors fell flat on their faces. Mr Bonavia can hardly expect to escape a similar fate.'

This voice can have the last word for now. It makes little difference, for the debate and the human judgements on Russia will not end there.

David Bonavia was born in Aberdeen in 1940 and went to Cambridge University, where he gravitated towards the study of Chinese. In 1967 *The Times* of London took him on as a staff correspondent for Vietnam, and after a year and a half in Saigon he was sent to Moscow. He had studied Russian as a hobby while at school. Together with his Australian wife, Judy, he spent three years investigating the social order in the Soviet Union, a process which resulted in their expulsion by the authorities in May, 1972. Six months later he was appointed Peking Correspondent of *The Times*, the first British newspaper correspondent to hold this post since the Communists came to power in China.